Broadcasting in the European Union:
The Role of Public Interest in Competition Analysis

Broadcasting in the European Union: The Role of Public Interest in Competition Analysis

Ingrid Nitsche

T·M·C·ASSER PRESS
The Hague

Published by T·M·C·ASSER PRESS
P.O.Box 16163, 2500 BD The Hague, The Netherlands

Sold and distributed in North, Central and South America
by Kluwer Law International,
101, Philip Drive, Norwell MA 02061

In all other countries, sold and distributed
by Kluwer Law International, Distribution Centre,
P.O.Box 322, 3300 AH Dordrecht, The Netherlands

ISBN 90-6704-131-9

T.M.C. Asser Instituut - Institute for Private and Public International Law, International Commercial Arbitration and European Law
Institute Address: R.J. Schimmelpennincklaan 20-22, The Hague, The Netherlands; P.O. Box 30461, 2500 GL The Hague, The Netherlands; Tel.: (31-70)3420300; Fax: (31-70)3420359; URL: www.asser.nl
The T.M.C. Asser Institute was founded in 1965 by the Dutch universities which offer courses in international law in order to promote education and research in the fields of law in which the Institute specialises: private international law, public international law including the law of international organisations, international commercial arbitration and the law of the European Union. The Institute discharges this task by organising educational programmes, by the establishment and management of documentary compilations and by undertaking academic research, in some cases in cooperation with international organsations and academic institutions, as well as by the dissemination of information deriving therefrom and by the publication of monographs and series. The Institute organises *Asser College Europe*, a project in cooperation with East and Central European countries whereby research and educational projects are organised and implemented.

PREFACE

In the last century, the media decisively shaped the way we view society and how people form their political opinions. How states regulate the media, and especially television broadcasting, reveals much about a society and its opinion elite. For European states, maintaining and fostering a wealth of different national cultures through the media has always been a high priority, but at the same time, an effort has been made to introduce the notion of a European culture and/or identity. This concept was meant to underpin economic integration and complement the achievements of the internal market. In Europe, content regulation and a corporatist broadcasting structure prevailed against a more market-oriented approach that would restrict itself to the provision of a framework ensuring a reasonable level of competition. Public and economic competition have traditionally been defined as distinct concepts that do not necessarily overlap. With the increased commercialisation of broadcasting from the 1960s and 1970s onwards, however, tension between the traditional role of the public service broadcaster to educate and inform and the new commercial broadcasters that predominantly entertain increased, generating a debate on the application of competition law to what has traditionally been viewed as a public service task. In particular, the qualification of television broadcasting as a service in the sense of the EC Treaty and the application of the competition rules and more recently state aid rules have been viewed with suspicion by some Member States. They were and continue to be reluctant to accept alleged 'intrusion' into their national broadcasting order by the European Courts. Yet, public interest concerns are also, to some extent, acknowledged in the case law of the Court of Justice and the Court of First Instance.

This book is partly based on research carried out for my PhD. thesis under the supervision of Jean Monnet Professor Gerte Reichelt. In May 1999, the thesis was accepted by the Faculty of Law of the University of Vienna. I am also especially grateful to Peter Muchlinski who was my teacher and tutor at LSE and first introduced me to the subject of EC Competition law. Moreover, I have to thank Klaus Wiedner for being a helpful and understanding supervisor during the *stage* which I was able to complete in 1998 in the EC Commission's Legal Service. I am indebted to many friends and colleagues who helped me to develop and refine my arguments through their ideas and critiques. In particular, I would like to thank Michael Hofstötter, Vincent Kronenberger, Christoph O. Meyer and Volker Schlechtriemen for their comments and advice. However, the usual disclaimer applies as to my responsibility for remaining mistakes and omissions. I would also like to thank Avril McDonald who language edited the book, the T.M.C. Asser Instituut for its interest in and support of my research and T.M.C. Asser Press for accepting it for publication. I dedicate this book to the memory of my grandparents.

Bonn, March 2001 INGRID NITSCHE

TABLE OF CONTENTS

ABBREVIATIONS

ARD	Arbeitsgemeinschaft der Rundfunkanstalten Deutschlands
BBC	British Broadcasting Corporation
BKartA	Bundeskartellamt (German Cartel Office)
BT	British Telecom
BVerfG	Bundesverfassungsgericht (German Constitutional Court)
CFI	Court of First Instance of the European Communities
CMLRev.	Common Market Law Review
COM	Commission of the European Communities
Denv. J. Int'l L & Pol'y	Denver Journal of International Law and Policy
CPN	Competition Policy Newsletter
C&R	Computer und Recht
EBOR	European Business Organisation Review
EBU	European Broadcasting Union
ECLR	European Competition Law Review
ECHR	European Convention on Human Rights
ECR	European Court Reports
ELR	European Law Reporter
ELRev	European Law Review
EPG	Electronic Programming Guide
EuR	Europarecht
EuZW	Europäische Zeitschrift für Wirtschaftsrecht
fn	footnote
Fordh. Int. L.J.	Fordham International Law Journal
FT	Financial Times
GATS	General Agreement on Trade in Services
Hastings Int. & Comp. L.Rev.	Hastings International & Comparative Law Review
HMSO	Her Majesty's Stationary Office
ICLQ	International and Comparative Law Quarterly
IJCLP	International Journal of Competition Law and Policy
JCMS	Journal of Common Market Studies
JV	Joint Venture
JZ	Juristenzeitung
LIEI	Legal Issues of European Integration
LJIL	Leiden Journal of International Law
LSE	London School of Economics
NJW	Neue Juristische Wochenschrift
OJ	Official Journal
RIDE	Revue Internationale de Droit économique
RIW	Recht der Internationalen Wirtschaft
RTDE	Revue trimestrielle de droit européen
SME	small and medium-sized undertakings
SpuRT	Sport und Recht

TV	Television
Vol.	Volume
WTO	World Trade Organisation
ZDF	Zweites Deutsche Fernsehen
ZEuS	Zeitschrift für Europäische Studien
ZUM	Zeitschrift für Urheber- und Medienrecht

Part I
THE ECONOMIC AND POLITICAL CONTEXT

Chapter 1
INTRODUCTION

1.1. General Remarks

Audio-visual media and, in particular, television constitute a major economic force within the European Union and globally. An average European spends about three hours a day watching television, and 98 percent of European households own a TV.[1] Despite the increasing use of new media, television can still be regarded as the most widely used and most influential medium,[2] with a substantial potential for economic growth and for the creation of highly skilled jobs.[3] Its economic development is closely connected to the unprecedented technological change witnessed over the last ten years. The television industry has moved from a system of limited frequencies in the days of terrestrial television towards cable and satellite and ultimately into the so-called 'digital age'. Set-top-boxes, conditional-access-systems, pay-TV and near-video-on-demand provide for a variety of new television services open to consumers.

Most importantly, the number of frequencies has become – at least with respect to the technically possible – virtually unlimited. It will be demonstrated that this development is changing the regulatory conditions for the audio-visual media. Broadband cable can potentially supply three different services: television, telephone and access to the Internet. The borders between different technical devices are becoming blurred, and it is already technically possible to use personal computers to watch television and access the Internet from a TV-screen. Currently, the discussion within the EU focuses on how this growing convergence between telecommunications, media and information technology sectors will and should affect future regulation in these areas.

1.2. The Significance of 'European' Culture and Identity

Apart from these technological and economic aspects, until the 1980s, television in Europe was viewed as a predominantly cultural issue to be regulated at nation state level. Most Member States operated national public service broadcasters and did not, or only partly, expose television to market forces. This was due to, first, the paramount importance of safeguarding national cultures and, second, the important

[1] Communication from the Commission on the principles for the Community's audiovisual policy in the digital age, 657 *COM* (1999), p. 3.

[2] Yet citizens regard the radio as a more reliable source of information than television or the press. Source: Eurobarometer No. 48, Oct.-Nov. 1997.

role attributed to broadcasting in a democratic society, namely, to ensure freedom of expression and pluralism of opinion. Even with the emergence of private broadcasting, television remained subject to tight regulation in most Member States.

The importance of broadcasting for a democratic society was expressly recognised by the Protocol on public service broadcasting to the Treaty of Amsterdam:

> the system of public broadcasting in the Member States is directly related to the democratic, social and cultural needs of each society and to the need to preserve media pluralism.

It should be noted that the term 'culture' did not appear in the Treaty of Rome. It was later included in the fourth recital of the Preamble of the Treaty on European Union (Treaty of Maastricht). The Heads of State of the (then) 12 Member States emphasised their desire '...to deepen the solidarity between their peoples while respecting their history, their culture and their traditions, ...'. Article F(1) determined that 'the Union shall respect the national identities of its Member States..' Member States have been reluctant to focus on a European cultural policy and emphasised instead the significance of the diversity of national and regional cultures for Europe as a whole. It has been argued that the deepening of European solidarity should neither come at the expense of national cultures nor should it be achieved through the promotion of European culture.[4] On the other hand, the importance of such a 'European' culture *vis-à-vis* the US[5] has been emphasised and there has been an extended discussion on the importance of broadcasting thereof.

If we pursue the idea of a 'European identity' further, we ought to acknowledge opinion polls demonstrating that 'Europe' has in the past been a mainly élitist concern.[6] It appears that the European Union has so far been unable to develop into an entity with which citizens of Member States can easily identify. Most Europeans still define themselves primarily in terms of their national or regional identity and show little enthusiasm for the notion of a 'European culture' and/or 'European identity'. Yet, some recent studies suggest that something akin to a 'European public sphere' might be evolving, which could underpin a process of transnational opinion and identity formation.[7]

---

[3] Employment opportunities in the information society: using the potential of the information revolution, 590 *COM* (1998) final.

[4] J.M.E. Loman, K.J.M. Mortelmans, H.H.G. Post and J.S. Watson, *Culture and Community Law. Before and after Maastricht* (1992) p. 190.

[5] See *infra* at 3.5.3.

[6] See e.g., Eurobarometer 1996, top decision-maker survey.

[7] P.R. Schlesinger, 'Changing spaces of political communication: The case of the European Union', 16 *Political Communication* (1999), pp. 263-279; D. Kevin and P.R. Schlesinger, 'Can the European Union Become a Sphere of Publics?' in E.O. Eriksen and J. E. Fossum, *Democracy in the European Union: Integration Through Deliberation?* (2000) pp. 206-229; C.O. Meyer, 'Towards a European public sphere? Transnational Investigative Journalism and the European Commission's Resignation', in B. Baeren/J. Rauppi, *Transnational Communication in Europe. Practice and Research* (2000). For a reluctant approach see e.g., K.M. Meessen, 'Potlitische Identität in Europa', 6 *Europarecht* (1999) pp. 701-712.

Numerous efforts have been made to define 'culture' in the context of broadcasting, in particular, a distinct 'European' culture. Or does this term merely signify the diversity of Member States' national cultures? *Baumann*[8], for example, refers to the concept of a 'scientific' European cultural identity in the literature, which is not simply the sum of cultural events in Member States and/or regions but a form of 'transnational unity', drawing from achievements such as the industrial revolution, the enlightenment and the idea of universal human rights, as a natural result of Christian-European history. Conversely, a European Parliament report argued that, under the Treaty', cultural diversity and pluralism come under the heading of cultural aspects',[9] i.e., it is the very *diversity* that constitutes European cultural identity.

As *Schlesinger* has pointed out, it might be misleading to consider Europe as having a single national culture and identity. In practice, the EU's media policy favours, for instance, the interests of the dominant ethnic groups (the Germans, British and French).[10] The whole discussion about the dangers of 'Americanisation' only masks the fact that the allegedly 'European' view has quintessentially served French interests of trade intervention.[11]

Indeed, the issue of 'Americanisation', portrayed as posing a threat to European local culture, must be viewed against the background of trade relations with the United States. The EU external trade deficit with the US on the audio-visual market approaches seven billion Euros; US productions achieve between 60 and 90 percent market share in the Member States, whereas European productions only account for between one and two percent in the US market.[12] Hence, one should be cautious about taking the 'Americanisation' argument at face value. When it comes to broadcasting, cultural and economic aspects appear closely interlinked and should be assessed in relation to each other.[13] As Dyson and Humphreys put it: 'Public-service broadcasting was a European institution *par excellence*; broadcasting and culture were intimately wedded together in the minds of the broadcasting élite.'[14]

---

[8] 'Die Dienstleistungsfreiheit auf dem Gebiet der audiovisuellen Medien im Rahmen des GATS im Spannungsfeld von Marktfreiheit und kutureller Selbstbestimung der Staaten der Europäischen Union', (1998) p. 106.

[9] Fayot and Schinzel (rapporteurs), 'Report of the committee on Culture, Youth, Education and the Media on the Commission Green Paper Pluralism and Media Concentration in the Internal Market', 92 *COM* 480-C3-0035/93, A3-0435, 5 January 1994.

[10] 'From cultural defence to political culture: media, politics and collective identity in the European Union', in 19 *Media Culture & Society* (1997) pp. 369, 382.

[11] Ibid., p. 376.

[12] Communication from the Commission on the principles for the Community's audiovisual policy in the digital age, 657 *COM* (1999), p. 9.

[13] It is worth noting that the former communist countries of Eastern Europe appear less concerned about protecting their local culture from American audiovisual products. See for example Mr. *Puchalsky*, Director of Czech Television, in a speech on 2 Dec. 1999 at the 11th European Film and Television Forum, Prague.

[14] 'Introduction: politics, markets and communication policies', in *The Political Economy of Communications, International and European Dimensions* (1999) p. 21.

1.3. **The Role of Competition Law**

Within the framework of EC law and the EU's media policy, audio-visual media have been assigned somewhat of a 'hybrid' role. One the one hand, the Court of Justice decided in 1974 that broadcasting was a service,[15] i.e., an economic activity falling fairly and squarely within the ambit of Article 49 (ex-Article 59) of the EC Treaty. On the other hand, the EU never denied the cultural importance of broadcasting. The tendency to emphasise cultural aspects was further reinforced by Member States' reluctance to let the EU interfere with their national media policy. The unsolved contradiction between these two positions caused disagreement over how far broadcasting could be regarded as 'special', and whether its particular characteristics justified an exemption from Article 49 (ex-Article 59) of the EC Treaty and/or its provisions on competition (Articles 81, 82 (ex-Articles 85 and 86) EC) and state aid (Article 87 (ex-Article 92) EC). Consensus has not yet been reached on how to balance these conflicting positions. Media and competition/internal market law tend to be treated as two different sets of legal regimes. The early judgements on broadcasting were delivered almost 20 years ago when states' broadcasting monopolies were still widespread.[16] Despite the emergence of private broadcasting, it was not until broadcasting enterprises in Europe started to merge on a large scale[17] that the media turned into an important issue for competition law. Even today, there is still a certain uneasiness about the application of competition law to the audio-visual sector, especially expressed by public broadcasters.

It has been submitted, in particular by some German authors, that competition law is not an appropriate tool to handle the public interest and cultural aspects of audio-visual media, to maintain media pluralism, and guarantee freedom of expression. For example, *Frey* argues that all measures designed to maintain media pluralism would fall foul of the free movement of services,[18] and that competition law is not suitable to deal with the issue of media pluralism.[19] However, such an approach appears to underestimate the potential benefits of competition for the media market. As *Mestmäcker* correctly puts it, competition law can contribute to pluralism by preventing market concentration and by providing for a range of independent suppliers.[20] Moreover, *Temple Lang* recognises a certain gap between media and competition law as well as between lawyers trained in one of the two disciplines,

---

[15] See Case 155/73, (1974) ECR 409.

[16] Case 155/73, *Sacchi* (1974) ECR 409.

[17] See, for example, *RTL/Veronique/Endemol* (HMG), *OJ* 1996 L134/32; Nordic Satellite, *OJ* 1996, L 053/20; *Kirch/Bertelsmann/Premiere OJ* 1999 L 53/1; *Deutsche Telekom/Beta Research, OJ* 1999 L 53/1.

[18] D. Frey, *Fernsehen und audiovisueller Pluralismus im Binnenmarkt der EG* (1999) p. 76.

[19] Ibid., p. 126.

[20] E.-J. Mestmäcker, *Recht und ökonomisches Gesetz. Über die Grenzen von Staat, Gesellschaft und Privatautonomie* 2nd ed. (1984) p. 254.

suggesting that an effort should be made to bring competition law to the attention of media lawyers.[21]

The concept of 'competition' as used in this book is deliberately broad in that it also covers internal market issues within the context of audio-visual policy. EC competition law regards restrictions on competition in the light of the obstacles they represent to trade between Member States.[22] It should be analysed in conjunction with the four freedoms,[23] which also act as a means to prevent distortions of intra-community trade. Thus, the four freedoms and Competition law are interlinked as they both act as a means of economic integration.[24] Broadly speaking, 'Competition law' can be understood as encompassing all laws that effect the conditions of competition.[25] Under the Treaty provisions, however, the free movement of goods applies to restrictions on the internal market resulting from Member States' actions, whereas restrictions resulting from private traders are subject to competition rules.[26]

This book aims to show that public interest considerations and competition are not irreconcilable in the field of audio-visual policy, and that the Court of Justice successfully fits public interest considerations, such as the maintenance of media pluralism and the promotion of local culture, into its analysis. Competition law should be regarded at least as an additional tool to deal with issues of media concentration and pluralism. Unlike content regulation, it does not interfere with consumer choice.

Adam Smith acknowledged the existence of a state's duty in a free-market-economy to maintain public undertakings and institutions that would not generate enough profits for someone or a small group but *can be useful for society as such*.[27] The pivotal question is whether a certain service is useful for the public and should be supplied from public sources although demand might not be large enough to recoup the costs of providing it.[28] Some authors appear to cut this discussion short by simply asserting the need to provide (and often also publicly finance) certain services. In contrast, the case law of the Community courts makes clear that there

---

[21] J. Temple Lang, *Media, Multimedia and European Community Antitrust Law*, Fordham Corporate Law Institute (1997) pp. 81 et seq.

[22] D.G. Goyder, *EC Competition Law* (1998) p. 503.

[23] The free movement of goods (Art. 28, ex-Art. 30), free movement of persons (Art. 39, ex-Art. 48)), freedom to supply services (Art. 49, ex-Art. 59) and freedom of establishment (Art. 43, ex-Art. 52).

[24] The so-called ordo-liberal concept of integration, see for example J. Weiler, 'The Transformation of Europe', 100 *Yale Law Journal* (1990) p. 2403 and Gerber, 'Constitutionalising the Economy: German Neo-liberalism, Competition Law and the "New Europe"', 42 *American Journal of Comparative Law* (1994) p. 25.

[25] D.P. Fidler, 'Competition Law and International Relations', 41 *ICLQ* (1992) pp. 563-589, p. 564.

[26] W. Kilian, *Europäisches Wirtschaftsrecht* (1996), p. 98.

[27] A. Smith, 'The Wealth of Nations', p. 687, quoted in Mestmäcker, *Recht und ökonomisches Gesetz. Über die Grenzen von Staat, Gesellschaft und Privatautonomie*, 2nd ed. (1984) p. 131.

[28] See for example the discussion about financing BBC digital television. *Financial Time online*, 3 November 1999, 'BBC: Digital' will need £730m more by 2007', 26 November 1999, 'BBC: MPs attack over spending on News 24', 21 December 1999, 'BBC: Kaufmann brings little festive cheer'.

needs to be a causal link between the financing of a public service and the public interest.

1.4. **Industrial Policy and External Aspects**

> Competition policy aims to offset market failure arising from scale economies and market power. Industrial policy is designed to offset other sources of market failure which arise in the production process.[29]

In an economist's definition of 'industrial policy', the aim of competition policy is to counter market failure. Consequently, both policies do not contravene but supplement each other. However, a more populist view conceives of competition, particularly on the global scale, as a struggle for dominance not only between companies, but also between nations, necessarily producing winners and losers. Although this view has been heavily criticised by some economists[30] who point out that it contradicts traditional theories of free trade,[31] it became increasingly accepted during the late 1980s and early 1990s in the US[32] and has impacted EU Audio-visual policy, which envisages international trade as a race between trading blocks:

> The danger is if Europe fails to take advantage of the opportunities provided by convergence, it could be left behind as other major trading blocks reap the benefits of a more positive approach.[33]

This fear of being left behind in the 'competitive race' is also apparent from the external elements of the EU's audio-visual policy. Whereas the 'internal' dimension of the EU's audio-visual policy deals with problems of harmonising Member States' national laws and how this affects their national culture and/or identity, the external dimension focuses on a 'European' culture whose protection has repercussions on external trade relations in the field of audio-visual media. This second aspect is often referred to in the context of 'Americanisation', i.e., the cultural pollution thesis, arising from the fact that the majority of European consumers watch American fiction programmes and Hollywood movies. This fear about the dangers of 'cultural imperialism' also materialised in EC secondary legislation. The 'Tele-

---

[29] D. Begg/S. Fischer/R. Dornbusch, *Economics*, 4th ed. (London, McGraw-Hill, 1994) p. 307.

[30] See, for example, P. Krugman, *Peddling Prosperity, Economic Sense and Nonsense in the Age of Diminishing Expectations* (1995).

[31] The benefits of international trade were first formulated by the English economist David Ricardo (1772-1823).

[32] See for example M. Porter, *Competitive Advantage of Nations'* (1990); R. Reich, *The Work of Nations: Preparing Ourselves for 21st Century Capitalism* (1992).

[33] Green Paper on the Convergence of the Telecommunications, Media and Information Technology Sectors, and the Implications for Regulation towards an Information Society Approach, 623 *COM* (1997) at point II1, 'Impact on economic and industrial competitiveness'.

vision Without Frontiers' Directive[34] introduced in its Article 4 a quota providing in part that:

> Member States shall ensure where practicable and by appropriate means, that broadcasters reserve for *European works*, within the meaning of Article 6, a *majority* proportion of their transmission time, excluding the time appointed to news, sports events, games, advertising and teletext services. (italics added)

The US has asserted that the EU, with this provision, violated the GATT,[35] in particular, the most-favoured-nation (MFN) clause. This argument failed to impress European politicians, who took the view that television is a service and not a product, as claimed by the US, and thus did not fall within the ambit of the GATT. But even if this was the case, it is argued that the GATT does not limit the EU's legitimate right to protect its culture. The 'cultural exception'[36] is based on the notion that certain 'cultural products', for example, movies, books and records, are excluded from the GATT.[37] These legal considerations were complemented by European politicians' statements; for example, François Mitterand, then French President, invoked 'the right of every country to create its own images. A society which abandons the means of depicting itself would soon be an enslaved society'.[38]

This debate should be viewed in the context of the European audio-visual market and its structure. Compared to the US, it is fragmented along national, and, in particular, linguistic lines and relies on small-and-medium-sized enterprises (SMEs). Consequently, European governments have been less reluctant about mergers or collaborations between undertakings, and have sometimes even supported 'strategic alliances' because they expect large entities to achieve economies of scale and scope more easily. The case of *Kirch/Bertelsmann/Premiere*[39] serves as an example in the broadcasting sector. In this case, German officials were much less concerned about the creation of a potential monopoly for digital TV than the Commission as long as digital television was introduced in Germany and not dominated by foreign investors.[40] It seems that the innovator, entrepreneur and risktaker deserve some

---

[34] Council Directive 89/552/EEC of 3 October 1989, Coordination of Certain Provisions Laid Down by Law, Regulation, or Administrative Action in Member States Concerning the Pursuit of Television Broadcasting Activities, 1989 *OJ* L 298, 23, as amended by Directive 97/36/EG of 30 June 1997, 1997 *OJ* L 202, 60.

[35] See, for example J. Filipik, '"Culture Quotas": The Trade Controversy over the European Community's Broadcasting Directive', 28 *Stanford Journal of International Law* pp. 324, 337 et seq.

[36] The principle basis is Art. IV GATT, but Art. XX may also be relevant.

[37] J. Filipik, op. cit. n. 35 at p. 351.

[38] Cited in Goodell, 'The French Revolution', *Premiere* 26 May 1994.

[39] *OJ* 1999 L 53/1.

[40] The two mergers would have created the framework for digital Pay-TV in Germany, but as Premiere would have achieved a monopoly position as a programming platform, Beta research for technical services and Deutsche Telekom regarding cable transmission, the operations were prohibited. See General Report on the Activities of the EU 1998, point 219 and EU-Bulletin 5-1998, point 1.2.64.

immunity from competition[41] and therefore industrial policy has often favoured 'national champions' that are potentially better equipped to compete in global markets. This is a highly contentious issue even within the Commission services; for example, in the civil aviation sector, Directorate Generals (DG IV) (competition) and DG III (industry) in the *Aérospatial-Allen/De Haviland*[42] merger disagreed as to whether or not the merger should be prohibited,[43] the former arguing for the strict application of competition law, the latter invoking industrial policy arguments.

Regarding the film and broadcasting industry, DG X[44] (responsible for audio-visual policy) initiated the MEDIA I and II programs to support and promote the European audio-visual industry by funding film projects, creating distribution networks and providing training schemes. Recently, the Commission suggested a new MEDIA PLUS program[45] to succeed MEDIA II,[46] which elapsed at the end of 2000.[47]

It is plain that an industrial policy aimed at creating large and powerful groups of undertakings or conglomerates can run into conflict with competition law, because concentrated and oligopolistic markets inherently contradict the functioning of competition within the EU. The contentious question remains whether competition law could constitute a better alternative for coping with unfair trade practices than *dirgiste* intervention. It appears that DG X's media policy[48] and DG IV's competition policy are often contradictory and difficult to reconcile with each other. The EC lacks a coherent media policy, but this is hardly surprising given that the Commission is not a homogenous and hierarchical institution, nor does it advocate a unified policy in other fields.[49]

1.5. **The European Audio-Visual Framework**

As a starting point, it is worth mentioning that broadcasting in the EU was not harmonised until the late 1980s. When the Treaty of Rome was first drafted, its

---

[41] R. Whish, *Competition Law*, 3rd ed. (1993) p. 9.

[42] *OJ* 1991 L 334, 42, (1992) CMLR M2.

[43] Finally, it was prohibited, because the Commission decided it would create a not merely temporary dominant position.

[44] The numbering has been abolished under the new Commission taking office under President Prodi in 1999.

[45] Communication from the Commission on the principles for the Community's audio-visual policy in the digital age, 657 *COM* (1999) p. 24. Council Decision of 20 December 2000 on the implementation of a programme to encourage the development, distribution and promation of European audiovisual works (MEDIA Plus, 2001-2005).

[46] *OJ* 1995 C 321/25.

[47] See *infra* at 3.5.2.2.

[48] Council Directive 89/552/EEC of 3 October 1989, Coordination of Certain Provisions Laid Down by Law, Regulation, or Administrative Action in Member States Concerning the Pursuit of Television Broadcasting Activities, 1989 *OJ* L 298, 23; amended by Directive 97/36/EG of 30 June 1997, *OJ* 1997 L 202, 60.

[49] R. Collins, *Broadcasting and Audio-Visual Policy in the European Single Market* (1994) p. 18.

authors did not consider broadcasting as being covered by any of the freedoms or subject to market forces even within the Member States' legal regimes. Neither primary nor secondary Community law expressly referred to television until the Television without frontiers Directive was adopted in 1989, based on (then) Articles 57(2) and 66 EC Treaty. But even before that, Community institutions, and in particular, the Court of Justice, were faced with problems of cross-border broadcasting. In the absence of specific secondary legislation, these cases were merely decided on the basis of Article 49 (ex-Article 59) EC Treaty. It was suggested that the harmonisation of broadcasting legislation by the legislature was for a long time lagging behind technical and economic developments, and there is still disagreement over the extent to which broadcasting falls into the Community's competence and which aspects remain for the Member States to regulate.

It was not until the Maastricht Treaty, which created an express Community competence for culture by inserting Title IX 'culture' (now Title XII) into the EC-Treaty, that this problem became regulated by primary law. The new provision in Article 128 (now Article 151)(2) subparagraph 4 EC Treaty particularly referred to the 'artistic and literary creation, including in the audio-visual sector'. The Community's contribution to the Member States' culture is, according to Article 128(5) (now Article 151) limited to the adoption of 'incentive measures, *excluding any harmonisation* of the laws and regulations of the Member States' (emphasis added).[50] Hence, this provision excludes a Community competence to harmonise the cultural aspects of broadcasting. However, since Article 128 (now Article 151) provides in paragraph 4 that 'the Community shall take cultural aspects into account in its action under other provisions of this Treaty', media regulation can be based on the freedom to provide services (Article 52(1), ex-Article 63(1))[51] or the freedom of establishment (Article 46(2), ex-Article 56(2)).[52]

Assuming a community competence in the field of broadcasting potentially causes problems under Member States' constitutional laws. For example, the highest German court (*Bundesverfassungsgericht)* took a generally reluctant approach toward the constitutional character of Community law in its so-called Maastricht-Judgement.[53] There was an extended discussion over whether the German government's approval of the Television without Frontiers Directive was unconstitutional.[54] Finally, the *Bundesverfassungsgericht* decided that the Community was competent to

[50] D. Frey, *Fernsehen und audiovisueller Pluralismus im Binnenmarkt der EG* (1999) p. 28.

[51] The 'Television Without Frontiers' Directive was based thereon. See *infra* at 3.5.3.

[52] See *infra* at 6.4.1 the discussion on the proposed Anti-Concentration Directive.

[53] BVerfGE 89, 155-213, see D. Dörr, 'Die Maastricht-Entscheidung des Bundesverfassungsgerichtes und ihre Auswirkungen auf die Medienpolitik', 1 *ZUM* (1995) pp. 14-20.

[54] See, for example, C. Degenhart, 'Rundfunkordnung im europäischen Rahmen', (1992) *ZUM* pp. 449-456; J. Martin-Pérez de Nanclares, *Die EG-Fernsehrichtlinie* (1995) pp. 29 et seq.; E. Steindorff, *Grenzen der EG-Kompetenzen* (1990) pp. 40 et seq.

regulate the areas of the right to reply, commercials, sponsoring and the protection of minors.[55]

As already mentioned, harmonisation regarding the cultural aspects of audio-visual media is precluded by Article 151 (ex-Article 128)(5)) EC Treaty. Hence, it does not come as a surprise that initiatives in this sector often take the form of so-called 'soft law', in particular, recommendations and notices. MEDIA I (MEDIA 92), for example, covered, *inter alia,* the training of professionals, the improvement of production and distribution, cinema production and stimulating financial investment. After the pilot stage was positively appraised by a group of experts, it was turned into a full scale program.[56] MEDIA I was later succeeded by MEDIA II (MEDIA 95) which was in turn replaced by MEDIA PLUS by the end of 2000.[57]

In addition to these 'soft law' measures, one needs to mention first and foremost the Television Without Frontiers Directive. It harmonises some issues on transnational broadcasting, most notably the question of who has jurisdiction over a given situation, in order to avoid more than one Member State having the competence to regulate a certain transborder transmission. The Directive is based on the principle of home control; generally, it is for the Member State from where the program originates to regulate the program content. The receiving Member State can only in very exceptional circumstances prevent the transmission into its territory, provided the program fulfils the conditions of the transmitting state. After some preliminary rulings on the question of which criteria apply in establishing jurisdiction over a broadcaster, it was clarified in the amendment that, *inter alia*, its place of establishment was decisive (Article 2(2) of Directive 97/36/EC[58]). However, Member States may nonetheless impose stricter rules on the 'national' broadcaster under their own jurisdiction (Article 8 of the Directive), i.e., so-called 'reverse discrimination'[59] is not prohibited.

Besides the 'European quota' in Article 4, the Directive also contains provisions on advertising, sponsoring and teleshopping (Chapter IV), defining these terms and limiting the maximum duration of advertisements. Chapter V (Article 22) regulates the protection of minors and Chapter VI (Article 23) the right to reply. These provisions impose minimum standards. The directive does not contain any specific competition rules or exceptions from the application of competition law in the audio-

---

[55] BVerfGE 92, 203 (241), *EG-Fernsehrichtlinie.*

[56] Council Decision 90/685/EEC of 21 December 1990 concerning the implementation of an action programme to promote the development of the European audio-visual industry (MEDIA) (1991 to 1995) *OJ* 1990 L 380/37. See also Communication from the Commission to the Council and Parliament on audio-visual policy, 90 *COM* 78 final.

[57] Communication from the Commission on the principles for the Community's audio-visual policy in the digital age, 657 *COM* (1999) p. 3. Council Decision of 20 December 2000 on the implementation of a programme to encourage the development, distribution and promation of European audiovisual works (MEDIA Plus, 2001-2005), *OJ* L 336/82, 30 December 2000.

[58] *OJ* L 202/60, 30 July 1997.

[59] See P. Beaumont/S. Weatherill, *EU Law,* (1999) Penguin Books, pp. 609 et seq.

visual sector: only in Rec. 2 the Directive generally refers to 'a system ensuring that competition in the common market is not distorted'.

Yet, as far back as 1992, the Commission acknowledged the problem of media concentration and issued the Green paper 'Pluralism and Media Concentration in the Internal Market: An Assessment of the Need for Community Action',[60] which extensively discussed the issue whether there was, in fact, need for community action at all or whether it should be left entirely to national regulators. In a notification to the Council and the Parliament,[61] the Commission arrived at the conclusion that there was indeed a need for Community action but the initial aim to present a draft directive was not further pursued. Neither within the Commission nor amongst Member States could agreement be achieved.[62] In 1996, Commissioner Mario Monti suggested a draft anti-concentration directive,[63] but it never reached the stage of adoption. Not could the Commission services agree on the text. A second attempt[64] was equally unsuccessful. Hence, despite the fact that the Commission identified a need for Community action in 1992, no specific anti-trust or merger regime applied to the audio-visual sector in the European Union until recently.

Thus, the audio-visual sector is only subject to the general rules on competition in the Treaty, most notably, Articles 81 (ex-Article 85, preventing concerted practices and fully-fledged cartels) and 82 (ex-Article 86, outlawing the abuse of a dominant position) and the Merger Regulation.[65] In the past, for example, private broadcasters invoked Article 81 to challenge the European Broadcasting Union (EBU),[66] an association of mainly public broadcasters, after EBU had refused them access to their system of cost-free internal program exchange of sports programs in particular. Surprisingly, Article 82 has not yet been applied to audio-visual media, although in times of media concentration the abuse of a dominant position could be expected to occur frequently. The fact that Article 82 has not yet been of much use is also related to the large amount of cases that have been reviewed under the Merger Regulation,[67] which is the tool to prevent dominant positions from emerging in the first place. Since its adoption, six Commission decisions were taken on the basis of the Merger Regulation within the first two years alone.[68] Generally, the present

---

[60] 92 *COM* 480 final.

[61] 94 *COM* 353 final.

[62] H. Kresse, 'Marktöffnung und Pluralitätssicherung. Eckpunkte zur effektiven Vielfaltsgestaltung im privaten Rundfunk', in H. Kresse, ed., *Pluralismus, Markt und Medienkonzentration: Positionen* (1995) p. 86.

[63] 96 *COM*, p. 396.

[64] 97 *COM*, p. 86.

[65] Regulation 4064/89 (1989) *OJ* L 395/1, as amended by Regulation 1310/97, (1997) *OJ* L 180/1.

[66] IV/32.524 Eurosport (1991) *OJ* L 63/32; IV/32.150 *EBU* (1993) L 184 /42, Case T-528/93, *Metropole*, Judgement of 11 July 1996, [1996] ECR II-0649, currently on appeal.

[67] See, for example, *MSG/Media Service*, (1994) *OJ* L 364/1; *Nordic Satellite*, (1996) *OJ* L 053/20;*Kirch/Bertelsmann/Premiere* (1999) *OJ* L 53/1; *Deutsche Telekom/Beta Research*, (1999) *OJ* L 53/1; *RTL/Veronique/Endemol* (HMG), (1996) *OJ* L 134/32 on appeal *Endemol/Kommission*, T-221/95.

[68] T. Jestaedt/J. Anweiler, 'Europäische Fusionskontrolle im Medienbereich', 18 *EuZW* (1997) p. 549.

trend indicates that competition law will become increasingly more important for the audio-visual media, and recent developments in the media industry need to be viewed against this background. National law on its own is too limited in scope to provide satisfactory regulation in a European (or indeed global) context, particularly when it comes to large cross-border mergers that could involve non-European undertakings.

1.6. **Aim and scope of this book**

At present, most of the literature in this area focuses on the audio-visual legal framework in the European Union,[69] in particular, on the Television without Frontiers Directive and aspects of television broadcasting within the common market.[70] This book builds on and extends this research agenda by analysing the key legal questions in their economic and political context. It focuses on the audio-visual sector from a competition perspective, taking special account of the Court of Justice's case law, and considering how cultural and competition aspects are balanced against each other. An effort will be made to identify, as far as possible, general principles from the case law, to contrast them with the Commission's media policy, and to highlight the contribution of competition law to a European media policy.

The book is divided into two parts: Part I deals with the audio-visual framework. Chapter 2 briefly discusses some of the economic implications of competition law in general, such as market structure and market definition. In addition, it focuses on the specific characteristics of broadcasting and to what extent it differs from 'ordinary' services. Chapter 3 examines policy options, gives a brief overview of some Member States' broadcasting systems and compares them with those of the US. This chapter also discusses the audio-visual policy of the EU and outlines the legal framework, including the Television Without Frontiers Directive.

Part II is designed to outline and analyse selected case-law on broadcasting, covering judgements of the Court of Justice, the Court of First instance and also to some extent Commission Decisions. Chapter 4 considers the notion of the 'legitimate general (or public) interest' in the application of Article 49 (ex-Article 59) EC Treaty and its application to broadcasting. Problems of cooperation and collusion between broadcasters under Article 81(ex-Article 85) are discussed in Chapter 5. It focuses on, *inter alia*, Joint Ventures under Article 81, aspects of digital television and the exchange mechanism set up by the European Broadcasting Union. Chapter 6 is dedicated to mergers, with a special emphasis on the German media market. It also deals with the formerly proposed EC anti-concentration directive. Public service broadcasting and the application of state aid rules are considered in Chapter 7.

---

[69] See, for example, D.B. Winn, *European Community and International Media Law* (1994).

[70] See, for example, H. Baumann, *Die Dienstleistungsfreiheit auf dem Gebiet der audiovisuellen Medien im Rahmen des GATS im Spannungsfeld von Marktfreiheit und kutureller Selbstbestimung der Staaten der Europaeischen Union* (1998), D. Frey, *Fernsehen und audiovisueller Pluralismus im Binnenmarkt der EG* (1999).

This chapter treats of public service broadcasting in relation to the notion of a public undertaking or an undertaking enjoying special or exclusive rights. It also offers some tentative conclusions on the application of EC state aid rules to Member States' public service broadcasting. Chapter 8 discusses the competition law implications of the broadcasting of sports events. It was clarified in the famous *Bosman*[71] ruling that sports as an economic activity is subject to the application of EC law. This has repercussions on the marketing of broadcasting rights by sports bodies. In particular exclusive transmission rights and the notion of collective selling will be assessed under the Treaty rules. Final conclusions are summarised in Chapter 9.

[71] Case C-415/93 [1995] ECR I-4921.

Chapter 2
ECONOMIC BACKGROUND

2.1. General Remarks

It is often claimed that television, and in particular public broadcasting, constitutes a distinct type of service that has to be treated accordingly, and which should not or only within certain limitations be exposed to market forces. Such remarks are to be found in legal publications often as a mere statement and not bolstered by further explanation or economic evidence, which leaves the picture incomplete. Hence, this chapter aims to explore some economic aspects of audio-visuals that should be acknowledged by lawyers dealing with the application of competition law to this field. Indeed, many arguments and discussions can only be understood within this context, as competition law, to a greater extent than other fields of law, concerns the application of economics. Thus, mutual understanding of economic and legal phenomena is essential. However, what makes applying economics in practice difficult is the potential uncertainty as to cause and effect, because economic models hardly ever provide the clear-cut and unambiguous rules that the lawyer seeks. Nonetheless, it may assist in applying the law and provide additional guidance. This chapter aims to provide some economic background information concerning audio-visuals.

2.2. Merit Goods

> Merit goods are goods that society thinks people should consume or receive, no matter what their incomes are[72] (...) regardless of whether they are wanted by each individual.[73]

There are two distinct reasons for merit goods: first, there permit the consideration of external effects. The individual demanding education, for example, will not consider that education also insures communication and social interaction – aspects that are valuable for society as such. It would, then, be prudent for society to encourage the provision of education (expecting that increased supply will also increase demand). Second, society believes that individuals sometimes do not act in their own best interests by, for example, having regular health checks. Thus the government may spend money on free health care because it recognises that otherwise individuals will act in a way they might subsequently regret. Hence, it has a

[72] Begg/Fischer/Dornbusch, op. cit. n. 29, p. 53.
[73] Ibid., p. 283.

certain paternalistic attitude. People may not actually want to go to school, but in their later life they might be glad that someone made.[74]

Merit goods should not be confused with public goods. Public goods are, when consumed by a person, still available for consumption by others. That appears paradoxical, because, in general, economics is all about the allocation of scarce resources, and 'normal' private goods, if consumed by one person, cannot be consumed by another. Governments are to a large extent concerned with the distribution of income, i.e., a society has to decide on what it wants to spend and what it will rather sacrifice.

By contrast, merit goods are goods that governments *want* the people to consume. They typically include health, education and food, and society agrees that everyone should have access to these basics. But merit goods are further characterised by society desiring the consumption of a *particular* good rather than another, e.g., the financing of a particular TV-program it considers valuable and not just any.

It cannot be denied that there is a certain resemblance between the concept of merit goods and public television.. European governments and EU institutions belief that 'quality' content should be broadcast, whether people actually want to watch it or not. Member States have introduced different systems of financing public broadcasting, such as funding it entirely by television licence fees, for example in the UK, or funding it partly by fees and partly by advertising, as in Germany or Austria. States are faced with the choices of how much to spend on public television and whom to charge for it. Anyone can have a perfectly sensible viewpoint on these issues, but translating these different opinions into a consistent approach that can be taken up by government and implemented is 'the impossible task of politics'.[75]

In the last couple of years, viewing habits have changed, and we have witnessed a transition from collective family viewing of two or three generalist TV channels to individual family members viewing alone, selecting from a much broader range of channels,[76] a development that already started with the use of VCRs.[77] Hence, the consensus on what society deems a program in the public interest and is prepared to finance appears to be narrowing. But this consensus constitutes a necessary precondition for characterising something as merit good. Thus it does not come as a surprise that public broadcasting, and the way it is financed, is increasingly questioned, and it seems legitimate to take the view that it does not qualify as a merit good anymore, and that in the absence of communal imperatives, individuals should be left to decide for themselves which type of program they prefer to watch.

---

[74] Ibid., p. 283.

[75] Ibid., p. 53.

[76] Green Paper on the Convergence of the Telecommunications, Media and Information Technology Sectors, and the Implications for Regulation towards an Information Society Approach, 97 *COM* p. 623 at point II3, 'The Consumer Perspective'.

[77] K. Dyson in K. Dyson and P. Humphreys, *Broadcasting and New Media Policies in Europe* (1988) p. 252.

2.3. **Market Structure**

When we talk about market structure we describe the behaviour of buyers and sellers in the market,[78] or in other words, 'market structure refers to the organisational main characteristics or dimensions of a market'[79] in terms of the degree of concentration, the existence of a homogenous product or product differentiation and barriers to entry (or exit) into the market. To establish these market characteristics, it is first essential to define the relevant market. Usually, all firms making the same or an interchangeable product belong to one market.[80] There exist a variety of models on market structure, ranging from the 'extremes' of perfect competition to pure monopoly. However, most markets are somewhere in-between, and a lot of industries, such as civil aviation or indeed entertainment, have become increasingly concentrated.

As already mentioned, market structure and undertaking's conduct is closely interlinked and finally results in a particular market performance. The interconnection between these three aspects has first been described as 'structure-conduct-performance-paradigm' by Joe Bain. It has been further explained by *Scherer & Ross*.[81] This model was later criticised for being too static, and it was subsequently established that not only market structure induces a particular conduct leading to specific performance but there are also repercussions within this circle, i.e., performance and conduct will result in a specific market structure.[82] The notion of game theory also influenced economist's understanding of competition and resulted in allowing them to analyse big businesses' strategic conduct. The so-called New Industrial Economics of imperfect competition believes that market structure and behaviour of incumbent firms are determined simultaneously. In particular, strategic behaviour has repercussions on market structure; it may, for example, erect barriers to entry. Aggressive advertising to build a brand and attract consumer loyalty will directly affect the market structure if it results in deterring entrance of potential competitors. Finally, the number of competitors in a market does not in itself indicate a certain market structure, but potential competition and the existence of entry barriers must equally be considered. For example, if barriers to entry are very low, even a monopolist might behave 'perfectly competitively'.[83] This represents a fairly wide interpretation of the term 'market structure' and it is also possible to define it more

---

[78] Begg/Fischer/Dornbusch, op. cit. n. 29, p. 132.

[79] J. Fejø, *Monopoly Law and Market. Studies of EC Competition Law with US American Antitrust Law as a frame of reference and supported by basic market economics* (1989) p. 39.

[80] See more detailed *infra* at 2.4.1.

[81] *Industrial Market Structure and Economic Performance*, 3rd ed. (1990) especially Chapters 1 and 2.

[82] Philips, 'Structure, Conduct and Performance – and Performance, Conduct and Structure', in J.W. Markham and G.F. Papanek, eds., *Industrial Organisation and Economic Development* (Boston, Houghton Mifflin, 1970).

[83] Begg/Fischer/Dornbusch, op. cit. n. 29, p. 169.

narrowly, focussing on the degree of concentration in the relevant market. Thus, high concentration does not necessarily lead to a certain conduct as other factors, such as entry barriers or heterogeneity of the product concerned, also have an impact on performance.

2.3.1. *Perfect Competition*

'Perfect competition' is used as a benchmark against which every free market system is ultimately measured because this model produces the very results that are intended in a free market economy. In a perfectly competitive market, resources are allocated efficiently. Generally, we distinguish between productive efficiency, ensuring that a good is produced at the lowest possible cost, and allocative efficiency, basically meaning that consumers get exactly the product they want. Both together result in the highest possible overall efficiency. In a perfectly competitive market, producers are mere price-takers and through their conduct cannot effect prices, which only cover production costs. Competition will also lead to permanent innovation because of constant pressure from other competing suppliers.

A perfectly competitive market is one in which both buyers and sellers believe that their own buying and selling decisions have no effect on the market price.[84]

The model of 'perfect competition' contains four elements: (1) many sellers and buyers, (2) a homogenous (or standard) product, (3) no barriers to entry or exit and (4) perfect information for consumers (completely transparent markets).[85] In a perfectly competitive industry, all firms must be making the same product, for which they must all charge the same price.[86] Within this definition there exists a range of possible broad and narrow definitions, the latter facilitating comparison between different systems. From the model of perfect competition it also follows that systems that do not comply with the conditions mentioned would not produce the desired results. Hence, such a market would not be what economists call 'pareto efficient'.[87] Yet, a market that fulfils all conditions but (2) is still a 'functioning market'.

---

[84] Ibid., p. 132.

[85] J. Fejø, *Monopoly Law and Market. Studies of EC Competition Law with US American Antitrust Law as a frame of reference and supported by basic market economics* (1989) p. 47; Whish, pp. 1 and 2; Begg/Fischer/Dornbusch, op. cit. n. 29, p. 133; S. Bishop and M. Walker, *The Economics of EC Competition Law* (1999) Sweet & Maxwell, pp. 17 et seq.

[86] Begg, Fischer and Dornbusch, op. cit. n. 29, p. 133.

[87] An allocation is pareto-efficient, it is impossible to move to another allocation which would make some people better off and nobody worse off. Ibid., p. 257.

2.3.2. *Workable Competition*

However, most markets are imperfectly competitive and only a few industries in the real world closely resemble the textbook model of perfect competition. Hence, there was room for a more pragmatic model. In 1940, *John Maurice Clarc* established his alternative concept of 'workable competition' and explained this theory in a famous article.[88] First and foremost, he did not believe that perfect competition would ever exist in the real world, and although he never rejected the concept altogether, he maintained that relying exclusively on this model might produce undesirable results in practice. In other words, some of the conditions considered as imperfections might have positive effect under special conditions in the real world. Hence, he suggested an alternative model for the most desirable forms of competition, which were possible in practice. His model of 'workable competition' or 'effective competition', as it is sometimes called, was taken up in the US and also by EC officials[89] and has since developed into the most important yardstick for EC Competition policy. It is also used by the Court of Justice, which explicitly introduced this concept in the *Saba/Metro*-case,[90] but refrained from defining it.[91]

2.3.3. *Pure Monopoly*

The opposite, limited, case of market structure to perfect competition is pure monopoly.

> A monopolist is the only seller or potential seller of the good in that industry.[92]

A monopolist will make supernormal or monopoly profits, which are pure profits after all costs have been deducted, including the opportunity costs of the owner's time and money. He has monopoly power and can raise prices above marginal costs and need not take into account the possibility of entry. In general, marginal costs equal marginal revenue for a monopolist. Unlike a producer in a perfectly competitive industry, he is a price setter.[93] Economists believe that unless there are severe barriers to entry, monopolies are not sustainable in the long run because the high profits will attract further entrants, which will subsequently result in price-cutting to a competitive level.

---

[88] J.M. Clark, 'Toward a Concept of Workable Competition', 30 *A.E.R.* (1940) p. 241.

[89] H. van der Groeben, 'Die Wettbewerbspolitik als Teil der Wirtschaftspolitik im Gemeinsamen Markt' Speech in the European Parliament, in 1965, pp. 10 et seq.

[90] *OJ* 1976 L 28/19.

[91] R.B. Bouterse, *Competition and Integration – What Goals Count? EEC Competition Law and Goals of Industrial Monetary and Cultural Policy* (1994) p. 24.

[92] Begg/Fischer/Dornbusch, op. cit. n. 29, p. 132.

[93] Ibid., p. 147.

Cases of pure monopoly are rare but often one competitor is more influential than others without holding a monopoly in the strict sense of the word. Market participants who can exercise 'market power' hold a so-called dominant position (Article 82 EC Treaty, ex-Article 86). The Court of Justice lay down the following legal test to establish dominance in the case of United Brands:[94]

> ... a position of economic strength enjoyed by an undertaking which enables it to prevent effective competition being maintained on the relevant market by offering it the power to behave to an appreciable extent independently of its competitors, customers and ultimately of its consumers.

With regard to broadcasting, the Commission has held that the decisive criterion to establish dominance is the incumbent operator's audience share.[95]

2.3.4. *Natural Monopoly*

Some industries have such a high minimum efficient scale that only one supplier can survive on the market; they are called natural monopolies. In fact, with such high economies of scale enjoyed by the monopolist there *should* only be a single supplier because a lot of small firms producing a small fraction each of total demand will be faced with enormous average costs. A single firm will undercut them and wipe them out.[96] Examples for such industries typically have very high fixed costs, such as railway or supply of natural gas. If there is a rail connection between X and Y, it would be unwise, not to say foolish, to built another one, considering the initial costs to be incurred by the potential competitor, whereas the costs of carrying additional customers are marginal. The costs for supplying gas to one additional consumer is infinitesimal compared with the initial investment.

It has long been discussed whether television constitutes a case of natural monopoly. In fact, in times of limited terrestrial frequencies and states' public broadcasting monopolies, such an argument appeared justified, at least for small countries with a limited audience. But in the meantime, market structure has developed rapidly in a different direction with the arrival of private terrestrial and cable television. The shortage of frequencies justifies qualifying television as a natural monopoly. More recently, however, the emergence of Pay-TV and digital TV directs our concern towards the industry's economies of scale. For example, the German Kirch-Group launched Pay-TV in Germany, but its channel DF1 failed to take off with consumers because they could chose from a range of free-TV channels and could not easily be attracted by the new service. Broadcasting sporting events and

[94] Case 27/76 [1978] ECR 207. The same definition was used e.g., in *Hoffmann-La Roche* [1975] ECR 461.

[95] Case IV/M.533 *RTL/Veronica/Endemol* [1996] *OJ* L 134/32, paras 17, 20.

[96] Begg/Fischer/Dornbusch, op. cit. n. 29, p. 150.

movies proofed a reliable way of attracting consumers to Pay-TV but, simultaneously, prices for these programs increased considerably. As a result, the initial investment to establish Pay-TV in Germany surged and Kirch was faced with the need to attract a financial heavy-weighted partner. First, he intended to merge with the German media group Bertelsmann, but the merger was prohibited by the EC Commission on the ground of potentially causing a sustained dominant position on the German Pay-TV market.[97] Finally, Kirch sold 25 percent of his shares to Rupert Murdoch.[98]

This case demonstrates the significance of new television services requiring substantial initial investment. The same applies to the launching of digital television that, while as a technology is fully developed, is nonetheless difficult to establish in the market because it also incurs high costs, for example, for decoder set-top boxes, that cannot easily be levied on viewers. Consumers are seldom prepared to pay these costs, preferring to remain with the choice of free terrestrial or cable programs they already have. So which lessons can we learn from the concept of natural monopoly for the television industry? A large minimum efficient scale will result, if not in a natural monopoly, at least in a market determined by only a few large providers, often called a concentrated market or oligopoly. In fact, this is the kind of market structure we are currently witnessing across several industries; i.e., there are merely a few comparatively large suppliers instead of many small undertakings.

2.3.5. *Oligopoly*

> An oligopoly is an industry with only a few[99] producers, each recognising that its own price depends not merely on its own output but also on the action of its important competitors in the industry.[100]

Oligopolistic competition, unlike perfect competition, is characterised by the strategic behaviour of the market participants. Every supplier takes its competitor's conduct into consideration when deciding on how to behave, e.g., which prices to charge. Thus, an oligopolist's behaviour lies half-way between being a pricetaker or pricemaker. A limited number of competitors jointly set the price, often without colluding in the strict sense. Competition is impeded fundamentally and markets operate inefficiently.[101] These theoretical considerations are further substantiated by economic evidence demonstrating a correlation between industrial structure and profit levels. It is suggested that profit levels increase with the concentration ratio

[97] *Kirch/Bertelsmann/Premiere OJ* 1999 L 53/1; *Deutsche Telekom/Beta Research, OJ* 1999 L 53/1.

[98] See, e.g., *Financial Times* online, 4 November 1999, 'Murdoch Master Plan for Europe'; Süddeutsche Zeitung online, 30 November 1999, 'Milliarden für das Pay-TV.'

[99] Usually up to ten.

[100] Begg/Fischer/Dornbusch, op. cit. n. 29, p. 156.

[101] R. Whish, op. cit. n. 41, p. 468.

of the relevant industry.[102] Although this evidence has been subject to critique,[103] it does give some indication of the characteristics of oligopolistic markets as to the conduct of oligopolists and their market performance.

In the broadcasting sector, most markets exhibit an oligopolist market structure with only very few large suppliers, such as Murdoch in the UK, Bertelsmann and Kirch in Germany and Berlusconi in Italy, alongside with still important and influential national public service broadcasters. Nevertheless, we should keep in mind that, formerly, broadcasting had been organised as a state monopoly and it makes sense to compare the previous monopoly to the current oligopolistic market structure.[104] *Noam* has scrutinised the effect on access to broadcasting markets and program quality by the emergence of private broadcasters and the abolition of the former public broadcasting monopolies. He suggests that, although conventional wisdom supposes that commercial broadcasting will lead to a 'race to the bottom', rational economics does not confirm this assumption. It will rather lead to diversity[105] and even give public broadcasters the chance to improve the quality of their program, because they, unlike private operators, need not maximise the amount of viewers.[106]

2.4. **Market Definition**

> Market definition is a tool to identify and define the boundaries of competition between firms.[107]

It is necessary to define the relevant market to establish the limits within which the competition analysis will be carried out. Whether someone is dominant on a specific market or whether a certain conduct affects trade between Member States can only be established with reference to a certain market. The relevant criterion is to establish, which undertakings compete with each other. Factors pertinent to market definition are the product concerned, the geographical area and temporal considerations.

---

[102] J. Bain, 'Relation of Profit Rate to Industry Concentration', 64 *Quarterly Journal of Economics* (1951) pp. 293-324.

[103] See, e.g., Weiss 'The Concentration and Profits Issue', in H.J. Goldschmid/H.M. Mann/F.J. Weston *Industrial Concentration: The New Learning* (1974); Y. Brozen, 'The Concentration-Collusion Doctrine', (1977) *Antitrust Law Journal* p. 826.

[104] Measuring the oligopolistic broadcasting market against a perfectly competitive market model would be a possible but entirely theoretical approach, as it hardly ever exists in the real world.

[105] E. Noam, 'Der Einfluß von Marktstruktur und Eintrittsschranken auf die Vielfalt der Fernsehprogramme', in (1977) E.-J. Mestmäcker, ed., *Offene Rundfunkordnung* (1988), at p. 208.

[106] Ibid., p. 212.

[107] Commission Notice on the definition of the relevant market for the purpose of Community competition law, *OJ* C 372, 9.12.1997.

2.4.1. *Product Market*

If all producers in an industry supplied the same product, say potatoes or wheat, establishing the product market would not be a difficult task. However, developed economies are often characterised by the production of differentiated products, such as branded or luxury goods or products targeting a particular group of consumers only. As the theory of perfect competition presumes a homogenous product, market structure in the real world may be at odds with the economic textbook concept and not fully applicable. As a rule of thumb we may say that the more heterogeneous a product is, the smaller the relevant product market will be. If we envisage the relation between Coca-Cola and a non-branded cola drink from a national retailer, can the two be considered 'the same product' to the extent that they belong to the same product market? To decide upon the relevant product market,[108] we first need to investigate the consumer's point of view. If the buyer of Coca-Cola under certain conditions switches to another cola, she considers these two products interchangeable and thus they belong to the same product market. The interchangeability of two goods can be measure by the so-called cross-price-elasticity of demand, that is, if prices for Coca-Cola increase do consumers switch to different brands of cola. If this is the case, then both products belong to the same product market because the price of one good influences demand for the other. If, on the contrary, a price increase for Coca Cola (or price decrease for another cola) does not effect demand for the other product, i.e., consumers still buy Coca Cola instead of switching to a cheaper drink, demand for Coca Cola is called inelastic and both goods constitute two distinct product markets. According to the Commission, 'the relevant product market comprises all those products and/or services which are regarded as interchangeable or substitutable by the consumer, by reason of the products' characteristics, their price and intended use'.[109]

In applying these criteria to the audio-visual sector, we need to consider the different types of television programs, such as news, fiction, sports programs and advertisements that can be transmitted via terrestrial, cable or satellite broadcasting, either analogue or digital, to name but a few. The European Commission in RTL/Veronica/Endemol stated that advertising constitutes a distinct product market,[110] but in the subsequent Decision in the Case of Bertelsmann/CLT[111] abandoned this distinction. In RTL/Veronica/Endemol,[112] the Commission clarified that

---

[108] Deciding on the relevant product market is of 'essential significance'. See Case 6/72 *Europemballage and Continental Can* v. *Commission*, [1973] ECR 215, 247; see also Cases 19 &20/74 *Kali und Salz und Kali Chemie* v. *Commission*, [1975] ECR 499.

[109] Commission Notice on the definition of the relevant market for the purpose of Community competition law, *OJ* C 372, 9.12.1997 at point II, referring to sec. 6 of Form A/B with regard to Regulation 17 and sec. 6 of Form CO with respect to Regulation 4064/89.

[110] *OJ* L 134/32, 5.6.1996.

[111] Comission Decision of 7.10.1996, IV/M.779.

[112] *OJ* L 134/32, 5.6.1996.

the broadcaster's audience share was of paramount importance in establishing if a broadcaster was dominant, regardless of whether, strictly speaking, a market for viewing television advertising in fact existed. In MSG/Media Service,[113] the Commission defined a distinct product market for Pay-TV as compared to Free-TV because the competitive conditions on the demand side are too dissimilar, and it subsequently maintained this distinction.

In the particular case of sports programs, it is suggested that not only do they constitute their own product market, distinct from other types of programs, such as news or game shows, but that there are various submarkets of particular types of sports,[114] for example, football or formula one racing. This argument is convincing as the transmission of the UEFA-Cup final, for example, is in the audience's view not regarded as interchangeable with other programs.

2.4.2. *Geographical Market*

To constitute one geographical market, conditions for suppliers and consumers in an area must be the same, or at least sufficiently similar. The Commission will first take a preliminary view of the scope of the geographic market based on broad indications, such as distribution of market shares and price differences at national or European levels. This hypothesis will then be checked against demand characteristics, e.g., national or local preferences of current patterns of purchases.[115] Generally, the Commission tends to take a broad view and to maintain that the whole common market forms the relevant geographical market.[116] But part of the common market where the incumbent products are not bought or sold to a significant extent will be disregarded.

Thus it is plain that elements such as transport costs, language barriers or consumer preferences need to be considered, because they may influence the conditions for buying and selling to an extent that will limit the geographical market. High transport costs will result in a good being less expensive if bought from a local supplier;[117] fresh dairy products can hardly be supplied from one end of the world to the other, and if I only speak German, I will not demand English or French newspapers or television programs. Apart from language barriers, differences in taste and production techniques remain significant in the single market and it appears that European consumers tend to be particularly conservative about food and

---

[113] *OJ* L 364, 31.12.1994, at paras 1 and 6.

[114] Judgement of the Restrictive Practices Court (in England and Wales), 28 July 1999, BBC/BskyB/ Premiere League, para 277.

[115] Commission Notice on the definition of the relevant market for the purpose of Community competition law, *OJ* C 372, 9.12.1997.

[116] See, for example, Case *Mitchell Cotts/Sofiltra*, *OJ* 1987 L41/31, [1988] 4 CMLR 11.

[117] For the significance of transport costs to limit the geographical market see, e.g., Commission Decision *Italian Flat Glass OJ* [1989] L 33/44, which was largely annulled on appeal in Cases T-68, T-77 and T-78/89 *Società Italaliano Vetro* v. *Commission* [1992] 5 *CMLR* 302.

its local peculiarities.[118] Local consumer habits and national regulation have repeatedly proven barriers to import, and Member States have been very reluctant to agree on mutual recognition *vis-à-vis* imported products.[119] However, it is noteworthy that the Commission, when deciding upon a geographical market for a merger or joint venture, will also consider the process of market integration, which would, in the short term, lead to wider geographic markets[120].

With regard to television, we must note that the markets remain largely national or comprise only a single language area, for example the UK and Ireland or Germany and Austria. But even extending the geographical market from the national to a language area is contestable as, for example, it was found that the Flemish-speaking part of Belgium was not sufficiently equal to the Netherlands to constitute one geographical market.[121] Prevailing cultural differences other than language may also limit the relevant geographical market. Sometimes, the Court has also left open the definitive scope of the geographical market embracing only one Member State or language area because a wider or narrower geographical market would not affect the substance of its judgement.[122]

2.4.3. *Temporal Market*

Market definitions may also change over time and it is necessary to consider its temporal quality; this may be due to fluctuating consumer demand according to the season.[123] Moreover, as mentioned above, the Commission takes a dynamic approach and considers the market against the background of single market integration[124], i.e., it will also include the potential danger of a sustained dominant position in its assessment. Especially with regard to broadcasting, the Commission in the Bertelsmann/Kirch/Premiere Case concluded that 'the intended concentration will give Premiere a dominant position on a *lasting basis* on the market in pay-TV in Germany'[125] (emphasis added) and thus prohibited the concentration.

---

[118] One could mention various food crises in the EU, for example, BSE, Dioxin and the ongoing discussion about genetically modified crops.

[119] As the most famous example may still serve the Case 120/78 *Cassis de Dijon* [1979] ECR 649.

[120] Commission Notice on the definition of the relevant market for the purpose of Community competition law, *OJ* C 372, 9 December1997.

[121] T. Jestaedt and J. Anweiler, 'Europäische Fusionskontrolle im Medienbereich', 18 *EuZW* (1997) p. 550, referring to Case IV/M.533 *RTL/Veronica/Endemol* [1996] *OJ* L 134/32.

[122] See, e.g., *Kirch/Bertelsmann/Premiere OJ* 1999 L 53/1; *Deutsche Telekom/Beta Research*, *OJ* 1999 L 53/1, at paras 22 and 101.

[123] This issue arose in the Case of United Brands 27/76, [1978] ECR 207, where it was suggested that the cross-elasticity of demand for bananas changed from season to season.

[124] Commission Notice on the definition of the relevant market for the purpose of Community competition law, *OJ* C 372, 9 December1997.

[125] *Kirch/Bertelsmann/Premiere OJ* 1999 L 53/1, para 100.

2.5. **Concluding Remarks**

> [...] [T]echnological change had [...] removed another major rationale for public regulation – the scarcity of frequencies. In this respect broadcasting no longer appeared to be a natural monopoly whose supply must be regulated. With so many possibilities for delivering broadcasting – videocassettes, cable, satellite, new terrestrial frequencies – the regulatory issues shifted to competition, efficiency and consumer preference. Broadcasting lost its distinctiveness as a field of activity and became subsumed in a wider consideration of the future information economy.[126]

Audio-visual policy and broadcasting regulation need to be assessed against the background of technological change and the industry's economic framework, in particular, market structure and the degree of competition materialising. Without considering the interaction between regulation, competition and policy, and by confining the analysis to the purely normative, one might actually miss the substantive problems broadcasting entails. The regulator enacts provisions motivated to remedy dysfunctional markets and achieve policy aims she deems desirable. Hence, to fully understand the legal framework, recourse to economic implications and the mutual influence between law and economics is indispensable.

[126] K. Dyson and P. Humphreys, 'Introduction: politics, markets and communication policies', in *The Political Economy of Communications, International and European Dimensions* (1988) p. 21.

Chapter 3
AUDIO-VISUAL AND BROADCASTING POLICY

3.1. Policy Options

> The broadcasting debate went to the very heart of how a democracy is informed.[127]

Audio-visual and broadcasting policy has always been a highly sensitive and contentious issue, not least because the last century witnessed how mass, organised propaganda was used to influence people's political opinions. Moreover, there is a close link between the media and the state as a political and cultural community. The current debate about media policy in the Member States and at the European level is still, to a certain extent, overshadowed by the reticence regarding unregulated broadcasting that prevails in most Member States. It is feared that it may 'mislead' audiences, gain political influence and result in an imbalance of information. There are a variety of policy options, ranging from outright content regulation to the virtually unregulated free play of market forces, and different regulatory systems employ various tools to achieve their policy goals. A state's media policy and especially its approach *vis-à-vis* broadcasting of foreign origin does not exist in an ideological vacuum and it can tell us much about the state of the society for which it is designed. As *Collins* put it:

> Debates about the media in Europe (...), involving culture as they do, are not only interesting because of what they reveal about different policies but also because of what they uncover about the complexes which the protagonists nurture about each other. In part, it is this which made the media policy debate so emotive and fractious.[128]

In general, social communication can be defined as transmission of a valued experience,[129] i.e., something is broadcast that is considered worth being brought to the attention of others; but it leaves unanswered the question of whose experience is more valued than others[130] and chosen as a program, because there is never enough airtime to transmit all the experiences of every individual. *Dyson* distinguishes between three basic concepts of social communication, which can each be linked to a

---

[127] K. Dyson in K. Dyson and Humphreys, P., *Broadcasting and New Media Policies in Western Europe* (1988) p. 62.

[128] R. Collins, *Broadcasting and Audio-Visual Policy in the European Single Market* (1994) p. 15.

[129] R. Williams, *The long revolution* (1965) p. 42.

[130] K. Dyson in K. Dyson and P. Humphreys, *Broadcasting and New Media Policies in Western Europe* (1988) p. 63.

distinct ideological background.[131] Social communication can be viewed as the protection of good taste (1), the distribution of information and the sharing of experience according to individual choice (2), or the distribution of information and the sharing of experience according to individual need (3). Social communications as the protection of good taste is conservative as it aims to maintain inherited values and to preserve the social order from disruption. It is a static concept which prescribes how people should view themselves and behave on the basis of tradition, whereas the second option refers to the individual's preference deriving from someone's personal interests. These interests may take different forms, from art exhibitions to game shows, and may clash with the content that spectators associated with the first concept expect. There can be a certain overlap where society and the individual share the same taste, but we cannot expect them to correspond to any significant degree. The third model differs from the second in the sense that it assumes that media content is insufficient, i.e., the public need to be informed about something without individually desiring it. The third notion holds that society agrees that some services (such as education or political information) are valuable and should be provided regardless of individual demand.[132] If the broadcaster aims to achieve all these needs, the result will be ambiguity if not contradiction.

Considering the model of society corresponding to each of the three concepts of social communication, the first envisages society as a hierarchical order with a 'natural' division into ranks. People of the highest rank possess the largest share of good taste and are correspondingly especially responsible to uphold and protect cultural excellence. Barbarism, provincialism and fragmentation of the social order are to be avoided. It is hardly surprising that this concept particularly appealed to the insecure German élite after World War II. The second model regards society as a competitive market without any 'natural' or fixed structure; society is viewed as composed of the interaction of autonomous and independent individuals. This model is characterised by a somewhat optimistic view of human nature and tends to equate social welfare with consumer welfare. Last is the model of society as a cooperative community, one large unit bound together by mutual dependence. The emphasis lies on facilitating communication between different groups and individuals by ensuring equal access to broadcasting and fostering a sense of solidarity instead of conflict.

Throughout this chapter, I will demonstrate according to which criteria various states shape their national media policy and how they relate to the models outlined above. Special emphasise will be give to the EU's media policy and particularities of the supra-national level.

---

131 Ibid., pp. 65 et seq.

132 This concept clearly resembles the rational for merit goods. See *supra* at 2.2.

3.2. **Public Service Broadcasting**

3.2.1. *Traditional Public Service Broadcasting*

Public broadcasting must make the popular worthwhile and the worthwhile popular.[133]

Before the emergence of private broadcasting, western European television was shaped as an 'ethic of comprehensiveness',[134] embracing multiple goals, such as education, information and entertainment; range, quality and popularity.[135] Public service broadcasters were given fairly broadly-worded mandates and a considerable amount of freedom and authority to perform their duty to provide audiences with a diverse and pluralistic program.

Definitions of public service broadcasting can be divided between 'inductive' and 'deductive' approaches, the former referring to public broadcasting via codification what *is* and the latter focusing on what it *ought* to be;[136] for example, *Blumler*[137] offer an inductive view whereas *Garnham*[138] and *Keane*[139] suggest a deductive, theoretical approach. *Tracy.*[140] identifies eight main characteristics of public service broadcasting, and his definition may also be considered deductive: (1) universality of availability, regardless of income etc. (2) university of appeal (something for everyone – from specialist to mainstream) (3) provision for minorities (4) serving the public sphere,[141] (5) commitment towards education (6) distance from vested interests (7) encourage competition in program quality rather than numbers of viewers (8) liberate rather than restrict the program-makers

Because of television's public service role, further scrutiny has to be directed towards the relation between broadcasting and politics. *Kelly* identified three systems regarding the interaction of television and a state's politics: (a) formally autonomous systems with mechanisms for distancing political organs from broadcasting, as, for example in Britain, Ireland or Sweden, (b) politics-in-broadcasting systems, in which the governing bodies of broadcasting organisations include party representatives and other social groups, e.g., in Germany, Denmark and Belgium, and finally, (c) politics-over-broadcasting systems, where state organs can directly

---

[133] Alasdair Milner, Director-General of the BBC in the 1980s, cited in J.G. Blumler, ed., *Television and the public interest. Valuable interests at stake* (1992) p. 11.

[134] Ibid., p. 7.

[135] T.J. Nossiter, 'British Television; A Mixed Economy', in *Research on the Range and Quality of Broadcasting Services* (1986) pp. 1-71.

[136] R. Collins, *From Satellite to Single Market. New Communication technology and European public service television* (1998) p. 53.

[137] Op. cit. n. 135.

[138] 'The media and the public sphere', in C. Calhoun, ed., *Habermas and the Public Sphere* (1992).

[139] *The Media and Democracy* (Cambridge, Cambridge Polity, 1991).

[140] *The Decline and Fall of Public Service Broadcasting* (1988) pp. 26 et seq.

[141] Public Service Broadcasting was meant to foster national identity and 'allow a nation to speak to itself', see R. Hoggart, 'The Public Service Idea' in *British Broadcasting: Main Principles* (1983) p. 5.

intervene into the broadcasting business, such as in Greece, Italy and France in the past.[142]

All of these concepts can be considered 'European' and differ from the US model, where from public broadcasting from the Thirties onwards enjoyed a much less influential role. The US approach to broadcasting could be characterised as follows: '[F]ree radio and a free democracy are inseparable; [...] we cannot be a controlled radio and remain a democracy; [...] when a free radio goes, so also goes free speech, free press, freedom of worship and freedom of education'.[143]

3.2.2. *A New Role for Public Service Broadcasting*

In Western Europe during the 1980s, the broadcasting sector experienced considerable change. New communication technologies (most notably cable and satellite) transformed the former monopolistic television systems into a service industry offering vastly expanded channel capacity and the possibility of simultaneous transmission.[144] The cultural mission became more ambiguous and the interpretation of the public service role of television in Britain was redefined:

> It is a good general principle that any service to the public should be designed to promote its satisfaction. If this principle is to govern the provision of a service, it can be shown that, provided certain conditions are fulfilled, the public are best served if able to buy the amount of the service required from suppliers who compete for custom through price and quality.[145]

Similarly, the concept of quality that had previously been merely assumed to automatically result from protecting broadcasting from market forces, had to be reassessed, and it was found that it has 'multiple meanings'.[146] It was, for example, suggested that quality was best understood as 'a relation between sets of [programme] characteristics and sets of [assessment] values', which cannot be reduced to some single criterion.[147] The decisive criterion is not that a particular quality criterion should prevail but that quality as such is a priority goal, and a wide-ranging spectrum of several types of excellence should be encouraged.[148] Against this back-

---

[142] M. Kelly, 'Influences on Broadcasting Policies for Election Coverage', in J.G. Blumer, ed., *Communicating to Voters: Television in The First European Parliamentary Elections* (1983) pp. 65-82.

[143] D. Sarnoff, 'Broadcasting in the American Democracy', in C.S. Marsh, ed., *Educational Broadcasting 1936* (1937) pp. 146-155.

[144] J.G. Blumler in J.G. Blumler, ed. (1882) p. 14, 15.

[145] Peacock Committee, *Report of the Committee on Financing the BBC* (1986) Cmnd 9824, London: HMSO.

[146] S. Ishikawa and Y. Murmatsu, 'Quality Assessment of Broadcast Programming: Resarch Subjects for the Future', 27 *Studies in Broadcasting* (1991) p. 209.

[147] K.H. Rosengren *et al*, 'Quality in Programming. Views from the North Studies' in *Broadcasting* (1991) p. 50.

[148] J.G. Blumler in J.G. Blumler (ed.), p. 31.

ground, public service television should no longer offer the whole range of programs the audience may desire but only provide services that the market could not supply, because demand was too weak. Thus, public broadcasting should compete on a *complementary* basis with private broadcasters by offering a truly different mix of programming.[149] Although assigning such a new role to public service television appears to make sense, some legal systems clearly chose a different way; for example, German media law[150] provides for a so-called 'basic supply' (*Grundversorgung*), maintaining that the whole program range and not only niche programs that cannot be produced by private broadcasters, must be offered by public service broadcasters. [151]

3.3. **Self-Regulation**

Besides broadcasting regulation in the strict sense of the word, covering a state's (or supranational body's) legislative measures by imposing restrictions and duties on broadcasters, growing concern is also directed towards self-regulation. This mainly results from tendencies from the so-called 'New Media', especially the Internet, computing and on-line publishing industries, where self-regulation from the very beginning played an important role. Traditional regulation of the 'New Media' often failed because it was even unclear which national authority was competent to regulate content.

3.3.1. *Self-Regulation at National Level*

If we scrutinise national regulation we can identify various aspects of self-regulation with regard to specific media such as the press, the broadcasting sector or new information and communication services directed at the public.[152] With regard to public service and commercial broadcasting, Greece and Italy, for example, employ codes of conduct for journalists.[153] A certain degree of self-regulatory character can also be ascribed to the United Kingdom,[154] where the Broadcasting Standards Commission exercises outside control by drawing up a Code of Guidance on Fairness and Privacy Matters (Fairness and Privacy Code).[155] In the public service

---

[149] J.G. Blumler & Hoffmann-Riem in J.G. Blumler, ibid., p. 206.

[150] See in detail *infra* at 3.4.3.

[151] See, for example, E.-J. Mestmäcker, ed., *Offene Rundfunkordnung. Prinzipien für den grenzüberschreitenden Rundfunk* (1988) p. 33.

[152] J. Bröhmer and J. Ukrow, *Self-Regulation of the Media in Europe. A Comparative Legal Study*, prepared at the request of the Federal Government for Cultural Affairs and the Media (1999) Saarbrücken.

[153] Ibid., p. 65.

[154] N. Mc Lean, 'Self-regulation in the Broadcasting Sector', (1998) *Council of Europe* SEM 3 no. 13.

[155] Bröhmer and Ukrow, op. cit n. 152, p. 66.

sector, most legislation prescribe a duty to the public broadcaster to serve the general public.[156] Austria is an interesting example of how far the freedom of the broadcaster to fulfil the role assigned to it, can actually reach. The Austrian Broadcasting Company (ORF) is a self-regulatory body and its tasks are regulated by the Austrian Broadcasting Law (*Rundfunkgesetz*).[157] As the ORF is bound by constitutional law and the sovereign, i.e., the Austrian people are at the same time the audience, it is taken for granted that the ORF will use its guaranteed liberties (only) to fulfil its programming duties.[158]

In the UK, the BBC is directed by the Board of Governors who are appointed by the Queen on the recommendation of the Prime Minister. It submits an annual report and is accountable to Parliament, which must also approve the licence fee, and consent is often preceded by a lively public discussion.[159] This acts as a system of checks and balances.[160]

However, it appears that self-regulation is a comparatively underdeveloped tool in the field of commercial broadcasting, and although on its face public service broadcasting employs self-regulatory measures as illustrated above, it is plain that the proximity to official authorities is very close. One can argue about whether this can, in fact, be qualified as self-regulation. For example, the Austrian Broadcasting Law (RFG), in Article 7, Sections 1 and 3, prescribes that most of the members of its Board of Trustees ('Kuratorium') are appointed by the Government, according to (party-) political aspects, and in Article 7, Section 2 that some members are to be named by the local authorities ('Länder'). The Prime Minster recommends the BBC's Board of Governor. Hence, ties with official authorities, and one might conclude with the political establishment, can expected to be rather close. This system is much less developed than self-regulation of the press, that in most countries is much more 'genuine' in the sense that it is distant from government.[161] Freedom of the press is a necessary precondition for functioning self-regulation and against the background of still heavily regulated national broadcasting systems. It does not come as a surprise that there is simply little room left for self-regulation.

---

[156] See e.g., Art. 7, sec. 1 of the Danish Broadcasting Law of 7 Jan 1994 in the version of 24 June 1994.

[157] *BGBl.* (Austrian Law Gazette) 1984/379, in the version of 1984/531 and 1985/563, as amended by 1987/606, 1991/10 and 1993/505.

[158] Bröhmer/Ukrow, op. cit. n. 152, p. 71.

[159] See, for example, the discussion about an additional levy of £ 24 to finance BBC digital television. *Financial Times online*: 'BBC: Digital will need £ 730 more by 2007', 3 November 1999; 'BBC; MPs attack over spending on News 24', 26 November 1999; 'BBC: Kaufmann brings little festive cheer', 21 November 1999.

[160] Bröhmer and Ukrow, op. cit. n. 152, p. 76.

[161] Ibid., p. 63. Although the printed press is subsidised in Austria and France.

3.3.2. *Self-Regulation in the EU*

The Commission's 'Green Paper on Regulatory Implications'[162] introduces self-regulation as an alternative to licensing in the IT and computing areas. It refers to some commentators, who argue for lighter regulation across the whole converged industry following the example of the Internet, where in the context of harmful content, the application of general law has given way to self-regulation. With increased convergence between the Internet, computing and broadcasting, these tendencies will also become significant with regard to the latter. The Commission highlights that this is not without risk for the Internal Market because of the potential technical divergence self-regulation may cause, and argues for some degree of coordination at Community level. Moreover, self-regulation would not provide sufficient guarantees to consumers.[163] In general, the Commission's approach in the Green Paper can be qualified as quite reluctant, and it is plain that self-regulation will merely be understood as complementary to traditional regulation. Additionally, the Council, in its conclusion of 27 September 1999,[164] recognises the role of self-regulation in new media services (rec. 3), and notes that it can usefully complement regulation in the context of future development (rec. 4). But it also clarifies in rec. 5 that 'public interest objectives and the choice of the best way to reach these objectives remains inherently the responsibility of Member States, without prejudice to Community law'.

It appears that both the Commission and the Council consider self-regulation not with regard to broadcasting but within the context of new media, most notably the Internet. Hence, it will become significant for broadcasting only if that convergence will advance considerably in the future, ultimately blurring the distinction between watching television 'the traditional way' and over the Internet. But even on this assumption, the role of self-regulation at Community level will be limited and will exclude public-interest considerations, which are likely to remain exclusively within the Member States' competence.

3.4. **Specific Country's Examples**

The following is intended as a brief overview, highlighting some of the characteristics of national media policies, starting with the US, because its media policy is distinct from European countries' approaches and thus provides a valuable contrast.

---

[162] Green Paper on the Convergence of the Telecommunications, Media and Information Technology Sectors, and the Implications for Regulation towards and Information Society Approach, 97 *COM* 623.

[163] Ibid., point IV.2.2. 'Market entry and Licensing'.

[164] Council Conclusion on the role of self-regulation in the light of the development of new media services, *OJ* 1999 L283/3.

3.4.1. *Media Regulation in the US*

A strong reluctance about any state interference into the media or the kind of content regulation that is common in Europe prevails in the US. Freedom of speech and, resulting from it, the free press, is protected by the First Amendment and governmental supervision of the media is considered irreconcilable with this provision:

> Indeed, entrusting government with the power to assure media access entails at least three dangers; the danger of deterring those items of coverage that will trigger duties of affording access at the media's expense; the danger of inviting manipulation of the media by whichever bureaucrats are entrusted to assure access; and the danger of escalating from access regulation to much more dubious exercise of governmental control.[165]

Thus, there is little government intervention into the media. At the federal level, it was first introduced with the Interstate Commerce Commission (1887), which was later preceded by the Federal Radio Commission (1927) and, since 1934, the Federal Communications Commission (FCC).[166] With the Federal Communications Act 1934 (FCA),[167] Congress established a governmental expert agency to occupy the field of telecommunications at the federal level, governed by a single regulatory regime.[168] In the common law tradition, regulation is not so much governmental action directed towards a specific, well-defined aim (as may be the case in Europe) but much more a process to solve conflicts without envisaging a certain outcome.[169] In other words, it is open as to the achievable solution, which should first and foremost be acceptable for all parties involved. It is less important that formally established principles are observed in such a solution.

Within the FCC, only a small fraction (the Mass Media Bureau, about 350 of its total 1800 employees) deals with radio and television. Regarding its substantive provisions, it is noteworthy that the FCA forbids foreigners from owning a US television station,[170] he or she must first become a US citizen.[171] Moreover, formerly, cross-ownership between press and broadcasting undertakings was prohibited and one undertaking could not operate more than two stations within the same market, that is, more than a broadcasting and a radio station respectively (duopoly-rule). However, since 1992, these provisions have been somewhat watered down.

---

[165] L. Tribe, *American Constitutional Law*, 2nd ed. (1988) p. 1002.

[166] H.J. Kleinsteuber, 'Regulierung des Rundfunks in den USA. Zur Kontrolle wirtschaftlicher Macht am Beispiel der FCC', *Rundfunk und Fernsehen* No. 1 (1996) p. 31.

[167] 47 U.S.C. § 151 (1934).

[168] *Cooperative Communications, Inc.* v. *AT&T Corp.*, 867 F. Supp. 1511 (D. Utah 1994).

[169] Kleinsteuber, op. cit. n. 166, p. 29.

[170] Sec. 310 (a) FCA.

[171] K.M. Mc Donald, 'How would you like your television: with or without borders and with or without culture – A new approach to media regulation in the European Union', in 22 *Fordh. Int. L J* (1991) pp. 99, at 2016.

The so-called fin-syn-rules (financial interest and syndication rules) prevented the three largest networks, CBS, NBC and ABC, from vertically integrating and setting up large production companies; instead, network-independent companies produced the important TV-serials.[172] These restrictions were gradually abandoned by 1995[173] on the grounds that, first, increasing convergence enhances competition, which, in turn, necessitates new alliances and, second, media concentration in Europe must be counterbalanced by US media undertakings.

Besides the formal regulatory framework, it is well-known that media undertakings in the US are also faced with numerous private interests and pressure groups – so-called media watchdogs – which aim to ensure fair and balanced information.[174] In a case in the 1950s, a TV station transmitted discriminatory programs and the FCC was finally forced by the Court of Appeal to deny it a licence.[175] Citizens' actions have repeatedly been successful in intervening into FCC decisions.[176] Consumer groups called on regulators in Washington to block the AOL/Time Warner merger because they saw Internet competition endangered.[177] The general openness and transparency of the FCC, which is typical of most US-regulatory bodies, acts as an additional tool of public control.[178]

In addition to the specific sector regulation by the FCC, the broadcasting industry is also subject to general anti-trust control. Competition law in the US has had a much longer tradition than in Europe and goes back as far as the Sherman Act of 1890, which was issued in reaction to large railway companies clustering in 'trusts' and establishing a dominant position on the market to the detriment of consumers. However, anti-trust measures in the telecommunication sector have not been taken on a regular basis although, for example, in 1982, the telephone-monopolist AT&T was forced to divest its conglomerate.[179] The case of Microsoft, where the US District Court of Columbia ordered divestiture of the company, is a more recent example.[180] Unlike *ex ante* EC merger control, under the Sherman Act, it is possible to break up companies that are found to be abusing their dominant position.

As to the relationship between the freedom of speech guaranteed in the First Amendment and competition law, the Supreme Court, in the landmark case of *US* v.

---

172 H.J. Kleinsteuber, op. cit. n. 166, p. 35.

173 D.L. Teeter and D.R. Le Duc, *Law of Mass Communications. Freedom and Control of Print and Broadcast Media* (1995) pp. 767 et seq.

174 S. Ruß-Mohl, 'Kontrolle der Kontrolleure', *Journalist* No. 2 (1994) p. 41.

175 *Office of Communication of the Church of Christ* v. *FCC*, 425 F.2d 543 (D.C.Cir. 1969).

176 Kleinsteuber, op. cit. n. 166, p. 39.

177 *Financial Times online*, 'AOL/TW merger faces test', 3 March 2000.

178 Ibid., p. 40.

179 H.J. Kleinsteuber, 'Telecommunikationspolitik und Deregulierung in den USA: Der Fall American Telephone & Telegraph (AT&T)', *Rundfunk und Fernsehen*, No. 2 (1987) pp. 151-168. The proceedings against Microsoft may serve as a more recent example.

180 Case annotation, 'Richter Penfield Jackson verurteilt Microsoft zur Spaltung', 9 *RIW* (2000) pp. 714-719.

Associated Press[181] decided that the First Amendment did not provide an exemption to the application of the Sherman Act; indeed, the opposite was true: the First Amendment presumed that a free flow of information and the exchange of opinions is not impeded by restrictions of competition by private parties. The First Amendment could not be read as affording private cartels the permission to interfere with the freedom of speech.[182]

The US media sector[183] has experienced fundamental change with the appearance of the broadband cable and increased convergence.[184] It is noteworthy that the US recently loosened the application of merger controls by abandoning restrictions on vertical integration; obviously to facilitate strategic alliances. In the light of harsh US criticism of 'projectionist' European audio-visual policy,[185] this appears somewhat contradictory and surprising.

3.4.2. *Broadcasting Regulation in the UK*

We aim to be the world's most creative and trusted broadcaster and program maker, seeking to satisfy all our audiences in the UK with services that inform, educate and entertain and then enrich their lives in ways that the market alone will not.[186]

3.4.2.1. The Legal Framework

The British Broadcasting system and, in particular, the British Broadcasting Corporation (BBC) as its main actor, is considered one of the most quality-oriented in the world and is often admired for the successful export of its programs. It also acted as a blueprint to the German System established after World War II and today still embodies a quite distinct and arguably well-developed approach towards broadcasting. The media landscape of the UK is to a large extent determined by its public service broadcaster, the BBC, which was established in 1927.[187] The BBC is strongly committed to its public service function, established by the Royal Charter as a legal basis. The Royal Charter was initially in force for ten years and has not been fundamentally changed subsequently, and can be described as enabling, rather than regulatory. It is granted from the Crown and accompanied by a licence from the Post-

---

181 327 US 1 (1945).

182 E.-J. Mestmäcker, *Recht und ökonomisches Gesetz. Über die Grenzen von Staat, Gesellschaft und Privatautonomie*, 2nd ed (1984), p. 260.

183 For a comprehensive analysis of the US Media's influence on foreign television see, for example, K. Segrave, *American Television Abroad. Hollywood's Attempt to Dominate World Televsion* (1998).

184 See in detail M. Esser-Wellié, *Das Verfassungs- und Wirtschaftsrecht der Breitbandkommunikation in den Vereinigten Staaten von Amerika. Zusammenhänge zwischen technischer Konvergenz und Wettbewerb* (1995).

185 See *infra* at 3.5.3.6.

186 'The BBC Beyond 2000 – our future role', see BBC online, http://www.bbc.co.uk/info/news/2000, visited 21 February 2000.

187 Its predecessor, the British Broadcasting Company, dates back to 1922.

master-General. The licence gives rather wide powers to the government although these have seldom been used.[188] Unlike other European public service broadcasters who are partly financed by advertising, it is entirely financed by the compulsory licence fee.[189] The BBC is obliged to fulfil its tasks of transmitting information, educational and entertainment programs, in that order of importance.[190] It carries full responsibility for its productions and is only bound by the duty to provide balanced and impartial news and political programs.[191] The first public television service was launched in 1936.

Commercial broadcasting in the UK, in the form of Independent Television (ITV), was introduced in 1954. Since the 1950s, the system of licensing private ITV corporations has essentially remained unchanged; the private ITV companies apply for licences which are granted for a period up to eight years for a specific area within the UK and, if successful, the licensee is granted a monopoly for the region. ITVs are obliged to include into their program 'proper proportions' of productions particularly interesting for the residents of that area.[192] The program content is regulated by the Independent Television Commission (ITC) on the basis of the Broadcasting Acts of 1990 and 1996. Notably, the Broadcasting Act of 1996 introduced ownership limitations based on audience share rather than the number of licences held. Holdings are restricted to 15 percent of audience share. Moreover, the 1996 Act introduced cross-media ownership rules between newspaper publishers and terrestrial TV licensees to ensure that they do not operate against the public interest.[193]

3.4.2.2. Policy Developments

From its birth in 1922, British broadcasting defined itself partly in opposition to the 'American experience'. The perception of the US broadcasting system – which was characterised by a large number of channels – was found to be 'a sort of chaos',[194] which was not desirable for the UK. Moreover, British broadcasting policy was influenced by distrust for what the opinion-élite called 'commercialism'. The pioneer of British television, John Reith, the first Director-General of the BBC, was

---

[188] S. Hearst, 'Broadcasting Regulation in Britain', in J.G. Blumler, ed., *Television and the Public Interest* (1992) p. 63.

[189] Ridder, *Die Rolle des öffentlich-rechtlichen Rundfunks im kommerzialisierten Mediensystem Zukunkftsstrategien der BBC* (1993) p. 155.

[190] V. Wiedemann, 'Der Zugang zum Rundfunk in Großbritannien', in E.-J. Mestmäcker, ed., *Offene Rundfunkordnung. Prinzipien für den grenzüberschreitenden Rundfunk* (1988) p. 90.

[191] See Home Office, ed., 'Broadcasting: Copy of the Licence and Agreement Dated the 2nd Day of April 1981 between Her Majesty's Secretary of State for the Home Department and the British Broadcasting Corporation' (1981) Preamble and Annexes.

[192] Wiedemann, op. cit. n. 190, p. 91.

[193] http://www.itc.org.uk/regulation/ownership/index.htm, visited 7 September 2000.

[194] Postmaster-General in a reply to a Parliamentary Question in April 1992, cited in S. Hearst, 'Broadcasting Regulation in Britain', in J.G. Blumler, ed., *Television and the Public Interest* (1992) p 62.

determined that broadcasting must not be used for entertainment purposes only.[195] In a personal memorandum, he wrote the oft-quoted sentence: 'He who prides himself in giving what he thinks the public wants is often creating a fictitious demand for lower standards which he will then satisfy.'[196] The BBC, from the very beginning, defined itself as committed to inform, educate and entertain.

Following its successful start, in 1936, the Ullswater Committee recommended extending the BBC Charter for another ten years.[197] With the beginning of the Second World War, government switched off the television service and had originally planned to take over the BBC, but ultimately shied away from this option, not least as a tribute to its special position. However, employees received detailed instructions on how to proceed in wartime. After the war, the BBC emerged strengthened, both at home and abroad, and television service resumed its activities in 1946. During the fifties, British broadcasting – which had won national trust – attracted the best minds and talents of the country, many of them Oxbridge-educated, which resulted in transforming British television into the Fourth Estate, a position denied to the British press, which has always been dominated by tabloids.

With the advent of a new conservative government under Winston Churchill during the Second World War, the forecast of the introduction of commercial television caused a great deal of national controversy[198] Commercial broadcasting was finally introduced in 1954, and although it was to be financed by advertising, it fell under the same public service obligation to inform, educate and entertain its audience.[199] In 1962, the Pilkington Committee recommended the award of a second television network to the BBC, and subsequently the new Channel BBC 2 was opened in 1964.[200]

With the major impact of the 1960s' youth culture on society, broadcasting changed considerably, BBC radio chose more 'modern' music, and, for the first time, games shows appeared on television. Although the legacy of Reith's vision remained strong within the BBC, two different groups – the 'pragmatists' and 'platonists' – could be distinguished.[201] The latter stressed the broadcaster's role to lead rather than to follow. The Pilkington Report of 1962 heavily criticised the triviality and debasement of standards that had followed the arrival of commercial

---

[195] S. Hearst, 'Broadcasting Regulation in Britain', in J.G. Blumler, ed., *Television and the Public Interest* (1992) pp. 62, 63.

[196] Quoted in A. Briggs, *The History of Broadcasting in the United Kingdom: The Birth of Broadcasting*, Vol. 1 (1961) p. 334.

[197] Ullswater Committee 'Report of the Broadcasting Committee' (1936) *Cmnd* 4798. London HMSO.

[198] S. 'Hearst, Broadcasting Regulation in Britain', in J.G. Blumler, ed., *Television and the Public Interest*' (1992) pp. 64 et seq.

[199] Wiedemann, op. cit. n. 190, p. 91.

[200] Hearst, op. cit. n. 188, p. 69.

[201] See the distinction in T. Burns, *The BBC: Public Institution and Private World* (1977).

television.[202] In contrast, the Hobart Papers[203] suggested a model of social communication as the satisfaction of individual preferences. They were based on Adam Smith's model of society as a competitive market and did not consider broadcasting as a 'public good' but believed in its duty to maximise consumer welfare, a concept best realised by 'pay-per-view' television. This view was later taken up by the Peacock Report of 1986,[204] which was heavily influenced by Samuel Brittan of the *Financial Times*. It criticised the inflation of broadcasting costs caused by the monopoly position of the ITV, and the BBC's arrogance and complacency.[205] Interestingly, the Report did not deliver the proposal to introduce advertising to the BBC, as the Prime Minister had wished, but instead focused on the key role to be accorded to subscription and 'pay-per-view'. This would discourage broadcasters from chasing mass audiences and lowering program standards.[206] The Report was heavily criticised, not least because it seemed too long term for political horizons, but it did play an important role in reshaping broadcasting policy in the 1980s.

3.4.2.3. Current Status

The UK is the first Western European country where pay television[207] played a more than negligible role in the broadcasting sector. The 1980s and 1990s were characterised by moving from a 'communitarian' to a market-based model. Notwithstanding this development, 'a chronic state of disagreement (...) reflecting the fluidity of modern society'[208] on what broadcasting should offer and how it should be regulated remains. The tendency towards a market-based concept has been reinforced by technological change, which facilitates defending the free-market approach. It also, to some extent, advocates rethinking the legacy of financing the BBC. The new Director, Gregory Dyke, is expected to cut back much of the structure put in place by his predecessor, Sir John Bird, who had reorganised the BBC in 1996 with the assistance of McKinsey consultants.[209] In particular, he intends to abolish the umbrella directorates embracing both television and radio, and introduce roughly 15 smaller directorates, focusing on particular areas, such as sport or education.[210]

---

[202] Pilkington Committee *Report of the Committee on Broadcasting 1960* (1982) HSMO London.

[203] W. Altman et al., 'TV: from monopoly to competition', 15 *Hobart Paper* (1962) Institute of Economic Affairs, London; S. Caine, 'Paying for TV', 43 *Hobart Paper* (1968) Institute of Economic Affairs, London; C. Veljanovksi/W. Bishop, 'Choice by cable: the economics of a new era in television', *Hobart Paper* 96 (1983) Institute for Economic Affairs, London.

[204] Peacock Committee *Report of the Committee on Financing the BBC* (1986) Cmnd 9824, London: HMSO.

[205] K. Dyson in K. Dyson/P. Humphreys, pp. 75, 76.

[206] Ibid., p. 77.

[207] The exclusive transmission of sports events facilitated the development of pay-TV and will in the light of future convergence between television and the Internet remain a decisive element. See e.g. *Financial Times online* 'BSky B and NTL both boost Sports Internet' 7.2.2000.

[208] K. Dyson in K. Dyson/P. Humphreys, p. 83.

[209] *Financial Times online* 24.12.1999; 'Media: BBC faces sweeping reforms'.

[210] *Financial Times online* 2.4.2000; 'BBC overhaul to free £ 100 for programmes'.

The BBC's claim for an additional levy of £24 for subscribers of digital television was rejected by Parliament. Government wants closer public scrutiny of the BBC in the future, and it will have to undergo public consultation before it introduces new services.[211] But, regardless of future developments in the field of television, the BBC still considers itself one of the core cultural institutions in the UK. It presumes that, even in the age of convergence, there will remain a place for public broadcasting, delivering trustworthy information and granting access to high-quality program to everyone.[212] This opinion is apparently also shared by the audiences, as the market share of BBC news programs has remained stable over the years.[213]

Regarding commercial broadcasting, Pay-TV, which has been especially successful in the UK as compared to other European states, will increase in importance. Digital television will be gradually introduced and, for example, the Pay-TV-provider BSkyB claimed that, by the end of 1999, digital already outnumbered analogue subscriptions.[214]

3.4.3. *Broadcasting Regulation in Germany*

3.4.3.1. The Legal Framework: 'Dual Broadcasting Order' (Duale Rundfunkordnung)

After World War II and the experience of propaganda in the 'Third Reich', the Allies considered establishing an independent broadcasting system of paramount importance to assist the transformation of Germany into a stable Western democracy. The BBC, in its public service role, served as a model but the actual shape of the German broadcasting order is unique. The underlying rational of the new system was the desire to embody and represent the diversity inherent in society.[215] Broadcasting was financed by user fees, and from the mid-50s onwards, supplemented by advertising revenue. After decades of intensive and controversial debate,[216] private radio and television stations finally started operating in Germany in 1984,[217] and the 'dual broadcasting order' was established. It should be stressed that, within the German Federal structure, the Federal Government itself has no jurisdiction over the broadcasting sector within Germany, because this falls into the competence of the formerly 11, now 16 states ('Länder'). Accordingly, broadcasting regulation is fractionated and treaties between the states – the so-called inter-

---

211 *Financial Times online* 21.2.2000: 'Tough love for the BBC'.

212 *Robin Foster*, BBC Director of Strategy and Development in a Speech on 2.12.1999 at the 11th European Television and Film Forum in Prague.

213 At about 5.2 m, see *Financial Times online,* 'ITV under fire', 2.3.2000.

214 *Financial Times online* 9.2.2000: 'BSkyB: Broadcaster expects rapid digital service growth'.

215 See in detail:H. Bausch, *Rundfunkpolitik nach 1945* (1980) Vol. 1, Munich, dtv.

216 P. Humphreys, 'Media and Media Policy in West Germany: The Press and Broadcasting since 1945' (1990) New York, p. 195 et seq.

217 W. Hoffmann-Riem, 'Protecting Vulnerable Values in the German Broadcasting Order' in: J.G. Blumler, ed., 'Television and the Public Interest' (1992) Sage Publications, New York, p. 43.

state treaties[218] (*Rundfunkstaatsverträge*) – are necessary to facilitate co-ordination.

In general, the Federal Constitutional Court has had a decisive influence in shaping German television regulation. Its case law on Article 5 of the German Basic Law (*Grundgesetz*) provides for the basic right of freedom of communication. The Federal Constitutional Court consistently held that the legislator should specify the structure of the broadcasting order by law, which must ensure the free formation of individual and public opinion.[219] It clearly envisaged a broadcasting order that is generally referred to as 'internal pluralism' (*Binnenpluralismus*).[220] The underlying idea is a corporatist model whereby political, religious and other social groups are represented in the broadcasting authorities. The Court assumes that this will result in balanced information and ensure that a broad range of opinions is available for the viewer/listener. Broadcasting is thus viewed as a democratic process where all relevant groups need to be represented. This approach can be contrasted with the concept of 'external pluralism' (*Außenpluralismus*[221]), where the main concern is to create economic conditions where potentially everyone interested can start broadcasting, without any government interference.

In a judgement of 1981,[222] the Court held that private broadcasting and the 'dual order' was not anti-constitutional in itself, but the way that the subject is approached, i.e., asking if commercial broadcasting is *allowed* at all, demonstrates the Court's reluctance *vis-à-vis* private broadcasting. Trying to preserve constitutional continuity and ensure the effective application of the law, the Court developed a hybrid regulatory concept. Commercial broadcasters were regulated by a system derived from a public organisational model which was inspired by a social purpose. This resulted in a tension between two inherently different regulatory approaches. Arguably, the broadcasting debate has opened up the contradictions inherent in the German 'social market economy'.[223]

Mestmäcker contrasts German with US jurisprudence and concludes that, whereas US-Courts considered independent private television as fulfilling the freedom of speech safeguarded in the First Amendment, the German Federal Constitutional Court held that private broadcasting endangered pluralism and that, even those who,

---

[218] See in more detail e.g., W.D. Ring, *Medienrecht. Rundfunk. Neue Medien, Presse* (München, Verlag für Verwaltungspraxis, 1990).

[219] BVerfGE 61, Judgment of 28.2.; BVerfGE 71, Judgment of 27.7.; BVerfGE 73, Judgment of 5.6.; BVerfGE 81, Judgment of 16.6.

[220] See e.g. H. Baumann, *Die Dienstleistungsfreiheit auf dem Gebiet der audiovisuellen Medien im Rahmen des GATS im Spannungsfeld von Marktfreiheit und kutureller Selbstbestimung der Staaten der Europaeischen Union* (1998) Berlin, p. 155.

[221] Ibid., p. 155.

[222] BVerfGE 81, Judgment of 16.6.

[223] V. Porter, and S. Hasselbach, *Pluralism, Politics and the Marketplace. The Regulation of German Broadcasting*, (1991) London and New York, p. 185.

technically don't receive public broadcasting, have to pay for it.[224] German public service television is obliged to offer the widest variety of programs possible (*Vollprogramm*)[225] to cater for all groups of viewers. The Federal Constitutional Court held that, within the dual broadcasting order, public broadcasting must fulfil the 'basic supply' (*Grundversorgung*) with television programs and that public broadcasters must thus be enabled to fulfil this task by receiving the necessary financial contribution.[226]

3.4.3.2. The German Broadcasting Discussion

Broadcasting has been a 'hot issue' in German legal and political debate for years. The representatives of a 'market-reluctant' approach, for example, repeatedly claimed that, between the functioning of a broadcasting market and economic competition, *strictu sensu*, 'structural differences'[227] prevailed which would justify a specific approach to broadcasting. This is also mirrored by the assertion that public competition can exist without economic competition[228] and that it may even be easier to guarantee diversity in a system protected from market forces. It is presumed that pluralism is better achieved by 'internal pluralism' because 'external pluralism' is open to the outcome of the interaction process and hence cannot guarantee a balanced pattern of the opinions represented. The fact that the same obviously does not apply to the press is justified by the inherent differences between the two media.[229] In particular with regard to the free movement of services (now Article 49 EC Treaty), some authors questioned whether the European approach offers guarantees of pluralism equivalent to the German legal framework[230] as well as its validity in the light of German constitutional law.[231] This approach, and its apparent desire for content-regulation, have been criticised as a paternalist and élitist concern, which imagines viewers as immature and 'telly-glued' recipients.[232]

On the other hand, market-oriented writers stress the tendency of the German system to encourage political intervention in the broadcasting sector. In particular,

---

[224] E.-J. Mestmäcker in E.-J. Mestmäcker, ed., 'Über den Einfluss von Ökonomie und Technik auf Recht und Organisation der Telekommuniktaion und der elektronischen Medien' in: *Kommunikation ohne Monopole II*, (1990), p. 152.

[225] D. Frey, *Fernsehen und audiovisueller Pluralismus im Binnenmarkt der EG*, (1999) Nomos, Baden-Baden, p. 146.

[226] BVerfGE 74, 297.

[227] See e.g., W. Hoffman-Riem, *Rundfunkrecht neben Wirtschaftsrecht. Zur Anwendbarkeit des GWB und des EWG-V auf das Wettbewerbsverhalten öffentlich-rechtlichen Rundfunks in der dualen Rundfunkordnung*, (1991) Baden-Baden, p. 183.

[228] Ibid., p. 27.

[229] U. Kische, in U. Kischel *Rundfunkfreiheit und Rundfunkmonopol* (1999), pp. 86, 87.

[230] D. Frey, op. cit. n. 225.

[231] See e.g., J. Rüggeberg 'Rundfunk als Wirtschaftsgut – Die Europäische Wirtschaftsgemeinschaft im Zugriff auf den öffentlich-rechtlichen Rundfunk' 83 *Verwaltungsarchiv* (1992) p. 350.

[232] See e.g., J. Lau, 'Das Fernsehen als Feind der Kutlureliten. Ein Selbstgespräch' 9/10 *Merkur. Deutsche Zeitschrift für europäisches Denken* (1995) p. 890.

Mestmäcker claims that the alleged danger of powerful 'media moguls' influencing public opinion are merely used as a pretext to support the influence of various interest groups in the local media authorities.[233] Moreover, he doubts if the broadcasting system in fact produces the desired results, and criticises that the mere assertion of freedom of opinion and pluralism on the grounds of corporatist interaction as prescribed by law do not necessarily translate into social reality.[234] Adopting the same line of reasoning, *Hoppmann* argues that competition between opinions and the media *inter se* cannot be isolated from each other; economic and publicist competition are interlinked and ideas essentially need to be proven in reality and must be open to rejection, which is not possible in an inflexible system.[235] Social scientists, in particular, point out that the legal concept of 'internal pluralism' is not supported by empirical evidence, which manifests a different pattern.[236] However, the relevant authorities neither seem interested in research about how the media function in the real world[237] nor in rethinking the regulatory framework.

3.4.3.3. Current Developments

Compared to the UK, pay-TV has found it much more difficult to penetrate the German market, largely because of the great variety of programs already offered by German Fee-TV, including special channels for news, music, children and sports and public and commercial general channels.[238] Thus, when the Munich-based Kirch-Group launched its pay-TV channel DF1, it failed to attract enough subscribers and finally had to close it down by the end of 1997. Rival provider Bertelsmann, with its Pay-TV-channel 'Premiere', only reached break-even after 7 years of operating the channel.[239] Kirch's intended alliance with the German Bertelsmann-group was

---

[233] E.-J. Mestmäcker, *Recht und ökonomisches Gesetz. Über die Grenzen von Staat, Gesellschaft und Privatautonomie* (1984) 2nd ed., p. 252.

[234] E.-J. Mestmäcker in E.-J. Mestmäcker (ed.) *Offene Rundfunkordnung. Prinzipien für den grenzüberschreitenden Rundfunk*, (1998) Verlag Berteslmann Stiftung, Gütersloh.

[235] E. Hoppmann, 'Meinungswettbewerb als Entdeckungsverfahren' in: E.-J. Mestmäcker, ed., *Offene Rundfunkordnung. Prinzipien für den grenzüberschreitenden Rundfunk*, (1998) Verlag Berteslmann Stiftung, Gütersloh, pp. 176, 177.

[236] E. Noelle-Neumann, 'Medienwirkung und Medienpolitik' in: E.-J. Mestmäcker, ed., *Offene Rundfunkordnung. Prinzipien für den grenzüberschreitenden Rundfunk*, (1998) Verlag Berteslmann Stiftung, Gütersloh, pp. 495-504; E. Noelle-Neumann, 'Das Reizwort "Ausgewogenheit". Über gruppendynamische Prozesse im Rundfunk-Journalismus' in *Franfurter Allgemeine Zeitung*. 8.5. 1981, p. 7. For a critique on both the traditional public service broadcasting system and an open-market-approach see L. Hachmeister, 'Wer hat Angst vor unabhängigem Fernsehen? Zum neuen deutschen Desinteresse am "dritten Weg"', 22 *Funk-Korrespondenz* 1996, pp. 11, 12.

[237] H.M. Kepplinger, et al. 'Medientenor und Bevölkerungsmeinung. Eine empirische Studie zum Image Helmut Kohls' in: 38/2 *Kölner Zeitschrift für Soziologie und Sozialpsychologie* (1986), pp. 247-279.

[238] J. Kleinsteuber/M. Rosenbach 'Digitales Fernsehen in Europa: Eine Bestandsaufnahme', 1 *Rundfunk und Fernsehen* (1998) p. 30.

[239] Ibid.

frustrated by the Commission's prohibition; he later involved Silvio Berlusconi.[240] and, more recently, sold 25 percent of his assets to Rupert Murdoch.[241] Whereas introducing Pay-TV in the 1990 involved difficulties in Germany, the introduction of commercial television and the transformation of viewer habits over the last 20years certainly had an impact: market shares of the public service broadcasters ARD and ZDF decreased to between 12-14 percent[242] from market shares of around 70 per cent in the early 1980s. Only in households without a cable or satellite-connection were market shares of around 25 percent retained.[243]

While the influence of public service broadcasting is declining, the inherent tensions and contradictions within the German broadcasting system have not been resolved. Based on the case law of the Federal Constitutional Court, pluralism remains a static concept, still heavily influenced by the experience of propaganda and demagogic abuse in the Third Reich.[244] Most scholars still define freedom of opinion and expression as a synthesis of monopoly and market, and presume that public freedom is best fulfilled by public service broadcasters.[245] Apart from objections that the underlying rational of the system is no longer substantiated by social reality, and that consumers/viewers are less dependent on protection against 'damaging' broadcasting content, this position also raises concerns regarding its compatibility with EC competition law and state aid. As public broadcasters are allocated the role of the 'basic provider' of a whole range of programs, including entertainment similarly produced by commercial television stations, the question arises if this is reconcilable with EC competition law. Moreover, public service broadcasting is also partly financed by advertising revenue, which will need to be analysed in the light of the Treaty's rules on state aid.[246]

3.5. **Broadcasting and Audio-Visual Policy in the EU**

As has been demonstrated by the examples of the UK and Germany, European states have employed a different approach toward media regulation than the US. In Europe, the term regulation is much broader, generally embracing all kinds of government interference.[247] As compared to the US, it very often lacks a specific regulatory body and does not clearly distinguish between operative and regulatory tasks. Informal procedures prevail and many systems also involve corporate aspects of

240 Source: *Medienspiegel,* (1999) 23/13, p. 4.
241 *Süddeutsche Zeitung online*, 'Milliarden für das Pay-TV', 30.11.1999.
242 Source: *Medienspiegel,* (1999) 23/41, p. 8.
243 Ibid., p. 8.
244 See detailed in G. Herrmann,*Rundfunkrecht* (1994), p. 63 et seq.
245 See e.g., U. Kische, in U. Kischel *Rundfunkfreiheit und Rundfunkmonopol* (1999), p. 76.
246 On public service broadcasting and state aid see *infra* chapter 7.
247 J. Francis, *The Politics of Regulation. A Comparative Perspective* (1993) Oxford, p. 5.

self-regulation.[248] These national traditions have repercussions for shaping an audio-visual policy at the European level.

3.5.1. *Different Approaches within the Commission*

> The Community's audio-visual policy is not the product of a single and unified Community vision of the audio-visual sector. Rather it is the result of the tortuous interaction of differing priorities and perspectives of several distinct power centres, notably the Member States of the Community, the European Parliament and rival power centres within the Commission of the European Communities itself.[249]

Because EU broadcasting and audio-visual policy is often characterised as contradictory and fragmented, it is useful to trace some of the different approaches identifiable within the Commission's services. Several DGs are involved in the audio-visual sector, namely, former DG III (Industrial Affairs), DG IV (Competition), DG X (Audio-Visuals, Communication and Culture) and DG XIII (Telecommunication Industries and Innovation). DG III was the lead directorate for the Community's most striking innovation in the media field, the 'Television without Frontiers' Directive. DG IV's competition policy has a profound impact on the audio-visual sector. DG XIII is concerned with the 'hardware' of broadcasting, dealing with different means of telecommunication (including satellites and television standards, such as HDTV). Finally, DG X has special responsibility for the audio-visual industries and hosts the MEDIA programs.[250] *Collins* identifies different orientations in the various DGs and suggests that DG III and especially DG IV have a markedly more liberal market orientation than the other DGs concerned with broadcasting and audiovisuals. Those preferring more intervention (*dirigists*) often describe the formers as 'ultra liberal'. In particular, DG X's audio-visual policy takes the industrial policy viewpoint, with MEDIA I and II and the new MEDIA plus program providing for a framework designed to assist the European audio-visual industries. These ideological differences are mirrored in the market-oriented DGs III and IV, primarily using English, and DG X and XIII, usually using French. The distinction can also be drawn along the north-south divide: normally the UK agrees with Ireland and the Netherlands, sometimes also with Germany, whereas France and Greece are usually to be found at the other end of the policy spectrum.[251]

The differentiation between 'dirigists' vs. neo-liberal and diversity vs. unity is finally also expressed in the terminology used. In the mid-nineteen eighties, Com-

---

[248] G. Majone ed. *Deregulation or Re-regulation? Regulatory Reform in Europe and the United States* (1990) London, p. 2.

[249] R. Collins, *Broadcasting and Audio-Visual Policy in The European Single Market* (1994) London, John Libbey & Comp., p. 27.

[250] Ibid., p. 18.

[251] R. Collins, *Broadcasting and Audio-Visual Policy in The European Single Market* (1994) London, John Libbey & Comp., p. 20.

munity documents started to differentiate between broadcasting and audio-visual policy.[252] Seemingly inconsequential, these different terms signify radically different policy priorities and political interests. From 1986 onwards,[253] those who viewed the creation of a single market as the major priority sailed under the banner of 'broadcasting policy', whereas those who sought the protection of the European film and video production industry chose 'audio-visual policy' as their motto. Usually, the European Parliament's Hahn-Report[254] is quoted as the birth of community broadcasting policy, and it is probably best known for its advocacy of pan-European television and the use of television as an instrument of European unification. Contemporary Community policy stresses the diversity throughout Europe, which is mainly a consequence of failing to successfully introduce transnational broadcasting in the 1980s.

3.5.2. *Current Audio-Visual and Broadcasting Policy*

Strictly speaking, a European audio-visual policy has existed only since 1988, when the Council of Ministers formally testified at its Rhodes meeting to the importance of cooperation in developing Europe's cultural identity.[255] Subsequently, audio-visual policy evolved gradually – often in an unpredictable way – and we can further distinguish two different concepts advocated: one the one hand, the single-market concept as envisaged by the 'Television without Frontiers' Directive stressed the unity of the EU and the need to develop a 'European culture' to assist European unification. On the other hand, it is claimed that the significance of European culture is its diversity and that there is no such thing as a single 'European culture' or 'European identity'.[256]

3.5.2.1. The dirigist Approach

Under the Treaty of Rome, the Community did not enjoy any significant powers in the field of audio-visual policy. Television was considered a service by the Court of Justice,[257] and the case law of the audio-visual sector mainly developed along the same lines as the four freedoms, in particular, the free movement of services and the freedom of establishment.[258] When the Treaty of Maastricht entered into force

[252] See in detail R. Collins, *Broadcasting and Audio-Visual Policy in The European Single Market*, (1994) London, John Libbey & Comp., p. 83.

[253] The first document to expressly mention 'audio-visual policy' was Information Memo P-26, March 1986, *COM* (86) 146.

[254] *Report on Radio and Television Broadcasting in the Community on behalf of the Committee on Youth, Culture, Education and Sport* (The Hahn Resolution) PE Document 1-1013/81.

[255] *The European Community Policy in the audio-visual field. Legal and political texts (1990)* Office for Official Publications of the European Communities, Luxembourg.

[256] See already above at 1.2.

[257] Case 155/73, *Sacchi* [1974] ECR 409.

[258] See detailed *infra* chapter 4.

on 1 November 1993, it included in Article 128 (now, after amendment Article 151) an innovation for the audio-visual sector: 'Action by the Community shall be aimed at encouraging co-operation between Member States and, if necessary, supporting and supplementing their action' in such fields as 'artistic and literary creation, including the audio-visual sector'. However, harmonisation is explicitly excluded in Article 128(5) (now Article 151(5)).

Within this framework, as has already been highlighted, DG X takes a fairly market-reluctant approach:

> Films can be seen as an area where business and the arts meet: economic and cultural factors are inextricably linked. It may be that the community devotes more attention to audio-visual production than purely economic considerations might warrant but there are other industries, which serve as precedents ...[259]

The Commission's Communication for the Community's audio-visual policy in the digital age,[260] in recital 11, stresses as the 'fundamental goals of its audio-visual policy to encourage the production and distribution of European works, by establishing a secure and stable legal framework to guarantee the freedom to provide audio-visual services, on the one hand, and through appropriate support mechanisms on the other'. The 'Green Paper on the Regulatory Implications'[261] also refers to economic and industrial competitiveness and the 'danger that if Europe fails to take advantage of the opportunities provided by convergence, it could be left behind as other major trading blocks reap the benefits of a more positive approach'.

In such statements one can easily identify the *dirigist* or interventionist point of view dominating in DG X. The industrial policy's ideas of strengthening a domestic industry[262] by taking an active role in promoting these industries, although originally developed in the nation state, have also succeeded at the supranational level. DG X's two MEDIA programs and the new MEDIA plus program were designed to promote the European television and film industry by offering organisational assistance and funding.

3.5.2.2. The MEDIA Programs

Throughout the 1980s, the European Parliament and the Commission had proposed measures to support the European audio-visual sector. These initiatives resulted in the MEDIA (Measures to Encourage the Development of the Industry of Audio-visual Production)[263] program, which started its pilot phase in 1986. The Council

---

[259] *Audiovisual Policy. Current Situation and Prospects* http://www.europa.eu.int/scadplus/leg/eng/lvb/124109.htm, visited on 18 January 2000.

[260] *COM* (1999) 657 final.

[261] *Green Paper on the Convergence of the Telecommunications, Media and Information Technology Sectors, and the Implications for Regulation towards an Information Society Approach*, 97 *COM* 623 final.

[262] See also above at 1.4.

[263] Often also referred to as MEDIA 92.

decided to support MEDIA,[264] which reflects the interventionist assumption that structural change in the European market was required to enable European producers to achieve 'economies of scale'. The pilot stage lasted from 1988 to 1990 and terminated with the positive appraisal by a group of experts.[265] This committee of experts, often known as *Les Sages*, also stated that MEDIA was not a subsidy machine. The administrative costs were to be paid partly by the Commission and partly by the host country.[266] Subsequently, MEDIA was turned into a full-scale program, MEDIA I,[267] covering the training of professionals (1), improvement of production conditions (2), support of distributions mechanisms (3), support of cinema production (4), contribution to the establishment of a 'second market' (5) and stimulating financial investment (6). MEDIA has so far undergone three stages, MEDIA I[268] (1991-1995), MEDIA II[269] (1996-2000) and MEDIA plus[270] (2001-2005).

The training of professionals ('European Audio-visual Entrepreneurs', 'EAVE') aims to train television producers in economics and marketing to create a pan-European network for producers to promote European co-productions.[271] It is designed for European independent producers of any genre who are about to develop a project but is also open to those who are interested in the subject and have 'creative potential'. EAVE has also given birth to the European Producers Network, an international association to improve the exchange of information and to develop contacts.[272]

To improve production conditions and, in particular, to facilitate fund-raising, the European Script Fund ('SCRIPT') was founded. It lends money to producers working in any language of a Member State whose production is intended for distribution in any audio-visual medium, considering any form of fiction or drama material.[273] SCRIPT aims to encourage films with strong stories that will be successful across borders and preference is given to projects which are interesting for co-producers from a state other than the originating one. Applicants should in general be nationals of the EU but exceptions are possible.[274] The DOCUMENTARY

[264] Decision 90/38/EEC concerning the implementation of an action programme to promote the development of the European audiovisual industry (media) (1991-1995), *OJ* L 137, 20.5.1992.

[265] Encouraging Europe's Media Industry-a Review of MEDIA 92, COM (90) 132 final.

[266] MEDIA. Progress Report of the Pilot Project (1990), Media 92 of the European Communities, Brussels.

[267] Council Decision 90/685/EEC of 21 December concerning the implementation of an action programme to promote the development of the European audiovisual industry (MEDIA) (1991-1995), *OJ* L 380/37, 31.12.1990.

[268] Ibid.

[269] Implemented by Council Decision 95/564/EC of 22.12.1995, *OJ* L 321/33, 30.12.1995 and Council Decision 95/563/EC of 10.7.1995, *OJ* L 321/25, 30.12.1995.

[270] Council Decision 2000/821/EC, *OJ* L 336/82, 30.12.2000.

[271] MEDIA GUIDE, p. 13.

[272] D.B. Winn, *European Community and International Media Law* (1994), Graham & Trotman/Nijhoff, London/Dordrecht/Boston, p. 374.

[273] SCRIPT Guidelines, Art. 1, MEDIA GUIDE, p. 39.

[274] SCRIPT Guidelines, Art. 2, MEDIA GUIDE, p. 39.

('DOKU') program also comes under the heading of improving production conditions and specifically aims to strengthen the documentary genre by awarding loans to European Independent Producers. 'Independent' means that producers and directors must be unconnected with television companies.[275]

To improve distribution, the European Film Distribution Office ('EFDO') was set up. As 80 percent of European films remain in their originating country, EFDO aims to assist the distribution of European theatrical films.[276] Eligible are film with a minimum length of 60 minutes whose production company is based in the European Community or belongs to the European cultural sphere, excluding productions that are clearly advertising mediums or pornographic.[277] At least three distributors from at least three different Member States must submit an application on the basis of existing cooperation contracts between them.[278] EFDO operates a priority system, preferring films where the greatest number of distributors cooperates. Next come films of 'difficult' film export countries, i.e., all countries other than France, Germany and the UK.[279]

The SALLES program aims to improve the distribution of films in cinema and any professional cinema exhibitors, association of national and international organisations may become a member.[280] Furthermore, the European Film Academy ('EFA') was founded as a non-profit organisation to provide a meeting place for the European film sector. Membership is only offered to recognised film professionals, subject to prior invitation.[281] By 1992, EFA had established an annual European Master school lasting for five days and catering for young professionals.[282]

To establish a 'second market', the Memory-Archives-Programmes TV ('MAP-TV') aims to enhance the value of the European audio-visual archives. It helps to set up co-productions of archive-based creative programs.[283] Additionally, the LUMIER project was launched to invest in the permanent preservation of films.[284]

For the stimulation of financial investments, the Euro Media Guarantees ('EMG') was founded to offer European financial institutions an option to share the risk involved in financing a European audio-visual work by providing loan-guarantees. In general, the Commission describes the aims of the MEDIA program as the removal barriers and the initiation of cross-frontier cooperation, giving priority to

---

[275] DOCUMENTARY Guidelines, MEDIA GUIDE, p. 57.

[276] D.B. Winn, *European Community and International Media Law* (1994), Graham & Trotman/ Nijhoff, London/Dordrecht/Boston, p. 380.

[277] EFDO Guidelines, Art. B.II, MEDIA GUIDE, p. 129.

[278] D.B. Winn, *European Community and International Media Law* (1994), Graham &Trotman/ Nijhoff, London/Dordrecht/Boston, p. 381.

[279] Ibid., p. 381.

[280] MEDIA GUIDE, p. 225.

[281] MEDIA GUIDE, p. 232.

[282] Ibid.

[283] MAP-TV Guidelines, Art. 1; MEDIA GUIDE, p. 240.

[284] LUMIERE Guidelines, MEDIA GUIDE, p. 251.

SME operators and independents, respecting national different identities and avoiding any cultural uniformatisation.[285] It includes several initiatives for cooperation and network-building and its primary aim is to encourage production of audio-visual works that face difficulties to finance and market their product. It intends to promote SME's productions and works originating from disadvantaged (language) areas. At the Audio-visual Conference in Birmingham in April 1998, the majority of delegates thought that MEDIA II had to a large extent achieved its objectives. However, most people also opined that national and European politics could complement each other better if greater emphasis was placed on industrial and structural aims at the European level and on cultural goals at the national level. Professionals working in the audio-visual field also maintained that public support was 'more essential than ever'.[286]

MEDIA II elapsed by the end of 2000, and in the meantime, the Commission proposed a new 'MEDIA Plus' program[287] (from 2001-2005). In its proposal the Commission once more highlighted the great potential for job creation in the audio-visual sector.[288] As the European content industry is ill prepared for the challenges ahead due to its fragmentation and resulting undercapitalisation, action to remedy these weaknesses must be taken.[289] The support mechanisms need to take account of national diversity and be complementary to national and regional policy. The 'automatic mechanism' (first established by MEDIA II) based on market performance shall be maintained and an increase in the program's resources is intended. In the light of developing digital technology, support systems should be technological neutral.[290] As in the preceding programs, beneficiaries must generally provide at least 50 percent of the funding and the majority of the participants of training schemes must have a nationality other than that of the country where the training takes place.[291] Furthermore, the program shall also be open to the countries of Central and Eastern Europe (CEEC), Cyprus, Malta, Turkey and the members of the EEA, subject to a prior examination of the compatibility of their national legislation with the Community, especially the Television without Frontiers Directive.[292]

---

[285] R. Collins, *Broadcasting and Audio-Visual Policy in The European Single Market*, (1994) London, John Libbey & Comp., p. 97.

[286] Commission Report on the results obtained under the MEDIA II programme (1996-2000) from 1.1.1996 – 30.6.1998, *COM* (1999) 91 final, p. 7.

[287] Communication from the Commission to the Council, the European Parliament, the Economic and Social Committee and the Committee of the Regions concerning a proposal for a programme in support of the audiovisual industries (MEDIA Plus – 2001 – 2005), *COM* (1999) 657 final. Council Decision of 20 December 2000 on the implementation of a programme to encourage the development, distribution and promation of European audiovisual works (MEDIA Plus, 2001-2005), *OJ* L 336/82, 30.12.2000.

[288] Ibid., footnote 3.

[289] Ibid., p. 6.

[290] Ibid., p. 7.

[291] Art. 4 of the proposed Decision.

[292] Ibid., Art. 6, sec. 1-4.

Decision 200/821/EC introduced the new MEDIA plus programme and essentially followed the proposed Decision. In particular, the programme is also open to the associated countries of Central and Eastern Europe.[293] It entered into force on 1 January 2001 and contains an extension of the policy already embodied in MEDIA I and II. It takes up the suggestion voiced at the Audio-visual Conference in Birmingham in April 1998 to concentrate more on complementary support at the national/regional and European levels. However, even the new MEDIA program has not overcome certain weaknesses and contradictions of its predecessors; for example, the Commission, on the one hand, emphasises the fragmentation of the industry and, on the other hand, maintains its specific support for small language areas and SME producers.

3.5.2.3. The Public Interest

Public interest objectives, such as the universal accessibility of quality television programming, is regulated within the Member States and there is no express community competence in this field. Nonetheless, the problem of reconciling these interests with the Treaty, in particular the free movement of services, frequently arose before the Court of Justice. Dealing with this question, it has repeatedly held that public interest considerations in the field of broadcasting can, as a general rule, prevail over the free movement of services.[294] However, everything will depend on the concrete facts of the case, if the causality between the legitimate aim and the measures enacted can be demonstrated; the measures must be appropriate to achieve the goal and proportionate, i.e., the same must not be achievable by lesser means. Member States have in the past relied on public interest considerations, but the Court of Justice's analysis demonstrated that this was only a mere pretext to realise illegitimate aims, for instance, the protection of certain industries or undertakings from competition.[295] From the case law it is clear that it is insufficient to rely on the legitimate public interest aim, without *in concreto* defining it and demonstrating how the measure acts as a tool to achieve the intended goal. As with all exceptions from the four freedoms, it has to be defined narrowly.[296]

It appears that the Commission takes a narrower approach. In its Green Paper on the Regulatory Implications,[297] it emphasised the unchanged value of a public service mission in broadcasting. The Commission defined public interest objective as 'universal service obligation' to 'ensure the universal availability of defined services at an affordable price'. Therefore, it is indispensable to define public interest objectives in the first place. It further identified two different opinion on the issue: some consider this definition also essential in order to establish if these objectives

[293] Decision 2000/861/EC, rec. 35.

[294] See e.g. Case C-23/93, *TV 10*, Slg. [1994] ECR I-4795.

[295] See e.g. Case C-211/91, *Com.* v. *Belgium*, [1992] I-6757.

[296] See detailed *infra* chapter 4.

[297] *COM* (97) 623.

remain valid at all, others would not question the validity of the aim as such but admit that the way they are realised might evolve. Specific obligation may be placed on one or more operator(s) to guarantee these objectives, but the costs may be shared also with other market players.[298]

This is a quite far-reaching statement. The Commission indicated that the definition of the public interest objective is not entirely at the discretion of the Member States but that there are inherent limits to it in the Treaty. This ties in with the Court of Justice's case law. Moreover, it elaborates on the fact that, either, the realisation of the aim is *evolving* or, with convergence, public interest objectives might even *diminish*, depending on which point of view one takes. The Commission does not elaborate on the option to simply *maintain* the status quo, thus the presumption obviously is that public interest aims must be reassessed against the background of convergence and, if necessary, adapted to these changes. This only allows the conclusion that static national broadcasting systems not reacting to technological and market changes will be open to much criticism in the future.

3.5.2.4. Public Service Broadcasting

Assessment of public interest objectives has repercussions on how public service broadcasting is assessed under the Treaty. We have seen that there are restrictions in relying on public interest considerations in the sense that these objectives must be clearly defined and the ends and means must be proportionate. This at the same time acts as a limit to the powers and privileges of the public service broadcaster who was assigned the task to fulfil these objectives. Moreover, with the Treaty of Amsterdam a protocol expressly dealing with public broadcasting in the Member States was inserted.

> The provisions of the Treaty establishing the European Community shall be without prejudice to the competence of Member States to provide for the funding of public service broadcasting insofar as such funding is granted to broadcasting organisations for the fulfilment of the public service remit as conferred, defined and organised by each Member State, and insofar as such funding does not affect trading conditions and competition in the Community to an extent which would be contrary to the common interest, while the realisation of the remit of that public service shall be taken into account.[299]

The Television without Frontiers Directive, as the major regulatory initiative regarding broadcasting in the EU, did not mention public service broadcasting. Hence, this protocol is a valuable indicator of how Community law will treat national public service broadcasting and, in particular, its funding. It gives a similar picture as the Court of Justice's case law and the Green Paper on the Regulatory Implications.

---

[298] Ibid., point IV.3.

[299] *Protocol on the System of Public Broadcasting in the Member States*. See detailed *infra* at 7.1.7.

First, the Member State's competence to define the role of public service broadcasting, as a general rule, is emphasised and second, the limitations under Community law are set out: the funding of public service broadcasting must not distort competition and trading interest. Essentially, this entails a balancing test taking into account, on the one hand, the public service remit and, on the other hand, the internal market. Although public service broadcasting as such is legitimate, it should not distort competition in the internal market more than is necessary and proportionate.

3.5.3. *The 'Television Without Frontiers' Directive*

The Directive has already been subject to extended research both from a European and US perspective.[300] Thus, only a brief overview highlighting the significance of the 'Community quota' will be given. The lessons for European broadcasting and audio-visual policy that can be learned from the Directive will be examined.

3.5.3.1. Background and Genesis

With the technological changes of the early 1980s, most notably as cable and satellite communications becoming more widespread, the need for regulating cross-border broadcasting in the Community became more pressing. The Directive was one of the 279 measures proposed in the Commission's 1985 White Paper on Completing the Internal Market, the blueprint for 1992.[301] On the basis of the Hahn-Report,[302] the European Parliament in 1982 adopted the Resolution on Radio and Broadcasting in the EC,[303] in which the Parliament emphasised the need for Community action in the audio-visual field, in particular to harmonise rules on advertising (by enacting a 'code of conduct') and the protection of minors. The Resolution also discussed the establishment of a new, pan-European television channel to buttress European identity, a project that was never carried out. The Commission, in 1983, reacted to the proposal by producing an interim report on realities and tendencies and, in 1984, sketched the outlines of the Directive in its Green Paper on Broadcasting.[304] As for national legislation requiring harmonisation, the Green pa-

[300] S.S. Venturelli, *Liberalizing the European media: politics, regulation, and the public sphere* (1998); P.R. Schlesinger, 'Wishful Thinking: Cultural Politics, Media and Collective Identities in Europe'. 43/2 *Journal of Communications* (1999), pp. 6-17. M. Meckel, 'Kommunikative Identität und Weltöffentlichkeit: Theoretische Überlegungen zur Rolle der Medien im Globalisierungsprozeß'. 43/4 *Publizistik* (1998) pp. 362-375.

[301] Completing the Internal Market, White Paper from the Commission to the European Council, *COM* (85) 310 final 31.

[302] European Parliament, 'Hahn-Report', Doc. 1-1013/1981. For a general discussion on the influence of the European Parliament on audio-visual policy in the EU see 'Audio-visual policies of the Community. The role of the European Parliament', Research and Documentation Papers, Economic Series No. 10 (1987) 8.

[303] *OJ* 1982 C 87/110

[304] Television without Frontiers: Green Paper on the Establishment of the Common Market for Broadcasting. Especially by Satellite and Cable. *COM* (1985) 300 final.

per identified four broad areas where action was deemed necessary: advertising, the right to reply, and protection of minors and copyright. The final version of the Directive no longer includes provisions on copyright because authors' associations in the Member States could not reach an agreement.[305]

In the Green Paper, the Commission declared that television reached an impressive number of people in the Member States and was of extraordinary cultural significance.[306] Moreover, it specifically recognised that television broadcasting would 'play an important part in developing and nurturing awareness of the rich variety of Europe's common culture and historical heritage' and 'contribute towards a more widespread European identity'.[307] Also, the great threat of 'cultural domination' through television broadcasting was understood by recognising that the majority of films broadcast in Europe originated in the US.

The Green Paper of 1984 served as a guideline for the 1986 Commission's proposal.[308] Through the 'establishment of a general preference for the distribution of television programmes of all kinds produced within the Community',[309] the Community meant to take advantage of the cultural influence of television programming. Thirty percent of broadcasting time, excluding news, advertising, game shows and sports, was to be reserved for 'European works' and this percentage was later increased to sixty percent.[310] The 'European quota' gave rise to much controversy[311] until the Member States at the summit at Rhodes in 1983 agreed on the less precise term also used by the Council of Europe Convention.[312] Subsequently the quota on broadcasting of European works was reduced to more than fifty percent, and in October 1989 the Council finally adopted the 'Television Without Frontiers' Directive.[313] Belgium, fearing an adverse effect on its language policy, and Denmark

305 For a discussion of the proposed copyright provision, see M. Maggiore, 'Audiovisual Production in the Single Market' (1990) European Cultural Foundation & European Institute for Media, Europe 2000: A Report of the European Television Task Force, pp. 69, 70. Subsequently, Directive 93/83/EEC, *OJ* O 248/15, 6.10.1993 partly harmonised this field.

306 *COM* (1985) 300 final, at 23.

307 Ibid., at 28 and 32.

308 Proposal for a Council Directive on the Coordination of Certain Provisions Laid Down by Law, Regulation of Administrative Action in Member States Concerning the Pursuit of Broadcasting Activities, *OJ* 1986 C 179/4.

309 Ibid., rec. 15, preamble.

310 Ibid., rec. 15, Art. 2. See also V. Salvatore 'Quotas on TV Prgrammes and EEC Law', 29 *CMLRev.* (1992) 973.

311 France was the chief proponent of the 60 percent quota contained in the Proposed Directive. See P. Presburger/M.R. Tyler 'Television without Frontiers: Opportunity and Debate Created by the New European Community Directive', 13 *Hastings Int. & Comp. L. Rev.* (1990), p. 495, at p. 499.

312 R. Wallace/D.Goldberg 'The EEC Directive an Television Broadcasting', 9 *YEL* (1989) p. 175.

313 Council Directive 89/552/EEC of 3 October 1989 on the coordination of certain provisions laid down by Law, Regulation or Administrative Action in Member States concerning the pursuit of television broadcasting activities, *OJ* L 298/23, 17.10.1989 subsequently amended by Directive 97/36/EC of the European Parliament and of the Council of 30 June 1997, *OJ* L 202/60, 30.07.1997.

denying community competence in the field of television altogether,[314] voted against it.[315] The debates in the European Parliament indicated that one – if not the primary motivation of enacting the Directive – was to protect, preserve and promote European cultural identity through the use of television broadcasts.[316]

3.5.3.2. Guiding Principle

The overarching goal of the Directive is to create an Internal Market for broadcasting, allowing television programs to move unimpeded across borders. The Directive, in its Article 2(2),[317] set out as its cornerstone the country of origin or Transmission State principle. Member States shall not restrict retransmission for reasons which fall within the fields coordinated by the Directive. If a broadcaster gravely infringes the provision to protect minors in Article 22 and has disobeyed it at least twice in the last year, the concerned Member State must notify the broadcaster and the Commission in writing of the alleged infringement and of the state's intention to restrict the transmission on the next violation.[318]

3.5.3.3. Public Interest

The Directive includes several provisions that cover public interest issues in a broad sense, in particular, advertising, which is restricted for the sake of the consumer and the protection of minors. Television advertising shall be readily recognisable and separate from other programs, isolated spots shall remain an exception and subliminal techniques and surreptitious advertising shall be prohibited.[319] Moreover, maximum duration for advertising per day is laid down and advertising is prohibited in any broadcasting of a religious service. The Directive contains detailed provisions on the conditions when and how advertising can interrupt programs; for example, news, documentaries and children's programs under 30 minutes shall not be interrupted.[320] It also prohibits advertising interfering with human dignity and advertising containing an offensive or discriminatory message.[321] Member States shall take appropriate measures to ensure that broadcasters within their jurisdiction do not transmit programs 'which might seriously impair the physical, mental or

---

314 This view was also shared by the UK, Germany, the Netherlands and France.

315 T.M. Lupinacci, 'The Pursuit of Television Broadcasting Activities in the European Community: Cultural Preservation or Economic Protectionism?', 24 *Vanderbilt Journal of Transnational Law* (1991), pp. 113-154, at p. 122 and R. Wallace/D.Goldberg 'The EEC Directive an Television Broadcasting', 9 *YEL* (1989) p. 175.

316 Debates of the European Parliament, Pursuit of Broadcasting Activities, *OJ* 1989 (2-378), p. 118.

317 Moved to Art. 2a after amendment by Directive 97/36/EC.

318 Directive 89/552/EEC, Art. 2 (2) (a) – (d), moved to Art. 2a (2) (a) – (d) after amendment. See also C.B. Scott, 'European Unification – Broadcasting Law –Eastern Europe and the "Television without Frontiers" Directive: Radio Free Europe – Can Television Unify it?', 22 *Georgian Journal of International and Comparative Law* (1992) pp. 547-566, at p. 551.

319 Council Directive 89/552/EEC, Art. 10.

320 Ibid., Art. 11.

321 Ibid., Art. 12.

moral development of minors'. The Directive expressly mentions pornography or gratuitous violence.[322] The advertising of alcoholic beverages is strictly controlled[323] and the advertising of tobacco products[324] and prescription drugs[325] is prohibited.

3.5.3.4. The 'European works'-Quota

The most contentious provision of the Directive is the so-called 'European works' quota. Approval of the Directive closely followed the adoption of a similar text concerning broadcasting, the European Convention on Transfrontier Television.[326] Both the Directive and the Convention include provisions that call upon European broadcasters to reserve a 'majority proportion' of air time for 'European works'.[327] Article 4 of the Directive provides:

> Member States shall ensure where practicable and by appropriate means, that broadcasters reserve for European works, within the meaning of Article 6, a majority proportion of their transmission time, excluding the time appointed to news, sports events, games, advertising and teletext services.

As there are no limits to the overall quantity for works originating outside Europe it has been suggested that it would be more correct to speak of 'European content requirements' instead of a quota.[328]

Article 4 is worded rather loosely and the US critique that it violates the GATT was, on the European side, met by the assurance that this was more of a soft-law policy goal.[329] The majority requirement is to be achieved 'progressively', taking into account the broadcaster's various responsibilities to its viewing public.[330] Article 6 in 'a densely-worded, multi-layered series of provisions'[331] defines 'European works' as works originating from a Member State, a state which is party to the

---

[322] Ibid., Art. 22.

[323] Ibid., Art. 15.

[324] Ibid., Art. 13.

[325] Ibid., Art. 14.

[326] European Convention on Transfrontier Television, reprinted in Council of Europe, Explanatory Convention on Transfrontier Television (1990).

[327] Directive, Art. 4(1), Convention, Art. 10. See J. Filipek, 'Cultural Quotas: The Trade Controversy over the European Community's Broadcasting Directive' in: (28*) Stanford Journal of International Law* (1992) p. 325.

[328] *De Witte,* 'The European content requirements in the EC Television Directive – Five years after' (1995) *Yearbook of Media and Entertainment Law*, p. 101.

[329] France applies very strict quota-rules whereas Germany relies on the interpretation that the quota is not legally binding. See A. Schardt, 'Novellierung der Richtlinie "Fernsehen ohne Grenzen": Quoten ohne Ende?', 11 *ZUM* (1995) pp. 734-739, at p. 736.

[330] Ibid., Art. 4 (1). Compare also the Convention's nearly identical language in Art. 10 (1) '..[e]ach transmitting Party shall ensure, where practical and by appropriate means, that broadcasters reserve for European works a majority proportion of their transmission time, excluding time appointed to news, sports events, advertising and teletext services...'.

[331] J. Filipek, 'Cultural Quotas: The Trade Controversy over the European Community's Broadcasting Directive' in: (28*) Stanford Journal of International Law* (1992) p. 333.

European Convention on Transfrontier Television and 'works mainly made with authors and workers' residing in one or more Member State(s) or a State Party to the Convention. The defining characteristic of a 'European work' seems to be European control.[332]

3.5.3.5. Amendment by Directive 97/36/EC

The Directive gave rise to a range of comments by legal writers on both sides of the Atlantic. In Europe, legal discussion largely focused on the interpretation of the Directive, in particular, on the question of which areas were subject to harmonisation. In fields covered by the Directive, Member States enacted diverging legislation, thus questioning its harmonisation effect.[333] Article 26 contains a provision that, after five years, the Commission should submit a report on the application of the Directive and, if necessary, proposals to adapt it. By the end of May 1995, the Commission had produced a proposal[334] for an amending directive, which was preceded by a Green Paper on the European program industry.[335] The proposal contained an important alteration of the 'European quota' by suggesting the deletion of the expression 'where practical and by appropriate means' in Articles 4 and 5. However, it was subsequently not taken up and Articles 4 and 5 remained unaltered by the amending Directive.[336] Moreover, under the original Directive it was unclear how the criterion in Article 2(1)[337] to determine jurisdiction over a broadcaster had to be interpreted. The new Article 2 clarified that establishment was the decisive criterion, which essentially was a confirmation of the Court of Justice's case law.[338] Chapter IV on television advertising and sponsorship was extended to teleshopping and the Chapter on protection of minors was rearranged. However, the underlying principle of the Directive to provide for partial and minimum harmonisation is not altered by the amendment.[339]

---

332 Ibid.

333 See the examples given by *A. Schardt*, 'Novellierung der Richtlinie "Fernsehen ohne Grenzen": Quoten ohne Ende?', 11 *ZUM* (1995) pp. 734-739, at p. 735.

334 *OJ* 1995 C 185/4.

335 *COM* (94) 96 final.

336 Directive 97/36/EC of the European Parliament and of the Council of 30 June 1997, *OJ* L 202/60, 30.07.1997.

337 '(1) Each Member State shall ensure that all television broadcasts transmitted
– by broadcasters under its jurisdiction, or
– by broadcasters, who, while not being under the jurisdiction of any Member States, make use of a frequency of a satellite capacity granted by, or a satellite up-link situated in, that Member States, comply with the law applicable to broadcasts intended for the public in that Member State.'

338 Case C-222/94, *Commission* v. *United Kingdom*, [1996] ECR I-4025, Case C-55/96, *VT4 Ltd.* v. *Vlaamse Gemeenschap*, [1997] *ECR* I-3143; See also M. Schmitd-Vockenhausen, 'Revision der EG-Fernsehrichtlinie. Ein weiterer Schritt in eine europäischie Medienordnung?', 5 *ZUM* (1998), pp. 377-381, at p. 378.

339 B. Drijber, 'The Revised Television without Frontiers Directive: Is It Fit For The Next Century?', 36 *CMLRev.* (1999), p. 82.

3.5.3.6. The External Dimension

US critique of the Television Without Frontiers Directive focused on the 'European works' quota in Article 4, and it was also due to intensive American lobbying that the first proposal envisaging a 60 percent quota was not realised. The economic background is plain: the majority of fiction screened on European television and in cinemas originates in the US. Europeans prefer national productions, but if they chose to watch a foreign program they are most likely to opt for a US production. Several grounds have been suggested as an explanation. First, US productions enjoy huge economies of scale and can easily provide the greater demand for television broadcasting programs which occurred in Europe due to an increase of the numbers of channels in the 1980s.[340] The American audio-visual industry was simply much better prepared to penetrate the emerging Internal Market in television than its European counterpart. Second, American fiction tends to be 'universal' in a particular way. It manages to chose topics and tell stories relevant to people living in different cultural contexts, whereas European productions cannot be easily removed from their national background; they are much more embedded in a particular national environment, the only exception to some extent being UK-productions, which account for the majority of successful European audio-visual exports, obviously also for language reasons.

US American legal writers have focused on the question how the 'European works' quota relates to the GATT, in particular, if it violates the MFN obligation in Article I, the national treatment requirement of Article III and the ban on quantitative restrictions in Article XI.[341] Furthermore, Article IV of the GATT, which permits states to set screen quotas for films, has been considered[342] as a possible legal basis for an exemption. A majority of American writers are rather critical,[343] and conclude that the Directive violates the GATT, albeit admitting that the preservation of European culture and national identity constitute 'reasonable aims'[344] that

---

[340] Between 1980 and 1988, US productions sold to Europe increased five-fold; See P. Presburger/ M.R. Tyler, 'Television without Frontiers: Opportunity and Debate Created by the New European Community Directive', 13 *Hastings Int. & Comp. L. Rev.* (1990), p. 503.

[341] J. Filipek, 'Cultural Quotas: The Trade Controversy over the European Community's Broadcasting Directive', 28 *Stanford Journal of International Law* (1992), p. 323, pp. 346-349; O'Connell, 'Television without Frontiers: The European Union's continuing Struggle for Cultural Survival', 28/2 *Case Western Reserve Journal of International Law* (1996), p. 501, pp. 520-529.

[342] M. *Braun/ L. Parker,* 'Trade in culture: Consumable Product or Cherished Articulation of a Nation's Soul' in: *Denv. J. Int'l L & Pol'y*, Vol . 22:1 (1993) pp. 155-191, p. 183 et seq.; L.L. Garrett, 'Commerce versus Culture: The Battle Between the United States and the European Union Over Audiovisual Trade Policies', 19 *N.C.J. Int'L & Com. Reg.* (1994) pp. 553-577, at p. 573.

[343] See e.g., Ross, 'I love Lucy, but the European Community doesn't: Apparent Protectionism in the European Community's Broadcasting Market', 16 *Brooklyn Journal of International Law* (1990) p. 595.

[344] T.M. Lupinacci, 'The Pursuit of Television Broadcasting Activities in the European Community: Cultural Preservation or Economic Protectionism?', 24 *Vanderbilt Journal of Transnational Law* (1991) pp. 113-154, at p. 152.

need to be considered and can justify deviation from free trade principles.[345] Thus, the Directive and its quota appear problematic not so much because of the intended 'ends' but the 'means' employed to achieve its goal.

3.5.4. *Conclusion*

The European Union's television broadcasting policy is a mass of contradictions.[346]

The EU's broadcasting and television policy consists of various bits and pieces, pursuing different and partly irreconcilable aims. As a result of the different priorities of the Member States, within the Commissions services it lacks a coherent overall approach. A clear policy option as envisaged by *Dyson*[347] cannot either be deduced from the various policy documents ('soft law') nor from Community primary and secondary legislation. Article 151(6) EC (ex-Article 128 (8)) expressly excludes harmonisation of broadcasting legislation on cultural grounds. The Television without frontiers Directive was based on Articles 57(2) and 66 EC (now Articles 47(2) and 55) but it has been argued that considering the cultural objectives of the Directive, this was not a sufficient legal basis. In response to these arguments, it was claimed that several Member States provided for quota rules and that a level playing field for Community broadcasting was required. As the Directive's main goal was to achieve the Internal Market, it was, in the light of the Court of Justice's case law,[348] not necessary to have recourse to other provisions of the Treaty to specifically cover its 'cultural' aspects.[349]

Regarding the dispute between Europe and the US, a multi-level motivation on both sides can be observed. Although the US position could be considered 'hypocritical',[350] the outright protectionism in the Directive is certainly counterproductive to justify the pursuit of legitimate cultural aims. The Directive does not guarantee that the programs covered are capable of buttressing European culture and identity any better than American productions, because defining European works on the basis of establishment is a purely formal criterion.[351] Thus, the Directive is open to

---

[345] See e.g., J.D. Donaldson, 'Television without Frontiers; The continuing Tension between liberal Free Trade and European Cultural Integration'(1996) 20 *Fordham International Law Journal*, pp. 90-180, at p. 180.

[346] L.J. Dhooge, 'No Place for Melrose', 16 *New York Law School Journal of International and Comparative Law* (1996) pp. 279-336, at p. 334.

[347] See above at 3.1.

[348] See e.g. Case C-155/91, *Commission* v. *Council* [1993] ECR I-939.

[349] B. Drijber, 'The Revised Television without Frontiers Directive: Is It Fit For The Next Century?', 36 *CMLRev.*, (1999) p. 109.

[350] T.M. Lupinacci, 'The Pursuit of Television Broadcasting Activities in the European Community: Cultural Preservation or Economic Protectionism?', 24 *Vanderbilt Journal of Transnational Law* (1991) pp. 113-154, at p. 154.

[351] B. Drijber, 'The Revised Television without Frontiers Directive: Is It Fit For The Next Century?', 36 *CMLRev.*, (1999) p. 109.

criticism that cultural aspects are merely used as a pretext to disguise the pursuit of European trading interests. In general, the EU's broadcasting policy shows heavy influence by a 'European' tradition of (content) regulated broadcasting and a strong role for public service broadcasting.

Part II
BROADCASTING IN THE EUROPEAN UNION – A COMPETITION PERSPECTIVE

TELEVISION BROADCASTING AS A SERVICE

The EC Treaty does not make express reference to broadcasting,[352] however, over time the Court of Justice has developed considerable jurisprudence in this area. In case 155/73 *Sacchi*,[353] the Court of Justice for the first time had to decide on a case involving cross-border television broadcasting. An Italian court had applied for a preliminary ruling. It involved criminal proceedings against the manager of 'Telebiella', an Italian television broadcaster, who transmitted his program via cable and refused to pay the licence fee levied on every television set to the national broadcaster RAI. RAI held a television monopoly, and licences for cable television had not yet been issued. The defendant argued that it was in contradiction to EC Competition law (in particular Articles 2, 3-5, 37, 86 and 90 EC) to charge for television sets that are only capable of receiving cable television and not terrestrial RAI broadcasts. Essentially, he claimed that he was forced to pay for something he does not take advantage of. Furthermore, the Italian provision would inhibit television advertising and thus adversely effect imports.

The defendant relied on Article 30 EC (now Article 28 EC), characterising television broadcasting as an intangible good subject to the free movement of goods. The same would also apply to the (tangible) film material. The Advocate General admitted that intangibles such as electricity were capable of falling inside the ambit of Article 30 EC (now Article 28 EC) but claimed that in the case of television not the electricity but the transmission of the program was subject to the 'import'. Hence, he suggested, analogous to movies, considering television as a service. In its judgement, the Court held that 'in the absence of express provision to the contrary in the Treaty, a television signal must, *by reason of its nature*,[354] be regarded as provision of services',[355] (emphasis added).[356] The fact that services are normally provided for remuneration does not change its 'nature'. By contrast, 'trade in material, sound recordings, films...[357]', in other words, all tangibles of the television industry are subject to Article 30 (now Article 28). The Court, as compared to the Advocate General, emphasised the delimitation between the free movement of services and goods.[358] By characterising television programs as services, the Court implicitly answered the question if the Treaty is applicable to the audio-visual field in the first

---

[352] Except for Protocol 9 on the System of Public Broadcasting in the Member States annexed to the EC Treaty by the Treaty of Amsterdam. See at 7.1.7.

[353] [1974] ECR 409.

[354] This qualification was critiqued e.g., by V. Salvatore 'Quotas on TV Programmes and EEC Law', (1992) *CMLRev.* p. 967, p. 968.

[355] *Sacchi,* para 6.

[356] This qualification of television services as a service has been criticised by N. March-Hunnings, 'Annotation on Case 52/79 and Case 62/79' (1980) *CMLRev*. pp. 564-569, at p. 568.

[357] *Sacchi.,* point 7.

[358] See also N. March-Hunnings, 'Cable Television in Italy', (1975) *The Journal of Business Law*, p. 72.

place.[359] In its subsequent case law, the Court confirmed the qualification of television as a service.[360]

THE RELATIONSHIP BETWEEN MEDIA LAW AND COMPETITION LAW

Analysis often starts on the basis of the underlying assumption that media law and competition law are two separately coexisting sets of provisions. For example, *Hoffmann-Riem* distinguishes between publicist and economic competition and maintains that one can exist without the other.[361] He refers to the preamble of the Television without Frontiers Directive which provides that 'this Directive, being confined specifically to television broadcasting rules, is without prejudice to existing or future Community acts of harmonisation, in particular to satisfy mandatory requirements concerning the protection of consumers and the fairness of commercial transactions and competition'. From this wording, *Hoffmann-Riem* concludes that the EC recognises the distinction between media law and competition law.[362] This interpretation appears somewhat far-fetched, as it can also be interpreted as clarifying that television broadcasting is *additionally* to the specific rules in the Directive that are also subject to other community legislation, most notably the EC rules on competition. The Directive also refers to 'a system ensuring that competition in the common market is not distorted', and it is argued that media and competition law need to be understood as a comprehensive overall system; Competition law forms an integral part of media law.[363]

As the audio-visual field is subject to both sets of provisions, one cannot conclude that the Council agreed to a 'dualism'[364] between the two. Against this background, approaches trying to allocate television broadcasting to either specific media legislation or Competition law will fail. 'Special characteristics'[365] of television broadcasting must be taken into account within the framework of Competition law without, however, justifying any general and non-specific exceptions.

Part II is analyses how far the Court of Justice in its case law and Commission Decisions acknowledges public interest considerations in television broadcasting, in particular, aspects of cultural preservation, quality and pluralism.

---

[359] E.-J. Mestmäcker, ed., *Der Einfluß des europäischen Gemeinschaftsrechts auf die deutsche Rundfunkordnung* (1990) Baden-Baden, p. 36.

[360] See the cases quoted in D. Frey op. cit. n. 225, p. 31, footnote 36.

[361] W. Hoffmann-Riem, *Rundfunkrecht neben Wirtschaftsrecht. Zur Anwendbarkeit des GWB und des EWG-V auf das Wettbewerbsverhalten öffentlich-rechtlichen Rundfunks in der dualen Rundfunkordnung*, (1991) Baden-Baden, p. 27.

[362] Ibid., pp. 182, 183.

[363] See e.g., J. Temple Lang, *Media, Multimedia and European Antitrust Law*, (1997) Fordham Corporate Law Institute, pp. 81, 82, who suggests that antitrust issues still have to enter the awareness of media lawyers.

[364] W. Hoffmann-Riem, op.cit. n. 361, p. 183.

[365] Ibid.

Chapter 4
THE 'LEGITIMATE GENERAL INTEREST' AND BROADCASTING

4.1. The Concept in General

4.1.1. *Exceptions to the Freedoms in the Treaty*

First, it is useful to review why general interest considerations cannot be based on the exceptions to the freedoms provided by Treaty provisions, i.e., why the Court of Justice considered it useful to develop the concept of 'legitimate' or 'imperative' public interest in the first place. The legal framework of the Treaty provides for the free movement of goods, the basic rule in Article 28 (ex-Article 30) and an exception in Article 30 (ex-Article 36) EC. This structure of general rule and exception repeats itself for the free movement of services in Articles 49 (ex-Article. 59) and 55 (ex-Article 66, referring to Article 46 (1), ex-Article 56(1)). However, the exception for the free movement of good in Article 30 (ex-Article 36) is construed very narrowly and allows restrictions only on grounds of 'public morality, public policy or public security; the protection of health and life of humans, animals or plants; the protection of national treasures possessing artistic, historic or archaeological value; or the protection of industrial and commercial property' and by no means shall such a measure 'constitute a means of arbitrary discrimination or a disguised restriction'. Article 46(1) (ex-Article 56 (1)) contains an even narrower exception for the free movement of service on grounds of public policy, public security or public health. With regard to goods, the Court in Case 30/77 *Bouchereau*[366] stated:

> In so far as it may justify certain restrictions on the free movement of persons subject to community law, recourse by a national authority to the concept of public policy presupposes (...) the existence (...) of a *genuine and sufficiently serious threat* to the requirements of public policy affecting one of the fundamental interests of society.[367] (emphasis added)

Specifically in the field of broadcasting, the Court of Justice first applied an equally restrictive interpretation of Article 56 (now Article 46) in the Case of *Bond van Adverteerders*.[368] In this case, Dutch law provided for a total prohibition on adver-

---

[366] [1977] ECR 1999.

[367] Ibid., para 35; see also Case 116/82, *Commission* v. *Germany*, ECR [1986] 2519.

[368] Case 352/85, [1988] ECR 2085, see *infra* at 4.2.2.

[369] Ibid., para 34.

tising for cable television and restricted the use of sub-titling of foreign programs. By restricting advertising of cable television originating abroad, Dutch media law aimed to prevent the emergence of commercial cable television, which would compete with the national Dutch broadcasters. In particular, the national Court asked whether the measures could be justified on grounds relating to the public interest and proportionality. In the course of the proceedings, the German government claimed that Article 56 (now Article 46) was applicable. The Court disagreed and concluded that 'economic aims (...) cannot constitute grounds of public policy within the meaning of Article 56.'[369] The Dutch government's argument that, ultimately, the provisions were designed to pursue a non-economic objective, namely that of maintaining a non-commercial and pluralistic broadcasting system, did not succeed. The Court concluded that, as this aim could equally be achieved by less restrictive means, the Dutch law contravened the proportionality principle. It held that Article 56 (now Article 46) 'must be interpreted in such a way that its effects are limited to that which is necessary in order to protect the interests which it seeks to safeguard.[370] Hence, Article 56 (now Article 46) did, in practice, not provide an appropriate legal basis to justify public interest considerations, such as the maintenance of a pluralistic and non-commercial broadcasting system.

4.1.2. *Public Interest Concerns recognised as 'Mandatory Requirements'*

It has been claimed that, although Articles 30 (ex-Article 28) and 46 (ex-Article 56) are not applicable because they are too narrow to embrace a certain measure enacted by national legislation, non-economic aspects relating to the public interest should justify deviation from the basic freedoms. This has been suggested by some authors, for instance in the context of importing foodstuffs[371] or bookselling.[372] The Court has also developed possible exceptions which would be compatible with the free movement principle. It first established the concept of 'mandatory requirements' in its famous *Cassis*-judgement.[373] The Court in *Cassis* opened up an additional route to deviate from the free-movement-principle by stating that

> Obstacles (...) resulting from disparities between the nationals laws (...) may be necessary in order to satisfy *mandatory requirements* relating in particular to the

[370] Ibid., para 36.

[371] For a discussion, see e.g., Von Heydebrand u.d. Lasa, 'Free Movement of Foodstuff, Consumer Protection and Food Standards in the European Community: Has the Court of Justice Got it Wrong?', 16 *ELRev* (1991) p. 391

[372] See e.g., J.M.E. Loman/K.J.M. Mortelmans/H.H.G. Post/J.S. Watson, *Culture and Community Law. Before and after Maastricht,* (1992) Kluwer, pp. 101-106.

[373] Case 120/78 [1979] ECR 649. French Cassis de Dijon-liqueur containing 10-15 per cent of alcohol was prevented from entering the German market on the grounds that German law provided for a higher alcohol content to qualify a beverage as 'liqueur'.

effectiveness of fiscal supervision, the protection of public health, the fairness of commercial transactions and the defence of the consumer.[374] (italics added)

However, this non-exhaustive list is not to be understood as an opportunity to contravene the free movement of goods; to satisfy a mandatory requirement, a measure has to be compatible with Article 28 (ex-Article 30) in the first place.[375] Most importantly, it must apply equally to foreign and domestic traders, i.e., it must not be discriminatory. Otherwise, the concept of mandatory requirements is not available.

In the absence of harmonisation, trade barriers resulting from disparities in legislation can be justified. *Cassis* provides for a non-exhaustive list of 'mandatory requirements' which need to be satisfied to allow deviation from the free movement principle. Subsequently the Court in *Keck*[376] limited the application of Article 30 (now Article 28) to the extent that 'certain selling arrangements' are not covered by the free movement of goods, provided that they, first, apply to all traders operating within the national territory and, second, affect in the same manner, in law and in fact, the marketing of domestic and imported products.

Grounds of general interest (sometimes also called the 'general good' or 'overriding requirements') had been recognised by the Court in various fields, for example, the protection of professional rules,[377] the protection of intellectual property,[378] the defence of the consumer,[379] and the protection of workers.[380] Overriding requirements to justify rules likely to obstruct the exercise of free movement of goods must be interpreted with regard to the general principles of law, in particular fundamental rights.[381] In *Familiapress*,[382] the Court held that 'maintenance of press diversity may constitute an overriding requirement justifying a restriction on free movement of goods'.[383] Freedom of expression is also protected by Article 10[384] of

[374] Case 120/78, para. 8.

[375] P. Beaumont/S. Weatherill, op. cit. n. 59, p. 576.

[376] Cases 267 and 268/91 [1993] ECR I-6097.

[377] Cases 110 and 111/78, *Van Wesmael*, [1979] ECR 35, para 28.

[378] Case 62/79, *Coditel*, [1908] ECR 881.

[379] Case 220/83, *Commission* v. *France*, [1986] ECR 3663, para 20.

[380] Cases 179/80, *Webb*, [1981] ECR 3305, para 19, Case 62 and 63/81, *Seco*, [1982] ECR 223, para 14.

[381] Case C-260/89 *ERT* [1991] ECR I-2925, para 43.

[382] Case C-368/95, [1997] ECR I-3689.

[383] Ibid., para 18.

[384] '1. Everyone has the right to freedom of expression. This right shall include freedom to hold opinions and to receive and impart information and ideas without interference by public authority and regardless of frontiers. This article shall not prevent States from requiring the licensing of broadcasting, television or cinema enterprises.

2. The exercise of these freedoms, since it carries with it duties and responsibilities, may be subject to such formalities, conditions, restrictions or penalties as are prescribed by law and are necessary in a democratic society, in the interests of national security, territorial integrity or public safety, for the prevention of disorder or crime, for the protection of health or morals, for the protection of the reputation or rights of others, for preventing the disclosure of information received in confidence, or for maintaining the authority and impartiality of the judiciary.'

the European Convention on Human Rights and Fundamental Freedoms, which is, at the same time, one of the fundamental rights guaranteed by the Community legal order.[385] Thus, press diversity and freedom of expression are overriding public interest requirements also recognised by Community law.

The mandatory requirements doctrine was subsequently extended to the free movement of services. In its judgement in *Van Binsbergen*,[386] the Court of Justice held that

> ... taking into account the particular nature of the services to be provided, specific requirements imposed on the person cannot be considered incompatible with the Treaty where they have as their purpose the application of professional rules justified by the *general good* – in particular rules relating to organisations, professional ethics, supervision and liability – which are binding upon any person established in the state in which the service is provided ...[387] (italics added)

Although the Court uses different terms ('mandatory' or 'overriding requirements', 'general interest' or 'the general good'), the parallels are obvious. Certain barriers, resulting from differences in national regulation, must, in the absence of harmonisation, also be respected by EC law.

This basic principle, however, was applied rather restrictively by the Court in subsequent proceedings. National regulation impeding the provision of a cross-border-service is subject to the state's ability to demonstrate overriding concern regarding the public interest, which cannot be met by less restrictive means of trade.[388] For example, in the so-called 'tourist guide cases',[389] Member States relied on consumer interests to justify various professional requirements. In *Commission* v. *Italy*,[390] Italian law[391] provided that tourist guides accompanying groups of tourists to places other than museums or historical monuments needed a special license which could only be obtained subject to the passing of an exam. Obviously, this was a disadvantage for tourist guides accompanying groups from other Member States. In fact, they would in most cases have to hire an additional local guide who held this special qualification. The Court found that the law in question 'prevents both tour companies from providing that service with their own staff and self-employed tourist guides from offering their services to those companies for organised tours.'[392]

---

385 Case C 353/89, *Commission* v. *Netherlands*, [1991] ECR I-4069, para 30.

386 Case 33/74 [1974] *ECR* 1299; The case concerned a Dutch lawyer, who, during proceedings before a Dutch court, moved to Belgium and was thus denied the right to act as a lawyer before the court; Dutch law prescribing that a lawyer has to be established in the Netherlands.

387 Ibid., para 12.

388 P. Beaumont/S. Weatherill, op. cit. n. 59, p. 682.

389 Cases C-154/89, *Commission* v. *France*, ECR [1991] I-659, C-180/89, *Commission* v. *Italy*, ECR [1991] I-709 and C-198/98 *Commission* v. *Greece*, ECR [1991] I-727.

390 ECR [1991] I-709.

391 Official Journal of the Italian Republic No. 141 of 25 May 1983, p. 4091.

392 Case C-180/89, *Commission* v. *Italy*, ECR [1991] I-709, para 16.

However, in the view of 'specific requirements' relating to certain services, such rules did not contravene Article 59 (now Article 49) if they were objectively justified in the general interest, proportionate and not already safeguarded by legislation of the Member State of establishment.[393] The last condition is also known as prohibition on 'double-checking' of goods or 'secondary control' of a service.[394] The Court held that, although consumer protection and the conservation of the national historical and artistic heritage can constitute an overriding reason justifying a restriction on the freedom to provide a service, the requirements in question did not satisfy the proportionality-criterion.[395]

In the case of *Commission* v. *Germany*,[396] the Commission challenged the German insurance supervision law – which provided that insurance undertakings offering their services in Germany had to be established and authorised thereon the grounds that it had failed to fulfil its obligation to transpose into national law Council Directive 78/473/EEC.[397] The Commission considered the establishment criteria as violating this Directive and Articles 59 and 60 (now Articles 49 and 50). The Court referred to its well-established case law that specific requirements imposed on a service provider are not incompatible with Article 59 (now Article 49) and repeated the conditions (justified by the general good, applied in a non-discriminatory manner, no double-checking, proportionate[398]) already set out in *Van Wesmael* and *Commission* v. *Italy*. However, the Court acknowledged that 'the insurance sector is a particularly sensitive area from the point of view of the protection of the consumer'[399] and considered the proportionality test satisfied.

The most comprehensive definition of the 'general good' is provided by the Court in the *Gebhard* case,[400] also known as the 'Gebhard formula'. It consists of four main criteria:

> ... [N]ational measures liable to hinder or make less attractive the exercise of fundamental freedoms guaranteed by the Treaty must fulfil four conditions: they must be applied in a *non-discriminatory* manner; they must be justified by imperative requirements in the *general interest*; they must be *suitable* for securing the attainment of the objective which they pursue; and they must not go beyond what is *necessary* in order to attain it.[401] (italics added)

---

393 Ibid., para 17; Case 205/84, *Commission* v. *Germany*, [1986] ECR 3755, para 27.

394 Unlike domestic traders, who only have to comply with the regulatory regime of one Member State, importers must also observe the laws of the Member State into which they import a product. This makes cross-border trade potentially more difficult and costly.

395 Ibid., paras 20 and 24.

396 Case 205/84 [1986] ECR 3755.

397 *OJ* 1978 L 151/25.

398 Case 205/84 [1986] ECR 3755, para 27.

399 Case 204/85, para 30.

400 Case C-55/94 [1995] ECR I-4165.

401 Ibid., para 37, confirmed in Case C-19/92 *Kraus* [1993] ECR I-1661, para 32; *Centros* [1999] ECR I-1459, para 34.

Most contentious is probably the last criteria mentioned, the prohibition on measures that go beyond what is strictly necessary. Hence, public interest concerns can only be successfully advanced if the goal could not be achieved by less restrictive means, otherwise the measure will be held to be disproportionate. This is notably the case for Member State's legislation that provide for 'double checking',[402] for example, if a certain goal is already safeguarded by the legislation of the export country or, in the case of a service, the Member State of establishment of the service provider, rules of the import country or the country where the service is provided must not be applied if they ensure the same aim. In such a case, mutual trust requires that the importing Member State or the Member State where the service is provided are satisfied with the safeguard mechanisms of the exporting Member State or the Member State of establishment respectively.

The Court repeatedly recognised public interest concerns as such, which Member States relied on during proceedings, but in the course of the analysis finally strikes down national legislation with the proportionality test. This test can be further broken down into three elements, namely causation; proportionality, strictly speaking; and necessity; and is used in different areas of Community law.[403] For instance, in the field of food regulation, the Court has consistently held that labelling is sufficient to achieve the aim of consumer protection, and qualified content requirement as disproportionate.[404] This approach has been criticised for disguising what is, in fact, politics. Distinguishing between 'ends' and 'means' cannot be a value-free process and should arguably not be left to a Court.[405]

Although the Court in its case law used different terms ('mandatory requirements', 'overriding public interest concerns', 'the general good'), the essential elements boil down to a common set of criteria, which have to be fulfilled to render a regulatory national measure restricting the free movement principle compatible with Articles 28 (ex-Article 30) or 49 (ex-Article 59). Broadcasting constitutes a core field where this principle has been applied and further developed, as will be demonstrated by analysing the case law below.

---

[402] P. Beaumont/S. Weatherill, op.cit. n. 59, p. 541.

[403] J. Schwarze, *European Administrative Law*, (1992) London/Luxembourg, Sweet and Maxwell, p. 854 et seq.; see also G. De Burca, 'The Principle of Proportionality and its Application in EC Law', 13 *YEL* (1993) 113.

[404] If national food regulations, for instance, provide that sausages must consist of a certain percentage of meat, imported sausages need not comply with this requirement, as long as a lower meat content is indicated on the label; this would suffice to protect the 'reasonably circumspect' consumer. See e.g., also Case C-470/93 *Mars* [1995] ECR I-1923, where the Court found a breach of Art. 30 (now Art. 28). German consumer law prohibited the sale of chocolate bars with a wrapping indicating + 10 per cent, when the marked area on the wrapping was actually larger than an increase of 10 per cent. In fact the chocolate bar was 10 per cent larger, but the size of the differently coloured wrapping indicating the promotion did not comply with the increase of chocolate. However, the Court found the misleading wrapping irrelevant, because a 'reasonably circumspect consumer' would not be confused.

[405] *G. Majone, Evidence, Argument and Perusalsion in the Policy Proces* (London, New Haven, 1989).

4.2. Public Interest Concerns in the Case Law on Broadcasting – Free Movement of Services

4.2.1. *Case 52/79 Debauve*

In *Debauve*,[406] the Tribunal Correctionnel in Liége applied for a preliminary ruling under Article 177 (now Article 234) on the interpretation of Articles 59 and 60 (now Articles 49 and 50). In criminal proceedings before the Tribunal, the question occurred whether Belgian law, which prohibits the transmission of broadcasts 'in the nature of commercial advertising', was compatible with the free movement of services. Since 1966, Belgian law has required cable diffusion firms to blot out all commercials in foreign television programs.[407] Cable distributors had disregarded this prohibition and transmitted foreign programmes, *including* advertising transmissions. Belgian authorities turned a blind eye for some time, but in 1974, various consumer groups launched official complaints. In the course of the national proceedings, the Liége Tribunal was asked whether certain national rules, such as the Belgian law prohibiting advertising, contravened Article 59 (now Article 49) and if the latter provision had direct effect with regard to national legislation. It also emphasised that, because of geographical circumstances, foreign broadcastings could, in any event, be received by some Belgian households via terrestrial signal.

The Advocate General, in his Opinion,[408] stated that, although Belgian law comes inside the Treaty provision on services, and restricted the uninhibited cross-border circulation of broadcasting signals, the measure ultimately benefited from the public policy-exception in Article 56 (now Article 46). In contrast, the Court did not rule on the question if Article 56 (now Article 46) could be applied, but concluded instead that specific requirements could legally be imposed on service providers, as long as they were 'justified by the general interest and apply to all persons and undertakings' and are 'not subject to similar regulations' in the Member State of establishment.[409]

Unlike the Advocate General, the Court invoked the concept of 'general interest' instead of Article 56 and concluded that, in the absence of harmonisation of national broadcasting regulation, in particular with regard to advertising, restrictions resulting from legal disparities had to be accepted under Community law.[410] It was even legitimate to totally prohibit television advertising,[411] and the fact that some Belgian households will still be able to receive foreign programs containing adver-

---

[406] Judgement of 18 March 1980, [1980] ECR 833.
[407] T. Benett, 'The Debauve and Coditel Cases' (1980) *ELRev*. pp.224-232, p. 225.
[408] [1980] ECR 833.
[409] Ibid., para 13. This can be qualified as prohibition on secondary control; see *supra* at 4.1.2
[410] Ibid.
[411] Ibid., para 15.

tising as a terrestrial signal, does not mean that the measure was disproportionate.[412]

This judgement did not even foreshadow the legal and political controversy on broadcasting that would follow. However, already in this early judgement, the Court did not apply Article 56 (now Article 46), but chose the far more flexible case law which has developed the concept of 'general interest'.

4.2.2. *Case 352/85 Bond van Adverteerders*[413]

The *Gerechtshof* in Den Haag (Regional Court of Appeal) applied for a preliminary ruling to clarify if the Dutch Cable Regulation Act (*Kabelregeling*) violated Article 59 (now Article 49). Its Article 4 (1)[414] prohibited cable programs, including advertisements targeted at a Dutch audience, and subjected programs containing Dutch subtitles to an authorisation that had to be obtained from the Dutch minister. This legislation aimed to prevent circumvention of the Dutch restrictions on advertising by foreign broadcasters.[415] According to an explanatory note to the Kabelregeling, these restrictions were designed to prevent the indirect establishment of commercial television in the Netherlands, which would unfairly compete with national broadcasting.[416] Dutch advertisers complained that the advertising facilities in the Netherlands were too restricted.[417]

In its application, the Dutch court asked if the provisions of the *Kableregeling* under consideration were compatible with Article 59 (now Article 49) and if the general interest of maintaining a pluralistic and non-economic broadcasting system justified restriction of the freedom to provide services. In the proceedings before the Court, lengthy discussions took place regarding whether a television signal transmitted via cable is a single activity or whether it can be broken down into two or three independent supplies of services. The Advocate General, after discussing the parties' submissions, concluded 'that the programme is deliberately aimed at an audience on the other side of the frontier',[418] which entails a cross-border element

---

412 Ibid., paras 17, 18.

413 Judgment of 26. April 1988, [1988] ECR 2085.

414 'The use of an antenna system to relay to the public radio television programmes shall be authorized in the case of (...) c) programmes supplied from abroad via cable, over the air or by satellite, by or on behalf of an organization of group of organizations distributing the programme in the country in which it is established by means of a transmitter or a cable network provided that: the programme does not contain advertisements intended especially for the public in the Netherlands; the programme does not contain subtitles in Dutch, unless authorisation has been granted by the minister'.

415 G. Friden, 'The "Bond van Adverteerders" case and recent legal developments in EEC "television law"' (1990) *LJIL* pp. 231-238, at p. 232.

416 [1988] ECR 2085, para 5.

417 Under Dutch law, it was only possible to obtain advertising time from the *STER* (*Stichting Ether Reclame*), which held a monopoly.

418 Ibid., para 7 of the Opinion

sufficient to render Article 59 (now Article 49) applicable. Furthermore, 'a program broadcast in a Member State (...) must be regarded as a single provision of services even if that programme is supplied to viewers in another Member State by satellite or is distributed by cable.'[419] In the judgement, however, the Court stipulated that the distribution of a television program by a cable operator established in one Member State containing a program intended for the audience in another Member State 'comprises a number of services within the meaning of Articles 59 and 60 of the Treaty'.[420] The prohibition on subtitling, as contained in the Kabelregeling, restricted the freedom to supply a service[421] and was held contrary to be Article 59 (now Article 49).[422] Although the Advocate General and the judges disagreed on how many servicing activities were involved, both found a breach of Article 59 (now Article 49).

The Dutch government could not successfully rely on the public interest exception in Article 56 (now Article 46) because, even if the measure pursued the non-economic aim of maintaining a pluralistic broadcasting system, this goal could have been equally achieved by less restrictive means and thus the measure was disproportionate.[423] In any event, the economic aim of securing all advertising revenue to a public body, the STER, cannot constitute a grounds of public policy in the sense of Article 56[424] (now Article 46).

Interestingly, the Court did not touch upon the substantive question of the interpretation of the concept of public interest considerations,[425] as developed by its own case law. It confined itself to striking the measure down with the proportionality test. Unlike *Debauve*, it did not consider it necessary to justify Dutch national regulations. However, the Court confirmed *Debauve*, insofar as Article 56 (now Article 46) was of no use for defending the national regulation. The Court applied the proportionality test very narrowly, and although the judgement did not got as far as the Advocate General's Opinion[426] in eliminating the Member States' discretion to shape its broadcasting system, it raised concerns that Community law as applied by the Court intruded areas which the drafters of the Treaty never intended to cover.[427]

---

419 Ibid., para 8.

420 Ibid., Judgment, para 17.

421 It is noteworthy, that Art. 59 (now Art. 49) was for the first time held to also safeguard the export (and not only import) of a service. See G. Friden, 'The "Bond van Adverteerders" case and recent legal developments in EEC "television law"', (1990) *LJIL* pp. 231-238, at p. 237.

422 Case 352/85, *Bond*, para. 30 of the Judgment.

423 Ibid., para 36.

424 Ibid., para 34.

425 M. De Blois, Case Note on Case 352/85 Bond van Adverteerders, 27 *CMLRev.* (1990) pp. 371-381, p. 379.

426 See more detailed I., Schwartz, 'Broadcasting and the EEC Treaty' (1986) 11 *ELRev.*, p. 17 et seq.

427 See, e.g., M. De Blois, op. cit. n. 425, p. 371. See also E.-J. Mestmäcker, 'The EC Commission's Modernization of Competition Policy: a Challenge to the Community's Constitution', 1 *EBOR* (2000) pp. 499-542, pp. 511, 512.

4.2.3. *Cases C-288/89 Gouda and C-353/89 Commission* v. *Netherlands*

The factual background of *Gouda*[428] and *Commission* v. *Netherlands*[429] is very similar and, thus, the two judgements shall be discussed together. Moreover, the Advocate General delivered a joint opinion. Again, Dutch broadcasting law was subject to the Court's scrutiny. A new law, the *Mediawet*, had in the meantime, replaced the *Kabelregeling.*[430]

In the *Gouda* case, a Dutch Court applied for a preliminary proceeding basically questioning the legality of the *Mediawet* under Community law, in particular, its compatibility with Article 59 (now Article 49). The Dutch *Commissariaat voor de Media*, a media supervisory body, had imposed fines for relaying foreign television programmes which contained advertisements in the Dutch language.[431] *The Commission* v. *Netherlands* case was an infringement procedure under Article 169 (now Article 226), which the Commission initiated against the Netherlands on the grounds that the *Mediawet* violated the free movement of services. *Gouda* was an application for a preliminary ruling by the Dutch *Raad van State*, also concerning the application of the *Mediawet.*

The new Article 66 Mediawet[432] stipulated that cable television broadcasting that included advertising programmes had to fulfil certain conditions: *inter alia*, they had to be produced by a separate legal person and be clearly distinct from other programmes. Advertising was limited to five per cent of the total program time and generally prohibited on Sundays. The Dutch system was characterised by allocating airtime to different social groups, allegedly representing the main schools of thought in Dutch society. These bodies were, in principle, free to produce programmes themselves, however, they were obliged to use the facilities of the

---

[428] Judgement of 25 July 1991, [1991] ECR I-4007.

[429] Judgement of 25 July 1991, [1991] ECR I-4069.

[430] Staatsblad No 249 of 4 June 1987.

[431] J. Feenstra, 'Case Note on Cases C-288/89 Gouda and C-353/89 *Commission* v. *Netherlands*', 30 *CMLRev*. (1993) pp. 424-432, at p. 424.

[432] '(1) The operator of the cable networks may: (a) transmit programmes which are broadcast by a foreign broadcasting body by means of a broadcasting transmitter and which may, most of the time, be received directly in the area served by the cable network by means of a normal individual aerial with a reasonable standard of quality; (b) transmit programmes other that those mentioned in (a) which are broadcast by a foreign broadcasting body or a group of such bodies as broadcasting programmes, in accordance with the legislation in force in the broadcasting country. If such programmes contain advertisements, they may be transmitted solely provided that the advertisements are produces by a separate legal person, that they are clearly identifiable as such and such advertisements does not exceed 5 % of the total air time utilised, that the broadcasting body fulfils the conditions laid down in Article 55(1) and that the entire revenue is used for the production of programmes. Nevertheless, if those conditions are not fulfilled, such a programme may also be transmitted provided that the advertisements contained therein are not specifically intended for the Dutch public;...'

Nederlandse Omroepproduktie Bedrijf (Broadcasting Production Company) ('NOPB').[433]

The Court in its Judgements first acknowledges that, 'at the outset (...) the system set up by Article 61 of the *Mediawet* does in fact result in a restriction on the freedom to provide services in the Community within the meaning of Article 59 of the Treaty'.[434] The *Mediawet* contained 'a two-fold restriction on the freedom to provide services. First, they prevent operators of cable networks established in a Member State from transmitting radio or television programmes (...). Secondly, they restrict the opportunities offered to those broadcasting bodies to include in their programmes (...) advertising intended specifically for the public in that State.'[435]

In its analysis, the Court distinguished between conditions on the structure of the broadcaster and conditions directly relating to the advertisement. The former could not be regarded as objectively necessary.[436] In order to secure pluralism, the Court held that it was sufficient to confine these provisions to Dutch broadcasters. The restriction on broadcasting advertising 'may be justified by overriding reasons relating to the general interest'.[437] However, although the *Mediawet*, unlike its predecessor, the *Kabelregeling*, did not reserve *all* the advertising revenue to the STER, it still pursued the same (economic) objective, namely, to protect the STER from competition it would otherwise be exposed to.[438] As this very objective of the national legislation could never be justified under Article 56 (now Article 46), the new Dutch provisions were incompatible with the free movement on services, regardless of the actual degree of protection enjoyed by the public body.

The arguments put forward by the Dutch Government in *Commission* v. *Netherlands* – that the restrictions are necessary to ensure a smooth transition and avoid mass redundancies – were unsuccessful.[439] A protection from competition could not be claimed, as Article 59 (now Article 49) had became directly applicable with the expiry of the transitional period on 31 December 1969.[440] The reason why, in

[433] Art. 61 Mediawet: 'In order to ensure that the means of production are maintained, bodies which have obtained air time on the national network must spend with the NOPB each year all the amounts allocated to them under Articles 101 and 102 with regard to the production of radio programmes and a percentage determined by decree with regard to the production of television programmes'. Public broadcasters were obliged to obtain 75 per cent of their requirements for programme production facilities from NOPB.

[434] *Commission* v. *Netherlands*, para 22. The term 'restriction of the freedom to provide services' was by the Court interpreted as also covering discrimination on the grounds of establishment in another Member State. It was not required that the discrimination was based on a distinction between national and foreign broadcasters. See ibid. para 13 and already G. Marenco, 'The Notion of Restriction on the Freedom of Establishment and Provision of Services in the Case-Law of the Court', 11 *YEL* (1991) p. 128.

[435] *Gouda*, para 17, *Commission* v. *Netherlands*, para 38.

[436] *Gouda*, para 25.

[437] Ibid., para 27; as similar statement it to be found in *Commission* v. *Netherlands*, para 30.

[438] Ibid., para 29 and *Commission* v. *Netherlands*, para 47.

[439] *Commission* v. *Netherlands*, para 26.

[440] Ibid., para 27.

this case, the Dutch law was found to contravene Article 59 (now Article 49) was the fact that restrictions on advertising only applied to programmes targeting a Dutch audience, which suggested that they had projectionist character.[441]

4.2.4. *Case C-211/91 Commission* v. *Belgium*

Commission v. *Belgium*[442] involved a straightforward case of discrimination, a fact not even denied by the defendant, the Belgian government. Belgian law prohibited the transmission of a television broadcast from another Member State, in case the programme was not in the official language of the state of origin. It also contained further restrictions on broadcasting, such as a requirement for prior authorisation, and it defined in a discriminatory way the notion of 'own cultural productions' which constituted a compulsory part of the commercial programmes.

These provisions were found by the Court to constitute a barrier to the freedom to provide services, as they prevented television stations established in other Member States from transmitting in any but their own official language/s.[443] As they did not apply to Belgian television operators, the restriction was discriminatory[444] and in violation of Article 59 (now Article 49). It virtually excluded all but Dutch programmes originating from the Netherlands from penetrating the Flemish-speaking area of Belgium. The Belgian government relied on cultural policy objectives to justify the restrictions. It invoked the need to maintain pluralism in the printed press by ensuring all the advertising revenue for the national broadcaster. This argument failed to convince the Court, which found the Belgian legislation to 'restrict genuine competition with the national broadcasting stations'.[445] The objectives of maintaining 'pluralism in the printed press' and 'the viability of the national broadcasting stations' revealed to the Court economic aims such shielding national broadcasters from competition and reducing demand for television in Dutch,[446] and were incapable of benefiting from Article 56 (now Article 46).

This judgement reveals how the free movement and competition rules are interlinked. In this case, the Court assessed the criteria in Article 56 (now Article 46) with regard to their impact on demand and competition between public national and (foreign) private broadcasters. The national regulator is restricted on how to shape a national broadcasting system by the four freedoms. Although the decision is rather general and does not go into any detail regarding precisely which Treaty provisions had been violated, it confirms that no remedy on cultural grounds is available by a

---

[441] J. Feenstra, Case Note on Cases C-288/89 *Gouda* and C-353/89 *Commission* v. *Netherlands*, 30 *CMLRev*. (1993) pp. 424-432, at p. 430.

[442] Judgement of 16 December 1992, [1992] ECR I-6757.

[443] Ibid., para 5.

[444] Ibid., para 6. The restriction does not apply to Belgian television operators because it is targeted against broadcasters established in another Member State transmitting *into* Belgium.

[445] Ibid., para. 7.

[446] Ibid.

'general interest', if the national legislation is directly discriminatory. The Court was not afraid to counter cultural arguments, such as the protection of national heritage with economic consideration, when it suspected cultural arguments to be used merely as a pretext. Hence, although one cannot conclude that the latter, in the given circumstances, takes precedence over the former, the Court will not be satisfied with the mere claim that a national measure is designed to protect cultural, and in any event, non-economic goals. This approach, developed on the case law of the basic freedoms, will also be relevant for the financing of broadcasting and its relation to EC state aid law.[447]

4.2.5. *Case C-11/95 Commission* v. *Belgium*

Commission v. *Belgium*[448] was decided on the basis of the 'Television without Frontiers' Directive[449] before its amendment. It focused on the question whether the Directive had been correctly transposed into Belgian law, in particular, if a system of prior authorisation of a foreign television program was compatible with the Directive.[450] The Court held that the 'country of origin' principle demanded free circulation of television programmes within the internal market without being inhibited by an authorisation requirement.[451]

However, aspects of the case also related to cultural issues and how they were recognised by the Treaty. The Belgian government maintained that Articles 4 and 5 of the Directive – which basically contain the 'European works quota' – must be interpreted in the light of Article 128 (now Article 151) of the Treaty on culture and would thus justify additional control by the receiving Member State. The argument was not accepted by the Court because it 'does not in any way authorise the receiving state, by way of derogation from the system established by Directive 89/552/EEC, to make programmes emanating from other Member States subject to further control.'[452] Further, the principle of subsidiarity in Article 3(b) (now Article 5) could not be of any assistance to the Belgian government because it cannot interfere with the principle of free reception established by the Directive.[453]

---

[447] See *infra* Chapter 7.

[448] Judgment of 10 September 1996, [1995] ECR I-4114.

[449] Directive 89/552/EEC, *OJ* 1989 L298/23.

[450] See para 33 of the Judgment: 'Member States are to ensure freedom of reception and must not restrict retransmission on their territory of television broadcasts from other Member States for reasons which fall within the fields coordinated by the directive'.

[451] This was subsequently also clarified by the amending Directive 97/36/EC, *OJ* 1997 L202/60, inserting Art. 2a which expressly provides that 'Member States shall ensure freedom of reception and shall not restrict retransmission on their territory of television broadcasts from other Member States for reasons which fall within the fields coordinated by this Directive'.

[452] Para 50 of the Judgment.

[453] Para 52 of the Judgment. The subsidiarity principle only applies if both the Member State and the EC are competent to regulate a specific subject matter; see e.g., D. Dörr, 'Europäische Medienordnung und – politik' in: *Internationales Handbuch für Hörfunk und Fernsehen 1996/97*, (1996) p. 36 et seq.

As for the preservation of pluralism in the media, the Court left open the question whether the Directive had already harmonised the matter.[454] Indeed, Article 19 of the Directive stipulates that Member States may *under their jurisdiction*, lay down stricter rules 'taking into account in particular (...) the role of television providing information, education, culture and entertainment [... and/or] the protection of pluralism of information and of the media'. This could be read as excluding national regulations that aim to maintain pluralism in the media, that is, in its effect, which is not strictly limited to national broadcasters but also effects trans-border broadcasting. On the other hand, such far-reaching interpretation appears incompatible with the general principle of minimum harmonisation in the Directive; rec. 14 of the preamble expressly confirms that the independence of cultural developments in the Member States and the preservation of cultural diversity remain unaffected.

4.2.6. *Joined Cases 34-36/95 De Agostini*[455]

The three cases dealt with the application of Swedish consumer protection law to television broadcasting and its assessment under Community law. In the first case, the Swedish Consumer Ombudsman (*KO*) invoked a violation of Article 11 of the Swedish Broadcasting Law, resulting in a request for an injunction to prohibit the defendant, De Agostini, from marketing its magazine via broadcasting on the basis of the Swedish Marketing Practices Law. De Agostini, a Swedish company belonging to an Italian group active all over Europe, had advertised its children's magazine about dinosaurs on both a Swedish channel and a satellite channel emanating from the UK. The second and third cases concerned TV-Shop, a Swedish subsidiary of TV-Shop Europe, specialising in teleshopping. The pertinent goods were skin-care products and a detergent advertised on Swedish and satellite television. In all three cases, the KO considered the marketing to be contrary to the Swedish Marketing Practices Act 1975 (*Marknadsföringslagen, MFL*), in particular as violating provisions against misleading advertising (in cases two and three) and its prohibition against targeting children under 12 (in the first case). The Swedish Market Court referred the following questions to the Court: firstly, can Article 30 (now Article 28) or Article 59 (now Article 49) or the Directive 89/552/EEC be interpreted in the sense that they prevent a Member State from taking action against cross-border television advertising, and secondly, do these provisions preclude the application of a prohibition on advertising directed at children.[456] The reference

[454] In particular, the Court referred to Articles 10(1), 11(1), 17(1)(a) on advertising and sponsoring and Art. 19, which provides for the admissibility of stricter rules for national broadcasters.

[455] Judgment of 9 July 1997, [1997] ECR I-3843.

[456] A. Criscuolo, 'The "TV Without Frontiers" Directive and the Legal Regulation of Publicity in the European Community' (1998) *ELRev* pp. 357-363, p. 359.

had been originally directed to the EFTA Court but was subsequently withdrawn when Sweden acceded to the European Union on 1 January 1995.[457]

As in the *Commission* v. *Belgium*, the Court held that the 'transmitting state' or 'country of origin' principle as enshrined in Article 2 of the Directive allows secondary control on content only if another Member State manifestly, seriously and gravely infringes Article 22.[458] As to the second question, the Court[459] and the Advocate General in his Opinion[460] agreed that Articles 16 and 22 of the Directive contained provisions specifically devoted to the protection of minors. Hence, this field had been harmonised by the Directive and Member States may no longer apply their national regulation.

The answer to the first question was less straightforward. Council Directive 84/450/EEC concerning misleading advertising[461] ('the MAD Directive') established minimum criteria for determining whether advertising can be considered as misleading, and laid down minimum requirements of protection against such advertising. The *KO* argued that, due to the MAD Directive, the Television Directive did not apply because Rec. 17 of the Television Directive provides that it is

> ... without prejudice to existing or future Community acts of harmonisation, in particular to satisfy mandatory requirements concerning the protection of consumers and the fairness of commercial transactions and competition.

The *KO* reads this provision as excluding the notion of misleading advertising from the scope of the Television Directive. The Advocate General dismissed this argument and submitted that it simply means that acts of harmonisation such as the MAD Directive are not affected by the Television Directive. Hence, the latter, and most importantly, the 'transmitting state principle', which it enshrines, remained applicable to misleading advertising. The Advocate General's argument failed to convince the Court, which concluded that the Member States may still enact measures to ensure consumer protection against misleading advertising[462] under the condition that it does not, first, amount to secondary control and, secondly, prevent retransmission as such into its territory.[463] It held that misleading advertising was not governed by the Television Directive.

---

[457] See para 20 of the Opinion.

[458] 'Member States shall take appropriate measures to ensure that television broadcasts by broadcasters under their jurisdiction do not include programmes which might seriously impair the physical, mental or moral development of minors, in particular those that involve pornography or gratuitous violence ...' Art. 2(2) of the Directive contains a detailed procedure which must be complied with to restrict transmission on the basis of Art. 22.

[459] See paras 57-62 of the Judgment.

[460] See paras 56 and 57 of the Opinion.

[461] *OJ* 1984 L 250/17.

[462] Para 38 of the Judgment.

[463] A. Criscuolo, 'The "TV Without Frontiers" Directive and the Legal Regulation of Publicity in the European Community' (1998) *ELRev* pp. 357-363, at p. 361.

Of specific interest regarding the acknowledgement of public interest considerations are the Court's findings on the compatibility of the Swedish legislation with Articles 30 (now Article 28) and 59 (now Article 49). The Court, in citing *Leclerc-Siplec*,[464] identified a (partial) ban on advertising as selling arrangement in the sense of *Keck*,[465] a case that was intended to clarify and limit the scope of Article 30.[466] The Court and the Advocate General concluded that Article 30 (now Article 28) was not infringed, provided that the criteria laid down in *Keck* were met: a measure necessary to satisfy imperative requirements[467] restricting the free movement of goods was permissive if it, first, applied to all relevant traders operating within the national territory, i.e., was indistinctly applicable, and second, affected in the same manner, in law and in fact, the marketing of domestic products and those from other Member States.[468] The Court emphasised that it was for the national court to determine whether the advertising ban was necessary and proportionate in satisfying overriding requirements of general public importance.[469] In particular, unlike in other judgements, the Court did not comment on whether it considered the measure proportionate but confined itself to merely mentioning its significance. Hence, regarding the admissibility of national measures to prevent misleading advertising, the ultimate decision remained with the national court.

4.3. **Freedom of Establishment and Exclusive Broadcasting Rights**

As is apparent from the case law discussed in 4.2, the majority of the cases have been dealt with under the free movement of services. Yet, there has also been a recent judgement which affirms the compatibility of exclusive rights to broadcast advertising with the freedom of establishment and possible justification of a restriction by imperative reasons of public interest.

In *VTM* v. *Commission*,[470] the Court of First Instance (CFI) had to decide a case where Belgian law required authorisation of private broadcasting and that the head office be in the Dutch-speaking part of Belgium.[471] It also demanded that the program be broadcast to the Flemish community as a whole and that at least 51 per cent of the shares shall be controlled by publishers of Dutch-language newspapers and magazines. Moreover, only *one* approved television broadcaster may be authorised to broadcast advertising.

---

[464] Case C-412/93 [1995] ECR I-6097.

[465] Cases C-267 and C-268/91 [1993] ECR I-6097.

[466] J. Stuyck, 34 *CMLRev.* (1997), pp. 1445-1468, at pp. 1464, 1465.

[467] This term (sometimes also referred to as 'mandatory requirements') constitutes the corollary to 'the general interest' or 'overriding public interest' in the area of the free movement of goods. See *supra* at 4.1.2.

[468] See also *supra* at 4.1.2.

[469] Para 45 of the Judgment.

[470] Case T-266/97, [1999] ECR II-2329.

[471] This requirement was abolished following the Judgment in Case C-211/91.

Accordingly, the Flemish Government approved the Vlaamse Televisie Maatschappij ('VTM') and authorised it to transmit advertising. Later, the London-based broadcaster VT4, incorporated under English law, started broadcasting programs via satellite including advertising aimed at the Flemish community and lodged a complaint with the Commission. In its Decision[472] pursuant to Article 90(3) (now Article 86(3)) the Commission declared the Belgian provisions incompatible with Article 90(1) (now Article 86(1)).[473] This Decision was challenged by VTM before the Court of First Instance. Large parts of the Judgement discuss procedural issues. In substantive law terms, the CFI upheld the Commission Decision in its entirety.

The CFI found that the Belgian provisions were liable to hamper or render less attractive the exercise of the freedom of establishment in the sense of the *Kraus* Judgement, because they made it impossible for a company from another Member State wishing to broadcast television advertising from Belgium to establish itself there.

The requirement that 51 per cent of the shares be held by the Flemish press was justified by the Belgian Government due to the need to remedy the loss of advertising revenue which the Flemish press would suffer with the introduction of private commercial television. Thus, the idea was to grant the Flemish press preferential access to the shares of the private broadcaster VTM to at least partly remedy their loss of advertising revenue by the dividends paid by VTM. The Belgian Government maintained that this measure was necessary to maintain pluralism in the Flemish media. The Commission found this measure ill-suited to achieve the envisaged aim. As it was possible that a single undertaking could acquired the entire 51 percent stake in VTM, there was thus no causal link between the Belgian provisions and the objective of cultural policy and media pluralism.[474] Moreover, some publishers only entered the Flemish media market *after* the shares of VTM had already been divided. Thus, VTM's exclusive right merely favoured one group of publishers over another. The CFI also rejected VTM's argument that it is sufficient if the measure was introduced for 'acceptable reasons',[475] because

> '(...) if the applicant's argument were accepted, it would make it impossible to contest any State measure granting an exclusive right to an undertaking if the grant of that right was initially justified (...) by "acceptable reasons". It would also become impossible to apply the rules on the fundamental freedoms contained in the Treaty to a State measure granting an exclusive right to an undertaking even though the impediments created by that right were no longer justified by overriding interests relating to the public interest.'[476]

---

[472] Decision 97/606/EC, *OJ* 1997, L 244/18.
[473] For a detailed discussion of Art. 86 (ex-Art. 90) see chapter 7.
[474] Decision 97/606/EC, preamble, point 13, para 5.
[475] Case T-266/97, para 82.
[476] Ibid., para 109.

The relevant question was not if that measure had been justified at the time of introduction, but whether the exclusive right granted was *still* justified at the time of the proceedings. Finally, the measure was found not to be proportionate, because it could have been attained by granting subsidies to the press, as the Commission stated.

In sum, it appears that protecting a private company from competition to achieve cultural aims and foster media pluralism is not compatible with the common market. In this case, the CFI comes very close indeed to saying that conferring an exclusive right to broadcast television commercials was in itself a violation of Article 86(1) read in conjunction with Article 43.[477]

4.4. Conclusion

These cases cover a whole range of legal problems concerning the freedom to provide services, the free movement of goods, the freedom of establishment and aspects of interpreting the Television without Frontiers Directive. For the sake of deducing the Court's approach regarding issues of pluralism, protection of national culture and consumer interests in a broader sense, the case law has mainly been analysed according to the role it assigns to mandatory or specific requirements, sometimes also called overriding public interest concerns. Despite using an inconsistent terminology, the notion of public interest objectives can clearly be identified in the Court's case law on broadcasting both before and after the Television Directive entered into force. Whereas in *Debauve* the Court clarified that Article 56 (now Article 46) was not available, but public interest concerns could be and actually were justified as mandatory requirements, in *Bond* it held that a national measure allegedly designed to maintain a pluralistic broadcasting system was disproportionate. It essentially repeated this decision in *Gouda*, although the national legislation in question was arguably less projectionist than its predecessor in *Bond.*

In the case of direct discrimination in *Commission* v. *Belgium*, public interest as mandatory requirement was not discussed as this concept is only available for indistinctly applicable measures. The Court did not expressly decide whether and to what extent the Television Without Frontiers Directive may have harmonised public interest aspects, such as the preservation of pluralism. Surprisingly, in *De Agostini* the Court appeared more reluctant to interfere with the choice of the national regulator and, unlike in its earlier Judgements, left the necessity and proportionality tests to be decided by the national court. In *VTM*, the Court of First Instance found that Belgian law provided for an exclusive right to transmit television commercials, in violation of Article 86(1) read together with Article 43, because the causal link to the envisaged aim of pluralism was missing. What lessons can be learned from the Court's case law on broadcasting, in particular, the role it assigns to public interest

[477] See detailed Chapter 7.

concerns? It appears that it is of paramount importance whether the Court considers a measure ‘projectionist’, i.e., if the national legislation pursues an economic aim. Along the same lines, *Pullen & Ris*[478] emphasised that, very often, ‘consumer protection or preservation of natural culture are really nothing more than protectionism dressed up in more respectable clothing’. However, this is essentially a value judgement and there are no hard-and-fast rules to detect protectionism in a Member State’s national legislation. But if this is the case, the Court will find a violation of Article 49 (ex-Article 59) and/or Article 28 (ex-Art. 30), and neither Articles 46 (ex-Article 56) and/or 30 (ex-Article 36) nor the mandatory requirements doctrine will be available as a justification.

A Member State’s protectionist measures violate not only the basic freedoms but also distort competition within the common market safeguarded by Article 3 g.[479] Although the Court did not discuss this in any detail, it made clear that hindrances to the freedom to provide services and/or the free movement of goods must also be assessed with regard to their effect on competition between foreign and domestic broadcasters. The four freedoms and competition law both constitute tools to establish the internal market and are thus interlinked with each other. On the other hand, if a measure is justified by mandatory requirements and hence not protectionist, the hindrance to trade must be accepted because of overriding public interest concerns. The measure will then also be compatible with competition law.

The Community courts interpret the four freedoms and competition law in a way that is consistent with each other. If a measure is compatible with the former, it will not be held to violate the latter. The earlier case law on broadcasting, which concentrates on the free movement of services and contains hardly any express reference to competition law, is nonetheless a valuable source on how the Community courts envisage a European market for broadcasting.

---

[478] ‘Advocate General Reinforces the Principle of Country of Origin Control under the Television Without Frontiers Directive’, 8 *ECLR* (1996) pp. 453-461, at p. 461.

[479] ‘a system ensuring that competition in the internal market is not distorted’.

Chapter 5
COLLABORATION BETWEEN BROADCASTERS

5.1. Application of Article 81 (ex-Article 85)

Article 81 (ex-Article 85) provides that a whole range of anti-competitive agreements between undertakings is prohibited and, if they cannot benefit from individual or block exemption under Article 81(3) (ex-Article 85(3), are automatically void by virtue of Article 81(2) (ex-Article 85(2).[480] Article 81 (ex-Article 85) is a general competition provision, applicable to all sectors but those explicitly exempt, such as, coal and steel,[481] agriculture[482] and defence industries.[483] The competition rules apply to some sectors subject to limitations, such as, road, rail, inland waterways, maritime and air transport.[484] Broadcasting is not mentioned and there is no block exemption for broadcasting/audio-visuals. Thus, the audio-visual sector does not benefit from general exemption. This was also confirmed by the Court of Justice, which decided that public and private broadcasting are subject to the general provisions on competition in the Treaty.[485] Hence, broadcasting and audio-visual media are generally subject to EC Competition law, and recognition of any 'special characteristics' of the sector is only possible within its framework.

5.1.1. *Article 81(1)(ex-Article 85(1))*

Article 81(1) reads as follows:

> 1. The following shall be prohibited as incompatible with the common market: all agreements between undertakings, decisions by associations of undertakings and concerted practices which may affect trade between Member Sates and which have as their object

[480] R. Whish, *Competition Law*, 3rd ed., p. 186.

[481] Applicable are instead Articles 65 and 66 ECSC Treaty.

[482] Art. 36 (ex-Art. 42) provides that 'The provision of the Chapter relating to rules on competition shall apply to production of and trade in agricultural products only to the extent determined by the Council within the framework of Articles 37(2) and (3) and in accordance with the procedure laid down therein, account being taken of the objectives set out in Article 33. The Council may, in particular, authorise the granting of aid: (a) for the protection of enterprises handicapped by structural or natural conditions; (b) within the framework of economic development programmes.'

[483] Art. 296(1)(b) (ex-Art. 223(1)(b)) authorises Member States to take necessary measures to protect their essential security interests connected with the production of and trade in arms, munitions, and war materials, provided that 'such measure shall not adversely affect the conditions of competition in the Common Market regarding products which were not intended for specifically military purposes'.

[484] See D.G. Goyder, *EC Competition Law*, (1998), pp. 76-85.

[485] *Sacchi*, Case 155/73, [1974] ECR 409

or effect the prevention, restriction of distortion of competition within the common market, and in particular those which:
directly or indirectly fix purchase or selling prices or any other trading conditions;
limit or control production, markets, technical development, or investment;
share markets or sources of supply;
apply dissimilar conditions to equivalent transactions with other trading parties, thereby placing them at a competitive disadvantage;
make the conclusion of contracts subject to the acceptance by other parties of supplementary obligations which, by their nature or according to commercial usage, have no connection with the subject of such contracts.[486]

The Court's interpretation of the conditions in Article 81(1) shall be assessed with specific regard to its application to broadcasters.

First, the notion of an undertaking in the sense of Article 81(1) has been defined rather broadly as '... any entity engaged in an economic activity',[487] which is unrelated to whether the entity possesses legal personality. The fact that an undertaking is not determined to make profits does not disqualify it as an undertaking.[488] In *Sacchi*, the Italian and German governments argued, albeit unsuccessfully, that because of the non-economic purpose of public broadcasting, it could not be regarded as an undertaking or, at least by virtue of Article 90(1) (now Article 86(1)), the rules on competition apply only insofar as they do not obstruct the performance of the particular tasks assigned.[489] The Court was not convinced by this argument, and although it admitted that Member States are entitled to confer an exclusive right to carry out broadcasting, it held that activities of an economic nature remain subject to Article 90 (now Article 86).[490] Regarding public undertakings, the Court implicitly found that broadcasters, including public service broadcasters qualify as undertakings in the sense of Article 81(1),[491] and refused to remove the broadcasting sector as such from the application of competition law.

Secondly, we need to define 'agreements, decisions and concerted practices', which are prohibited by Article 81(1). These terms have been given a very broad interpretation by the Court, which is not restricted to any kind of formal cartel but also embraces collusion which merely materialises as parallel conduct. 'Gentlemen's agreements' and simple understandings[492] are also be covered. Moreover, the Court does not always clearly distinguish between 'agreements', 'decisions' and 'con-

[486] Case 155/73, [1974] ECR 409.
[487] *Polypropylene OJ* 1986, L 230/1, para 99.
[488] R. Whish, op. cit. n. 480, p. 188.
[489] Ibid., para 13.
[490] In short, Art. 86 (ex-Art. 90) regulates to what extent the competition rules apply to public undertakings entrusted with special or exclusive rights. See also *infra* Chapter 7 on state aid.
[491] See already Case 41/69 *ACF Chemiefarma* v. *Commission*, [1970] ECR 661.
[492] See e.g., *Panasonic, OJ* 1982 L 354/28.

certed practices'.[493] . The relevant delimitation is between collusive and non-collusive behaviour.[494] If traders engage in parallel conduct because of market circumstances, for example in an oligopoly[495] the competition authority might be tempted to interpret this as proof of collusion. It requires great care to distinguish covert restricted practices from rational but innocent commercial behaviour.[496]

As will be demonstrated below, so far the question whether a certain conduct by broadcasters qualifies as collusive has not occupied the Court. However, with further concentration on the market, the likelihood increases that the problem might occur in the future. It remains to be seen, if there is a prospect of increased collusion between broadcasters. This might be the case if, for instance, the parties to a joint venture decided to coordinate conduct of the independent parent companies in areas not subject to the joint venture.

Thirdly, Article 81 prohibits conduct the *object or effect* of which is to restrict competition. This test was first applied in *Société Technique Minière* v. *Maschinenbau Ulm.*[497] The Court held that this was to be interpreted as requiring to establish, first, whether the measure had the **object** of restricting competition. If this was not the case, it is necessary to, secondly, proceed with investigating the conduct's **effect**. The term 'object' was given an objective meaning, disregarding the subjective intent of the parties.[498] In the case of market sharing, price fixing and export bans, the restriction is sufficiently grave to render the conduct *per se* illegal and no further investigation regarding its effect is necessary. Nonetheless, it might be appropriate to analyse how to establish the amount of any fine.[499] If a measures cannot be said to have as its objective the restriction of competition, its effect on the relevant product and geographical markets[500] has to be determined. For example, in *Brasserie de Haecht,*[501] the Court held that 'an agreement cannot be examined in isolation of the above content, that is, from the factual or legal circumstances causing it to prevent, restrict or distort competition'.[502]

Fourthly, to come within Article 41, a measure must adversely affect trade between Member States. The Court has adopted a fairly liberal interpretation of the inter-state trade clause, thereby allegedly widening the scope of the competition

493 A comprehensive definition on 'concerted practices' was given in the *Sugar Cartel* case: '...a form of co-ordination between undertakings which, without having been taken to the stage where an agreement properly so-called has been concluded, knowingly substitutes for the risks of competition practical co-operation between them which leads to conditions of competition which do not correspond to the normal conditions of the market ...' [1975] ECR 1916.

494 *Polypropylene OJ* 1986, L 230/1.

495 See *infra* at 2.3.5.

496 R. Whish,op. cit. n. 480, p.195.

497 Case 56/65 [1966] ECR 234, at 249.

498 See e.g., Cases 29 and 30/83, *Rheinzink,* [1984] ECR 1679.

499 R. Whish,op. cit. n. 480, p. 204.

500 For the issue of market definition see *supra* at 2.4.

501 Case 23/67 [1967] ECR 407.

502 Ibid., at 415.

rules in the Treaty. The test to be applied was first laid down in *Société Technique Minière* v. *Maschinenbau Ulm*.[503]

> ... it must be possible to foresee with a sufficient degree of probability on the basis of a set of objective factors of law or of fact that the agreement in question may have an influence, *direct* or *indirect*, *actual* or *potential*, on the patterns of trade between Member States. (italics added)

The language used is obviously borrowed from the case law on the free movement of goods, notably *Dassonville*,[504] where the Court defined 'measures having equivalent effect' to quantitative restrictions in the sense of Article 30 (now Article 28). In practice, in all but the most exceptional cases the Court found that inter-state trade was restricted. It employs a rather permissive test where indirect and/or potential distortions of competition are sufficient to bring Article 81(1) into play.

5.1.2. *Article 81(3)(ex-Article 85(3))*

The prohibition set out in Article 81(1) is supplemented by the conditions of individual exemption[505] contained in Article 81(3). It is for the Commission to apply and balance the two paragraphs of Article 81[506]. To qualify for individual exemption, a restricted practice falling into the ambit of Article 81(1) must fulfil the four conditions laid down in Article 81(3):

First, there must be a benefit for the production or distribution of goods or the measure must promote technical or economic progress. It is an interesting question if Article 81(3) can also be used for non-economic public interest considerations, such as social objectives.[507] In *Metro* v. *Commission*,[508] the Court held that stabilisation of employment might improve the general conditions of production and hence could be taken into account under Article 85(3) (now Article 81(3)). This was also confirmed in *Nutricia* v. *Commission*[509] and it appears that a teleological interpretation permits taking into account such wider considerations.[510]

---

[503] Case 56/65 [1966] ECR 234, at 249.

[504] Case 8/74 [1974] ECR 837.

[505] Formerly, a number of block exemptions for different types of agreements (e.g., franchising or exclusive distribution) and/or specific sectors, e.g., car distribution had been in force, which now have been replaced by Commission Regualtion EC No. 2790/1999 of 22. Dec. 1999 on the application of Art. 81(3) of the Treaty to categories of vertical agreements and concerted practices. *OJ* 1999, L 336/21.

[506] D.G. Goyder, op. cit. n. 484, p. 128.

[507] R. Whish, op, cit. 480, p. 229.

[508] Case 26/76 [1977] ECR 1875.

[509] Case 43/84 [1985] ECR 2545.

[510] R. Whish, op, cit. 480, p. 229.

Secondly, the measure must also 'allow consumers a fair share of the resulting benefit'. Not only the public but also undertakings qualify as 'consumers'.[511] The Commission gave the term 'fair share' a wide definition, and on several occasions, a measure was held incompatible with Article 81 because it failed to benefit consumers. With special regard to television, the Commission in *Screensport/EBU*[512] accepted that the establishment of the transnational satellite television channel Eurosport might be beneficial to consumers in the short term. This decision and the case on appeal shall be discussed in detail below.[513]

Thirdly, restrictions must not be indispensable. This negative conditions is essentially the proportionality test in Article 81(3). The measure must not entail greater restriction of competition than is necessary to procure the benefit in question.[514] Fourthly, the restriction must not result in an elimination of competition in respect of a substantial part of the product in question. For example, market sharing arrangements, dual pricing[515] and export bans will fall foul of this condition and thus fail to benefit from Article 81(3).

It has been extensively discussed whether the application of Article 81(3) amounts to something equivalent to the 'rule of reason' applied by United States' Courts. Apart from the general consideration that one should be careful to transfer a *terminus technicus* into another legal system, it appears that Article 81(3) is more rigid than a 'rule of reason'; it contains a cumulative series of four separate tests. There is no overall balancing of debits and credits, and if only one of the tests is not satisfied, Article 81(3) cannot be successfully relied on.[516]

5.2. **Joint Ventures (JVs)**

5.2.1. *Definition*

Undertakings sometimes have to acknowledge that, on their own, they cannot raise sufficient capital or lack the personal to carry out a certain investment. This is particularly the case in quickly developing high technologies, such as IT, telecommunications and the media. Particularly with the emergence of Pay-TV and digital technology – which are very capital-demanding areas – broadcasting undertakings increasingly look for partners to pool resources for large investments, not only for the development of technology (decoders etc.) but also for acquiring premium content, for example, transmission rights for sports events and feature films. To pursue

---

511 See e.g., *Re ACEC/Berliet Agreements OJ* 1968 L201/7.
512 *OJ* 1991, L 63/32.
513 See *infra* at 5.3.1.-5.3.3.
514 R. Whish, op, cit. 480, p. 230.
515 See Case 30/78, *Distillers,* [1980] ECR 2229.
516 D.G. Goyder, op. cit. n. 484, p. 145.

this aim, broadcasters often decide to stop short of a full merger and set up a JV covering only parts of their activities, while the parent companies remain independent. The term 'Joint Ventures' covers a wide range of activities, from market sharing and price-fixing arrangements reassembling a cartel to a virtual merger of certain activities, which the parent companies cease completely .[517]

5.2.2. *'Cooperative'* v. *'Concentrative' JVs*

This distinction was relevant under the original Article 3(2) of Regulation 4086/89[518] ('the Merger Regulation'). It provided that 'the creation of a joint venture performing on a lasting basis all the functions of an autonomous economic entity, which does not give rise to co-ordination of the competitive behaviour of the parties (...) shall constitute a concentration' within the meaning of the Merger Regulation. Thus, it was necessary to determine if the JV was 'full-function' and assess if it gave rise to co-ordination of the parties to the JV. Only if the first question could be answered 'affirmatively and the second negatively could the Merger Regulation became applicable. If the JV was full-function but gave rise to co-ordination, the JV was a so-called co-operative JV and remained subject to Article 85 (now Article 81).

The twofold test in Article 3(2) of the Merger Regulation and the resulting distinction between cooperative and concentrative JVs gave rise to much disagreement[519] and it was difficult to establish which type of JV would qualify.[520] Parties sought to draft their JV-agreement to bring it inside the definition of a 'concentration' in the sense of the Merger Regulation to benefit from its more expedient and probably also predictable assessment. Between 1990 and 1994, the Commission moved substantially in favour of broadening the definition of a concentration but still, many full-function JVs remained subject to Article 85 (now Article 81).[521] This situation has changed with the subsequent amendment of the Merger Regulation by Regulation 1310/97,[522] which shifted the relevant distinction solely to the notion of a 'full-function' JV and omitting the coordination test. Full-function JVs are now defined as 'performing on a lasting basis all the functions of an autonomous economic entity.'[523] Hence, the only JVs not subject to the Merger Regulation remain those that are not full-function or do not meet the threshold criteria in

[517] D.G. Goyder, op, cit. n. 484, p. 441.

[518] *OJ* 30.12.1989, L 395/1.

[519] See e.g., A.S. Pathak, 'The EC Commission's Approach to Joint Ventures: A Policy of Contradictions', 5 *ECLR* (1991) pp. 171-183; V. Korah, 'Collaborative Joint Ventures: the Competition Rules of the Common Market and the Invalidity of Contracts' (1991-92) 15 *Fordh. Int. L.J.*, p. 248.

[520] To facilitate the distinction, the Commission issued a Notice on the distinction between concentrative and co-operative JV. *OJ* 31.12.1994, C 385/1.

[521] D.G. Goyder, op, cit. n. 484, p. 426.

[522] *OJ* 1997, L 180/1.

[523] Para 11 of the 1998 Interface Notice, referring to the (new) Art. 3(2) of the Merger Regulation.

Article 1.[524] Accordingly, this chapter discusses JVs between broadcasters subject to Article 81, whereas full-function JVs shall be assessed in chapter 6 on mergers.

5.3. **The European Broadcasting Union and EC Competition Law**

The European Broadcasting Union (EBU) is an association of radio and television organisations set up in 1950 with headquarters in Geneva. It is a non-profit organisation but also engages in economic activities. EBU coordinates and supports television programme exchanges among its members (Eurovision) and supports any other form of cooperation. EBU has 68 active members in 49 countries situated in the European broadcasting area and 50 associate members in 30 countries outside the area.[525] The EBU members are the main European public broadcasters.[526]

5.3.1. *Commission Decision 93/403/EEC, IV/32.150 EBU/Eurovision System*

This Decision[527] deals with the legality of the EBU and the Eurovision System established amongst its members. The Commission starts with extensively elaborating on the situation of broadcasting and the development towards more competition with emerging private commercial operators. It emphasised the non-commercial aims of EBU and acknowledges the increased difficulties in acquiring transmission rights for sporting events. 'In some countries, the national EBU members compete at a growing disadvantage *vis-à-vis* commercial channels, which are in some cases backed by powerful media conglomerates ...'[528] Under scrutiny were the EBU's 'Statutes' and, in particular, its system of collectively obtaining broadcasting rights, most notably for sports programs. However, most of the Commission's observations are rather general, such as asserting that 'public mission-oriented channels normally show a broader range of sports than purely commercial channels'.[529] It highlights that the access scheme for non-members had, at the Commission's request, been altered to grant the latter live transmission rights for an event that is

---

[524] The Merger Regulation as amended by Regulation 1310/97 provides for a combined aggregate world-wide turnover of all the undertakings concerned of more than ECU 2 500 million, a combined aggregate turnover of each in at least three Member States of more than ECU 100 million and an aggregate Community-wide turnover of each of at least two of the undertakings concerned of more than ECU 100 million, unless each of the undertakings achieves more than two thirds of its aggregate Community-wide turnover within one Member State.

[525] A. Font Galarza, 'The Commission's Assessment of the Eurovision System pursuant to Article 81 EC', 2 *CPN* (2000), pp. 28-33, at p. 28.

[526] Ibid.

[527] *OJ* 1993, L179/23.

[528] Para 11 of the Decision.

[529] Para 19 of the Decision.

not broadcast live by the EBU members and deferred transmission rights for live broadcasts of EBU members.[530]

The Commission found a restriction of competition both between the EBU members *inter se* and *vis-à-vis* non-members, and distortions of competition were held to be particularly grave in the former case. 'As [a] result of the joint negotiation and acquisition of the rights within the framework of Eurovision this competition is greatly restricted if not, in many cases, eliminated.'[531] The Commission also acknowledged that the joint purchasing system[532] strengthens the negotiating powers of EBU.[533]

However, under Article 85(3) (now Article 81(3)), the Commission found the restriction justified, because it, first, improved production/distribution by reducing transaction costs and specifically benefiting small members by enabling collective purchasing as compared to separate negotiations.[534] Apart from economic advantages of rationalisation and cost-saving, 'as a result of reciprocity and solidarity any EBU member will feel obliged to produce the television signal for events taking place in its country, even if it is not itself interested in the event'.[535] The access scheme which provided the possibility for non-members to obtain deferred rights would be sufficient because most satellite and cable channels would not be able to incur the costs for live transmission anyway.[536] Secondly, consumers were granted a fair share of the benefit because they were able to access more high-quality sports programmes of both popular and minority sports. Thirdly, the restrictions were indispensable, as the same result could not be achieved by less restrictive means. Separate bids for television rights would obstruct the benefit of joint negotiations.[537] Fourthly, the system did not eliminate competition; only international events were covered and there was enough competition from independent broadcasters. As the Commission found all the conditions of Article 85(3) (now Article 81(3)) fulfilled, it granted individual exemption for the acquisition of sports broadcasting rights for five years.

5.3.2. *Joined Cases T-528/93, T-524/93, T-543/93 and T-546/93, Metropole*

In *Metropole*,[538] several commercial broadcasters (Metropole Television ('M6'), Reti Televissive Italiane ('RTI'), Gestevision Telecinco ('Telecinco') and Antena 3) brought an action for annulment of the EBU Decision (Commission Decision

[530] Para 37 of the Decision.
[531] Para 49 of the Decision.
[532] Sometimes also called a 'buying cartel'.
[533] Para 52 of the Decision.
[534] Para 59 of the Decision.
[535] Para 63 of the Decision.
[536] Para 66 of the Decision.
[537] Para 70 of the Decision.
[538] Judgment of the Court of First Instance, 11 July 1996, [1996] ECR II-649.

93/403/EEC[539]) before the Court of First Instance ('CFI'). In 1984, EBU had, for the first time, admitted a private television company as a member, the French broadcaster Canal plus, and in 1986 it had allowed TF1 to remain a member after privatisation.[540] M6 and Antena 3 had, without success, sought membership of the EBU.

The CFI, after considering arguments on the admissibility, assessed Decision 93/403/EEC regarding the application of Article 85(3)(a) (now Article 81(1)(a)).[541] The parties submitted that from the EBU's Statutes it did not appear that its members had to fulfil a particular public service mission. The discriminatory nature was confirmed by the admission of Canal plus.[542] Moreover, some EBU members did not in fact fulfil the conditions of the Statutes, whereas certain non-members complied with them.[543] The Commission admitted that there might be private television channels which did fulfil the conditions in question but submitted that it was not under an obligation to examine the application of the EBU Statutes on a case-by-case basis.[544] The CFI disagreed.

In the first limb of its initial plea, the plaintiff argued that the Commission had based its decision on an erroneous interpretation of Article 85(3) (now Article 81(3)). Its plea was upheld by the CFI, which found that the Commission was indeed under a duty to scrutinise individual cases if the membership rules were 'objective and sufficiently determinate so as to enable them to be applied uniformly and in a non-discriminatory manner *vis-à-vis* all potential active members'.[545] The data on coverage of the population and on programming and production were 'vague and imprecise',[546] the Commission should have concluded that it was not in a position to assess the indispensability of the restrictions.[547]

In the second limb of the plea, the parties submitted that the concept of a particular public mission purporting to be characteristic of EBU members has no place in the analysis under Article 85(3) (now Article 81(3)). The Commission observed that although the competition rules had to be equally applied to public and private undertakings, this did not exclude considering the particular features of the sector under Article 85(3) (now Article 81(3)). Moreover, the Decision was based on a 'public mission' only in the alternative, and this concept was to be assessed under Article 90(2) (now Article 86), which covers the notion of a 'service of general economic interest'. Again, the CFI was not convinced by the Commission's argu-

[539] See *supra* at 5.3.1.

[540] Joined Cases T-528/93, T-524/93, T-543/93 and T-546/93, *Metropole,* [1996] ECR II-649, para 8.

[541] '... which does not (a) impose on the undertakings concerned restrictions which are not indispensable of these objectives.'

[542] *Metropole,* para 85.

[543] Ibid., para 86.

[544] Ibid., para 90.

[545] Ibid., para 95.

[546] Ibid., para 97.

[547] Ibid., para 99.

ments. It took the view that being a public service broadcaster was 'the principle factor in defining the circle of beneficiaries of the exemption ...'[548] The CFI also ruled on the relationship between Article 90 (now Art. 86) and Article 85(3) (now Article 81(3)). It found that the Commission Decision had erronously taken over elements of Article 90 (now Article 86) into the analysis under Article 85 (now Art. 81). The CFI held that 'inasmuch as (...) Article 90(2) is not applicable, factors coming essentially within the ambit of that article cannot in this case constitute a criterion for the application of Article 85(3) in the absence of other justifications'.[549] However, it adds that '[a]dmittedly, in the context of an overall assessment, the Commission is entitled to base itself on considerations connected with the pursuit of the public interest in order to grant exemption under Article 85(3)'.

Thus, the CFI highlights that the public service obligations are primarily to be dealt with under Article 90 (now Article 86), but still there is also a certain fairly unclear relevance under Article 81(3). It is difficult to interpret the CFI's statement as anything but contradictory. If a public service obligation must be assessed under Article 86 (ex-Article 90) and cannot constitute a criterion for individual exemption under Article 81(3), how could it then be relevant for the overall assessment under Article 81? However, the judgement is clear insofar, as the Commission had failed to demonstrate that exclusivity was required to transmit sports events and to base its findings on economic evidence.[550]

5.3.3. *Commission Decision 2000/400/EC, IV/32.150 Eurovision*

Following the CFI's judgement in *Metropole*, the EBU appealed before the Court of Justice, supported by the Commission. The appeal is still pending. Moreover, the Commission on 26 June 2000 issued a new Decision.[551] The situation as compared to the background of Decision 93/403/EEC has changed with regard to the admission rules of the EBU. Since 1998, the EBU had altered membership rules and introduced rules for the continuing participation of former Eurovision members. This was necessary because, following the annulment of Decision 93/403/EEC, the commercial broadcaster Canal plus could no longer be a member. In addition to the 1993 rules on access to Eurovision Sport Programmes for EBU non-members, in 1999, the EBU adopted a set of sub-licensing rules relating to the exploitation of Eurovision rights on Pay-TV channels.[552]

The Commission identified the market for the acquisition of television rights to important sporting events as the relevant product market. It clarified that for certain premium sports events the market may be confined to the rights for a single tourna-

---

[548] Ibid., para 115.
[549] Ibid., para 117.
[550] Ibid., para 120.
[551] *OJ* 2000, L 151/18.
[552] These have also been submitted to the Commission and published in the *OJ* 1999, C 248/7.

ment, such as the Olympic Games or the Football World Cup.[553] However, the Commission finally decided that it was not necessary to exactly define the relevant product market. It identified a transfer of profits away from downstream broadcasters towards upstream rights owners. In the last ten years, EBU has lost significant market share and faced strong competition from European media groups, such as, Kirch, Mediaset, Bertelsmann, BSkyB and Canal plus. But it has retained a strong position in the acquisition of major international sports events, including, continuous the television rights for the Olympic Games.

The Commission's legal assessment is arguably better structured than it was in the annulled Decision 93/403/EEC but does not add very much in substantive terms. The argument under Article 81(3) (ex-Article 85(3) again focuses on the reduction of transaction costs, the benefit for small members, the extended coverage of sporting events and increased diversity of the programme. These objectives would be jeopardised by individual negotiations by the EBU members and in the light of the market structure and EBU's difficult position *vis-à-vis* its competitors, there was no danger that competition would be eliminated. The 1999 rules ensured that competition was not eliminated on the Pay-TV market. The Commission decided to grant individual exemption until 31 December 2005, because the EBU had already acquired the rights for the 2008 Olympic Games, and the negotiations for the 2012 Olympic Games would take place no sooner than 2006. Decision 2000/400/EC is currently on appeal before the CFI.[554]

5.3.4. *Commission Decision 1999/242/EC, IV/32.524 Screensport/EBU*

The EBU refused to grant Screensport, a commercial transnational satellite television sports channel registered in England that commenced service in 1984, sublicenses to sports events, for which the EBU or its members held exclusive rights. This caused Screensport to issue a complaint at the Commission, resulting in the *Screensport* Decision.[555] Screensport argued that the JV, with EBU and/or certain of its members, in setting up the sports channel 'Eurosport', violated Article 85 (now Article 81), which was the subject of this Decision.[556]

At the time of the Decision, the Eurosport consortium consisted of 17 public service broadcasters, including broadcasters from non-European states. Eurosport, like Screensport, was a transnational satellite television channel service dedicated

[553] The Commission stated that in free-to-air television one could not directly observe evidence on the price-elasticity of demand. Also Pay-TV normally involved monthly or annually subscription fees, which made it difficult for the consumer to switch. However, evidence form a study for DG Competition indicated that there was virtually no cross-elasticity of demand between the Wimbledon Finals and the Football World Cup. See footnote 11 of the Decision.

[554] Cases T-216/00, T-299/00 and T-185/00.

[555] *OJ* 9.3.1991, L063/32.

[556] The first aspect of the complaint was dealt with in separate proceedings, see Case IV/32.150 *EBU/Eurovision System supra* at 5.3.1.

to sport, established in 1989 on the basis of an agreement between EBU members and contractually linked to Sky Television, an English language satellite channel. According to the Shareholders Agreement, EBU and Sky equally shared ownership and management of Eurosport.[557]

EBU and its members provided exclusive broadcasts of sports events, to which they generally acquired the collective rights. Eurosport also had access to these rights, in fact, the channel was mainly set up to exploit them. The Eurosport consortium had emphasised that it represented an extension of its members and must thus be viewed as a public service channel. However, the viewing public tended to prefer Eurosport to Sky Television.[558]

Concerning the relevant market, the Commission distinguished between national public broadcasting, commercial broadcasting and the recently established direct-to-home broadcasting.[559] It emphasised the particular attraction of sports programmes and the increased competition in acquiring transmission rights. At the same time, sports organisations had become increasingly aware of the value of their events and prices had increased. However, although competition in bidding for broadcasting rights increased, public broadcasters and consequently Eurosport remained in a privileged position. Screensport claimed that setting up Eurosport had exacerbated its problem in gaining access to transmission rights, because unlike its direct competitor Eurosport, it was denied access to the resources of Eurovision.[560]

The parties are 'undertakings' in the sense of Article 85 (now Article 81) and the Shareholder Agreement to set up the Eurosport Consortium[561] qualifies as an 'agreement' in the sense of Article 85 (ex-Article 81). The Commission suspected that the JV was, *inter alia*, designed to get rid of a potential competitor, as there was evidence that Sky had planned to establish its own sports channel.[562] In the following analysis, the Commission detected a range of disadvantages Screensport was exposed to in comparison to Eurosport. Only Eurosport had privileged access to essential program content. It may select freely from a range of sports events and even chose to coordinate its program with EBU and/or it members.[563] Unlike Eurosport, which benefits from the reciprocity in the Eurovision system, Screensport had to pay for the services it was able to acquire. Moreover, the package deals obtained by Eurosport often result in the exploitation of only parts of the acquired rights. As an international sports channel like Screensport is particularly interested in a whole range of events, including minority sports, this results in valuable rights not being

---

[557] Para 21 of the Decision.
[558] Paras 32 and 33 of the Decision.
[559] Paras 34-37 of the Decision.
[560] Para 47 of the Decision.
[561] A consortium can be defined as a contractual form of a multinational enterprise. See P.T. Muchlinski, *Multinational Enterprises and the Law* (London, Blackwell, 1995), p. 64.
[562] Para 54 of the Decision.
[563] Para 61 of the Decision.

used.[564] Hence, the agreement restricted competition and fell foul of Article 85(1) (now Article 81(1)).

An individual exemption under Article 85(3) (now Article 81(3)) was not available because the same benefit of increasing consumer choice and offering a new service could also be achieved by a multiplicity of channels:[565] '... [P]riority must be given to ensuring that competition at all levels should remains as open as possible as to confer upon all potential market entrants an equal opportunity to compete.'[566] Consumers may in fact be better served by being able to make an 'informed choice.'[567] Finally, the restriction of competition was not indispensable.[568] The agreement thus failed to fulfil the conditions for individual exemption and the disadvantages outweighed the possible improvements.[569]

Neither could Article 90(2) (now Article 86(2)), be of any assistance to EBU's arguments.[570] Although the Commission did not question the public service obligation of the national broadcasters, it, doubted if these could be interpreted as extending to transnational activities.[571] But even if this was assumed, Article 85(3) (now Article 81(3)) was held not to interfere with these obligations. Moreover, the commercial character of the service had been admitted.[572] Although the Commission did not expand on the latter statement, it indicates that a public service obligation is of a national character and cannot be extended easily to transnational activities.

5.4. **Digital Television Platforms**

5.4.1. *Commission Decision 1999/242/EC, IV./36.237, TPS*

This Decision[573] concerns a JV for French Pay-TV platform. The parties to this project were the privatised French television channels TF1, the public operators France 2 and France 3, the commercial channel M6, France Telecom and Suez Lyonaise des Eaux, a company mainly active in the water and energy sectors, but also in communication. CLT, which had originally been a party subsequently withdrew its stake. *Télévision par satellite* (TPS) was introduced as a digital platform to market satellite Pay-TV. The parties first notified TPS under the Merger Regulation, but the Commission arrived at the conclusion that it did not qualify as a full-

[564] Para 65 of the Decision.
[565] Para 70 of the Decision.
[566] Para 71 of the Decision.
[567] Para 73 of the Decision.
[568] Para 74 of the Decision.
[569] Para 76 of the Decision.
[570] For a detailed analysis of the Community rules on state aid with regard to broadcasting see Chapter 7.
[571] Para 69 of the Decision.
[572] Ibid.
[573] *OJ* 2.4.1999 L 90/6.

function JV, because its management was not sufficiently autonomous. The board of directors appointed by the parties had to approve in advance any decision concerning changes in TPS' activities. Consequently, Article 81 was applicable and the parties applied for negative clearance and *in eventu* individual exemption under Article 85(3) (now Article 81(3)). TPS was also active in the acquisition of television rights and the distribution and operation of special-interest channels. It used the Viaccess conditional access system, licensed from France Télécom. It had also entered into agreements for sport and movie rights, but had only obtained a right for 'second window' of a sport event, after it had been broadcast by Canal plus. Moreover, Canal plus was said to hold about 87 per cent of Hollywood's output.[574] At the time of the Decision, satellite television accounted for 15 per cent of subscribers on the French market, cable for 28 and terrestrial broadcasting for 57 per cent.[575] The relevant market was the Pay-TV market in France, possibly also including other French-speaking areas in Europe[576] and without further distinguishing between analogue and digital transmission. Traditionally, Canal plus has had a strong position on the market, holding a market share from approximately 70 per cent. It faced competition from the AB group, with 100,000 subscribers in 1998 and TPS, accounting for almost 500,000 subscribers.

Three clauses in the agreement setting up TPS were scrutinised by the Commission. First, a non-competition provision relating to the distribution and marketing of Pay-TV in digital mode to French-speaking areas in Europe. Secondly, the parties had granted TPS a right of first refusal for the special-interest programmes or services they themselves operated and, thirdly, committed themselves to exclusively transmit their general interest channels on TPS.[577]

As TPS was not under the joint control of its shareholders, the Commission concluded that there was no apparent risk of coordination between the parties, which could violate Article 85 (now Article 81). However, a detailed analysis of the single clauses had to be carried out. The non-competition clause was found to be ancillary to the creation of TPS, i.e., the protection was considered necessary to successfully establish the new channel. Otherwise, the operation would have no chance to succeed on the market. Thus, this clause fell outside Article 85(1) (now Article 81(1)) during the first three years. As to the clause, which granted TPS priority rights to the parties' special-interest channels, the Commission held that it limited the supply of special interest channels and thus fell into the ambit of Article 85(1) (now Article 81(1)). The same applied to the exclusivity clause concerning the general interest channels. In agreeing to exclusively transmit their most demanded programmes on

[574] Decision 1999/242/EC, para 58.

[575] Ibid., para 31.

[576] The Commission left the question open, as already in Cases *MSG/Media Service, OJ* 1994 L 364/1, *Bertelsmann/CLT, OJ* 1996 C 364/3, *Bertelsmann/Kirch/Premiere, OJ* 1999 L 53/1.

[577] Originally, it was also intended to distribute the channels 'Arte' and 'La Cinqueme' via TPS but this clause was deleted on the Commission's request.

TPS, the parties restricted competition, because the general-interest channels were of paramount importance and accounted for 90 percent of all viewers.[578]

After finding an infringement of Article 85(1) (now Article 81(1)), the Commission considered possible justifications under Article 85(3) (now Article 81(1)). It held that the establishment of the platform resulted in, first, an increase in the number of special-interest channels, which qualified as an improvement in distribution and production. Secondly, the keen competition introduced to the market which resulted in special offers[579] and an increase of choice was held to also benefit consumers. Thirdly, the clauses in the agreement were indispensable in nature because, without exclusive access to the parties' programmes, TPS would have had to produce a large number of channels itself. There was simply no other way to penetrate the market and TPS still had a much weaker position in acquiring Hollywood rights than Canal plus. Fourthly, there was no elimination of competition. On the contrary, the introduction of a new platform 'has had an extremely favourable knock-on-effect on cable TV.'[580] A new competitor able to challenge Canal plus's predominant position had appeared. Hence, the four conditions of Article 85(3) were fulfilled[581] and individual exemption was granted for three years.[582]

5.4.2. *Commission Decision 1999/2935/EC, IV./36.539, BIB/Open*

The parties of the JV, BSkyB, BT Holdings, the Midland Bank and Matsushita Electric Europe launched the new service to introduce digital interactive television in the United Kingdom.[583] Put simple, BSkyB was to provide the broadcasting know-how, BT the network and the Midland Bank the financial resources. As the name indicates, it allowed suppliers from various sectors, from bank to supermarkets, to interact directly with consumers. Additionally, it granted access to a limited number of 'walled gardens' Internet sides, provided by a third party and e-mail.[584] BiB was intended to become active both on the digital interactive service and the related technical service market and it was planned to subsidise the retail price of set-top boxes and satellite dishes. Article 81 was applicable because the JV was not 'full-function'. Certain major decisions required consent of BSkyB's shareholders whose interest in BiB was at least ten per cent.

The Commission identified the market for digital interactive television services market as a separate product market from, on the one hand, other television ser-

---

[578] Decision 1999/242/EC, para 103.

[579] As reaction to the establishment of TPS, Canal plus lowered its subscription fee from FF 153 to FF 130 and launched special introductory offers. Ibid., para 119.

[580] Ibid., para 137.

[581] See *supra* at 5.1.2.

[582] Originally, the parties had intended to obtain exemption for 10 year, but the Commission considered that far too long.

[583] *OJ* 6.12.1999 L 312/1.

[584] Ibid., para 11.

vices, most notably Pay-TV and, on the other hand, high-street retailing. It appeared that it would be especially suitable to purchase perishable or bulky goods and that consumers would be willing to pay a premium for the convenience of home shopping. It was also distinct from shopping services accessible via a Personal Computer ('PC'), because television sets were ubiquitous, whereas only some 25 per cent of British households were equipped with a PC. Further, the suppliers considered Internet home shoppers as a different group of consumers that should be targeted separately.

The Commission confirmed its definition of a product market for the wholesale provision of technical services necessary for Pay-TV, comprising, essentially set-top boxes, conditionals-access services, subscriber management services and possibly also the electronic programme guide ('EPG'[585]). It identified *one* product market for technical services for Pay-TV and interactive television, but narrower product markets for individual technical services might exist. The market for customer access was limited to the traditional BT copper networks, excluding wireless and GSM networks. Because the service was adopted to the national taste in the UK, digital interactive television services and the market for related technical services were limited to this area.[586] Moreover, according to Council Directive 95/47/EC,[587] there was a specific regulatory regime in the UK, which justified limiting the geographical market to the UK. BiB was to introduce the new market of digital interactive television, a service that had previously not been provided. The peculiarity of the service lies in the interactivity made possible by a return path. Unlike terrestrial broadcasting, digital transmission does not face technical restrictions on the number of frequencies.

As to the Pay-TV market in the UK, about a quarter of households subscribed to a Pay-TV service.[588] The market was characterised by significant barriers to entry and the British Office of Fair Trading (OFT) had concluded that BSkyB was dominant in the supply of sports channels and held more than 90 per cent of the Pay-TV-rights for first-run major films. The various cable operators each use different technical services, but BSkyB's position on that market was secured by its strong position on the content market.[589] Most importantly, the set-top box[590] used by BiB would be using BSkyB's conditional access and accesses control and are thus tied to BSkyB's system. It did not contain a common interface but the Commission had required the parties to develop a Simulcrypt arrangement that contains interface ports for other telecommunication networks. The parties had also agreed to end the

[585] EPG is a navigation system listing channels and services designed to facilitate orientation for the consumer.

[586] As for Pay-TV, the Commission again left open if the geographical market would be extended to Ireland.

[587] *OJ* 3.11.1995, L 281/51.

[588] Para 66 of the Decision.

[589] Para 85 of the Decision.

[590] It also included a modem and a standardised slot for electronic payment cards.

exclusivity granted to BiB of the BSkyB EPG. However, there was a close relationship between BSkyB and BiB. The purchase of the equipment necessary to receive BSkyB enabled the consumer to access BiB services..[591] BiB was given a right of first refusal if shareholders provided digital interactive television services by means of a broadband system. The non-competition clause was limited to the business scope of BiB, and two separate legal entities for the operation of BiB and the subsidisation of the set-top box were created.

Article 81, and not the Merger Regulation, was applicable in this case, because there was a possibility of coordination between the parent companies in the relevant and neighbouring markets. Before the creation of the JV, BSkyB and BT had been potential competitors on the market for digital interactive services. The Commission in its Decision listed a whole range of clauses in the agreement that restricted competition and thus fell foul of Article 81(1),[592] most notably, the non-competition clause and the various close connections to BSkyB's technical services, such as the obligation to only promote set-top boxes that were BiB-compatible.[593]

The JV had an effect on trade between Member States because it could not be excluded that the service would be extended to Ireland. Even if this was not the case, the agreement made it more difficult for potential competitors from other Member States to penetrate the UK market.[594]

However, the Commission found all four conditions of Article 81(3) to be fulfilled. First, there was beneficial technical development, because a new service was offered which none of the parties could have achieved on their own. Secondly, this allowed consumers to access the new technology via their TV sets. Thirdly, there were no less restrictive means to achieve the same goal (indispensability). Fourthly, although the Commission first considered the combination of BT's and BSkyB's market power as a cause for concern for potential market foreclosure, these fears were successfully remedied by the conditions set out in the Decision. It was found that access for third parties, for example to BiB set-top boxes,[595] was sufficient and, in particular, other than BiB set-top boxes could be developed.[596] Thus, individual exemption was granted for a period of seven years. The Decision comprised ten conditions, which, *inter alia*, required BSkyB to grant third-party distributors access to its and BiB's services on a non-discriminatory basis and BT to divest its broadband cable television franchises.

---

591 Para 122 of the Decision. A clause that required consumers, who wanted to obtain BiB to also subscribe to BSkyB for at least 12 month, was removed from the agreement on the Commission's request.

592 See paras 145-152 of the Decision.

593 For example, the endeavours to ensure that all programmes broadcast on BSkyB's analogue satellite service will by simultaneously broadcast on its digital satellite service.

594 Para 156 of the Decision.

595 This was safeguarded by the legal separation of BiB, the subsidy mechanism and the supply of technical services to third parties. See paras 176-181 of the Decision.

596 Para 170 of the Decision.

Subsequently, BSkyB attempted to increase its shareholding in Open from its 32.5 percent stake, because, under the original structure of the JV, Open and not BSkyB controlled the 'return path' and the use of the set-top box.[597] It is unclear whether the other shareholders will agree to this attempt. However, increasing BSkyB's stake would alter the balance of the JV and cause new competition concerns. Hence, it would be for the Commission to reconsider its Decision.

5.5. **Conclusion**

The cases mentioned can give at least some guidance on how Community authorities balance aspects of competition and public interest considerations under Article 81 (ex-Article 85). It appears that the market structure will be of paramount importance to the analysis. *TPS* demonstrates that, for assessing the admissibility of an agreement, much will depend on the conditions of competition on the relevant market, the number of competitors and their market shares. Had there not been Canal plus, which has had an important first-mover-advantage in Pay-TV, the Commission could very well have reached a different conclusion and decided against an individual exemption.[598]

In *BIB/Open*, it appears that the Commission, after having virtually redrafted the agreement by numerous conditions, considered that the JV would not pose a threat to competition and decided to grant individual exemption for a comparatively long period of time. The Decision is characterised by a complicated fact pattern and one is left with the impression that it forms the product of lengthy negotiations between the parties and the Commission. Regarding its content, the Commission in its product market definition avoided to taking into account competition from Internet/ email-services accessed via PC. It did not closely examine if there could at least be a partial overlap that potentially enlarges the product market, but merely relied on the assumption that access via a TV-set or a PC were not interchangeable.

It should also be mentioned that the well-known and often criticised[599] contradiction between assuming potential competition under Article 81(1) and individually exempting the same JV under Article 81(3) also characterises the Decision in *BIB/Open*. This amounts to the JV essentially in itself infringing Article. 81(1).[600] It is simply against the laws of logic to establish a restriction of competition because two previously independent undertakings join forces, if later in the analysis it is established that the two undertakings could not have competed anyway, because

[597] *Financial Times online,* 'BSkyB chases Open prize', 30.5.2000.

[598] For example in the case of *Bertelsmann/Kirch/Premiere, OJ* 1999 L 53/1, a new platform tried to establish itself on the Pay-TV market in Germany as the first and, as was assumed, for some time only provider. The concentration was prohibited by the Commission. See D. Buschle, 'Freistellung vom Kartellverbot für den Markteintritt ins Pay-TV', 7 *ELR* (1999) pp. 305-308, at p. 308.

[599] See e.g., A.S. Pathak, 'The EC Commission's Approach to Joint Ventures: A Policy of Contradictions', 5 *ECLR* (1991) pp. 171-183.

none of them was able to incur the costs for the investment on its own. Such an interpretation of 'potential' competition goes too far.

The case law indicates that a rather permissive approach under Article 81(3) (ex-Article 85(3)) can also expected if a new service, such as a digital interactive programme is introduced. The Commission also had a positive view on strategic alliances in the Pay-TV sector, if the parties to the JV were active on different product markets. The Commission's approach changes when the parent companies' activities overlap in the same product and/ or geographical market.[601]

As to the inter-state effect of a *prima vista* national agreement, it was made clear in *Metropole* and *BiB* that the mere possibility that services be extended to other French or English-speaking areas in Europe suffices to render Community rules applicable. The Commission refrained from defining the relevant geographical market conclusively, but it appears that joint action by national broadcasters will also be subject to the Community authorities' scrutiny, unless the broadcasters in question only transmit in a language restricted to their territory and it cannot be expected that the broadcast will cross borders, which in the time of cable and satellite television is most unlikely.

Problems of public service broadcasting are, in the Treaty structure, to be analysed under Article 86 (ex-Article 90) but, as the case law demonstrated, they also have some significance under Article 81, particularly for the question whether individual exemption can be granted. Unfortunately, the CFI in *Metropole* remained rather vague and unclear and avoided stating, how and to what extent the characteristics of a public service obligation are to be treated under Article 81(3). It merely held that it has some relevance in the overall assessment, without substantiating its argument in any detail. Yet, it stressed that it will not suffice to globally assume some kind of altruism from the very status of a public service broadcaster, as the Commission did in the *Eurovision* Decision. The CFI in *Metropole* closely scrutinised whether the principles laid down were in fact adhered to. It required a mixed objective-subjective test that they were capable of being applied indistinctly, i.e., sufficiently precise and that no discrimination occurred in the application in a concrete case. In *Screensport*, the Commission indicated that a public service obligation is of a national character and it is doubtful if it can be extended to a transnational activity, in particular, if this activity is of a commercial nature.

---

[600] See e.g., *Vacuum Interrupters Ltd., OJ* 1977 L48/32.

[601] N. Nikolinakos, 'Strategic alliances in the pay-TV market: The TPS case', 7 *ECLR* (2000) pp. 334-339, at p. 338.

Chapter 6
MERGERS IN THE BROADCASTING INDUSTRY

The broadcasting industry is subject to the general EC merger regime, Regulation 4064/89.[602] Until today, no specific directive on media concentration at European level exists, although there have been several, albeit unsuccessful, initiatives.[603] Thus, this chapter mainly focuses on the application of the 'general' Merger Regulation 4064/89 to broadcasting enterprises.

6.1. The EC Legal Regime on Mergers: Regulation 4064/89

Before the adoption of the EC Merger Regulation, merger control in the Community was mainly based on Article 82 (ex-Article 86),[604] which generally outlaws the abuse of a dominant position.[605] However, there were several obstacles in using Article 82 (ex-Article 86) as an instrument for general merger control. It is aimed exclusively at the behaviour of firms already enjoying a dominant position. As it became evident in *Continental Can*,[606] Article 82 (ex-Article 86) could only be used if a dominant position was strengthened, and was of no use to prevent dominant positions from emerging in the first place.[607] Against this background, the Council of Ministers, after lengthy discussions, adopted Council Regulation 4064/89,[608] which introduced as a fundamental principle the 'one-stop-shop' rule for mergers. As a single authority, the Commission examines and assesses mergers having a Community dimension[609] within a strict timetable[610] and will prohibit

---

[602] *OJ* 30.12.1989, L395/1, as amended by Regulation 1310/97, *OJ* 9.7.1997, L 180/1.

[603] See *infra* at 6.4.

[604] In *PhilipMorris,* joined Cases 142 & 156/84 [1987] ECR 4487, the Court indicated, albeit ambiguously, that also Art. 81 (ex-Art. 85) could be used as a means of merger control.

[605] 'Any abuse by one or more undertakings of a dominant position within the common market or in a substantial part of it shall be prohibited as incompatible with the common market insofar as it may affect trade between Member States.'

[606] Case 6/72 [1973] ECR 215.

[607] A. Downs/J. Ellison, *The Legal Control of Mergers in the European Communities* (London, Blackstone Press, 1990), p. 7.

[608] For a good overview see e.g., M. Van Empel, 'Merger Control in the EEC' (1989) 13/1 *World Competition Law and Economics Review*, pp. 5-22.

[609] The Merger Regulation as amended by Regulation 1310/97 provides for a combined aggregate world-wide turnover of all the undertakings concerned of more than ECU 2 500 million, a combined aggregate turnover of each in at least three Member States of more than ECU 100 million and an aggregate Community-wide turnover of each of at least two of the undertakings concerned of more than ECU 100 million, unless each of the undertakings achieves more than two thirds of its aggregate Community-wide turnover within one Member State. On the calculation of the turnover see e.g., C. Jones & E. Gonzáles-Diaz, *The Merger Regulation* (London, Sweet & Maxwell, 1992) pp. 16-19.

[610] C.J. Cook/C.S. Kerse, 'E.C. Merger Control', 3rd ed., (2000) Sweet & Maxwell, p. 3.

mergers that lead to a dominant position, as a result of which efficient competition would be significantly impeded in the common market. Limited space prevents a coherent description of the Merger Regulation here, however, some general remarks and aspects particularly relevant for the case law on broadcasting shall be highlighted.

6.1.1. *Definition of 'Concentration'*

As already mentioned *supra* at 5.2.2, the Merger Regulation only applies to concentrations. After the unclear previous distinction between cooperative and concentrative JVs had been abolished, defining the notion of a 'concentration' has become crucial in determining if the Merger Regulation is applicable to the facts of a case. Rec. 23 of the Merger Regulation defines concentrations as 'operations bringing about a lasting change in the structure of the undertakings concerned'. Article 3 provides in more detail that 'a concentration shall be deemed to arise where two or more previously independent undertakings merge, or – one or more persons already controlling at least one undertaking, or – one or more undertakings acquire, whether by purchase of securities or assets, by contract or by any other means, direct or indirect control of the whole or parts of one or more undertakings.'

This definition covers a 'full merger' (Article 3(1)(a)), where all the rights and liabilities of one or more companies are transferred to another company,[611] as well as the acquisition or change of control (Article. 3(1)(b)). In the Merger Regulation, the term 'merger' is merely used for the first type of concentration and is thus defined narrowly. Such a merger in the sense of 'legal fusion'[612] or 'amalgamation'[613] is not very common, in particular in a common law jurisdiction,[614] and most concentrations are covered by Article 3(1)(b).[615] This provision refers to the acquisition of – joint or sole – control. A wider definition of 'merger' would render Article 3(1)(b) largely, if not completely, redundant.[616] 'Control' is, in Article 3(1)(b), defined as the 'possibility of exercising decisive influence'. Lesser degrees of influence, such as minority shareholders, are not covered, nonetheless they can be relevant too. In *MSG/Media Service*,[617] the Commission also took into account one of the parties' (Deutsche Telekom) 16.6 per cent shareholding in the main European satellite operator SES in assessing the competitive advantages MSG would enjoy in the markets concerned.[618]

611 Ibid., p. 27.
612 Notification form CO sec. 2, para 2.1(a) refers to a 'full legal merger'.
613 Commission Notice *OJ* 1988 C66/02, point 6.
614 Cook/Kerse, op. cit. n. 610, p. 28.
615 V. Korah, *An Introductory Guide to EC Competition Law and Practice*, (1997) p. 263.
616 Cook/Kerse, op. cit. n. 610, p. 27.
617 *OJ* 1994 L 364/1.
618 Cook/Kerse, op. cit. n. 610, p. 30.

To be covered by Article 3(1)(b), common control over the commercial strategy on a lasting basis is required.[619] However, there exists one major exception. Prerogatives exercised by a Member State *qua* public authority and not *qua* shareholder, do not qualify as control within the meaning of the Merger Regulation because they do not have as their object of effect the exercise of decisive influence on the business activity but are designed to protect the public interest.[620]

The Commission additionally issued a Notice on the concept of concentrations under the Merger Regulation[621] to provide further guidance on the interpretation of the term 'concentration'. Accordingly, a merger within the meaning of Article 3(1)(a) requires the establishment of a genuine common economic unit with a common economic management.[622] Regarding Article 3(1)(b), the concept of concentration is limited to changes in control and does not cover internal company restructuring.[623] In exceptional circumstances, control may also occur on a *de facto* basis due to economic dependence, for example, because of long-term supply agreements.[624] With specific regard to broadcasting, it may be significant if one operator depends largely on another's transmission rights for movies and/or sports events.

6.1.2. *Appraisal of a Concentration*

Concentrations above the thresholds[625] require appraisal to be compatible with the Common Market according to the following criteria:

> A concentration which does not create or strengthen a dominant position as a result of which effective competition would be significantly impeded in the common market or in a substantial part of if shall be declared compatible with the common market.[626]

If, on the other hand, a concentration does create or strengthen a dominant position, the Commission shall declare it incompatible with the Common Market (Article 2(3) of the Merger Regulation). The term 'dominant position' stems from Article 82 (ex-Article 86) and has constantly been defined by the Court of Justice as

---

619 Ibid., p. 32.

620 Ibid., It is doubtful if this provision does not contradict the principle of equal treatment of public and private undertakings laid down in Rec. 12 of the Merger Regulation.

621 *OJ* 1988 C66/02, replacing the previous Notice, *OJ* C 385/06, 31.12.1994.

622 Ibid., point 7. This, for example applies to the German *Gleichordnungskonzern* or the French *Groupement d'Intérêt Economique*.

623 Ibid., point 8.

624 Ibid., point 9.

625 Art. 1 of the Merger Regulation provides that concentrations have a community dimension, if the combined turnover of the undertakings involved exceeds 2500 million ECU world-wide and if the turnover exceeds 100 million ECU in at least three Member States, provided that at least two of the undertakings achieve a turnover within the Community of more than 25 million ECU. Moreover, none of the undertakings must achieve more than two thirds of their turnover in one and the same Member State.

626 Art. 2(2) of the Merger Regulation.

> a position of economic strength enjoyed by an undertaking which enables it to prevent effective competition being maintained on the relevant market by affording it the power to behave to an appreciable extent independently of its competitors, customers and ultimately of its consumers.[627]

Very often, the Commission does not simply prohibit a concentration but proposes some alterations of its structure, such as divesting part of its business. If the parties agree, the Commission than declares the concentration compatible with the Common Market, subject to these conditions.[628] This results in the Commission exercising considerable influence on shaping the concentration.

In assessing whether a dominant position is created or strengthened, Article 2(1) requires the Commission to take into account

> (a) the need to maintain and develop effective competition within the common market in view of, among other things, the structure of all the markets concerned and the actual or potential competition from undertakings located either within or without the Community';
> (b) the market position of the undertakings concerned and their economic and financial power, the opportunities available to suppliers and users, their access to supplies of markets, any legal or other barriers to entry, supply and demand trends for the relevant goods and services, the interests of the intermediate and ultimate consumers, and the development of technical and economic progress provided that it is to consumers' advantage and does not form an obstacle to competition.

Thus, it is apparent that the market structure will also play an important role for the assessment under the Merger Regulation.

The justification of non-economic considerations, which was included in an earlier draft of the Merger Regulation, was later deleted. Article 21 now expressly provides that the Commission has sole jurisdiction, and national competition authorities must not apply their national legislation to considerations having a Community dimension ('one-stop-shop principle'). Notwithstanding this provision, Member States may take appropriate measures to protect legitimate interests other than those taken into consideration by the Merger Regulation, provided that they do not contradict general principles or provisions of Community law (Article 21(3) of the Merger Regulation). This also covers legitimate general interest considerations, such as the plurality of the media and other unspecific public interests that are recognised by the Commission after notification by the Member State,[629] and could be of special relevance to mergers or acquisitions of control in the broadcasting sector.

---

[627] Case 27/76 *United Brands* [1978] ECR 207, para 38. It has been confirmed e.g., in Case 85/76 *Hoffmann-La Roche* [1979] ECR 461. For a detailed discussion of Art. 86 see R. Whish, op. cit. n. 480, pp. 253-282, G.D. Goyder, op. cit. n. 484, pp. 320-378.

[628] Korah, op. cit. n. 615, p. 268.

[629] Korah, op. cit. n. 615, p. 269; R. Whish, op. cit. n. 480, p. 725.

6.2. **Pay-TV in the European Union**

The number of merger proceedings before the Commission had increased considerably during the last year. Although limited space prevents a discussion of all of them, some selected decisions of particular importance shall be examined here, with a particular emphasis on the German broadcasting market. In particular, the Decisions *MSG/Media Service*[630] and *Kirch/Bertelsmann/Premiere*[631] shall be analysed in more detail.

6.2.1. *Pay-TV as a Separate Market: the Endemol Case*

In case T-221/95, *Endemol* v. *Commission*,[632] the Commission was requested by the Dutch government to scrutinise a JV between RTL, Veronica and Endemol to form the 'Holland Media Groep' (HMG). As the JV did not have a community dimension, this request according to Article 22(3) Merger Regulation was a necessary precondition to render the Commission competent to examine the concentration. Relying on Decision of 5.2.1996 the Commission prohibited the merger, the Decision being contested by the parties before the Court of First Instance (CFI). Moreover, the parties continued negotiations with the Commission and finally adapted the merger in such a way that the Commission granted permission according to Articles 8(2) and 22 of the Merger Regulation. Endemol ceased its participation in the JV and the remaining parties agreed to transform RTL 5 into a news channel. Consequently, Endemol remained as the only applicant in the proceedings before the CFI.

The first three pleas were concerned with procedural issues and, in particular, the question to what extent the Commission was competent to assess the JV.

In its fourth plea, the applicant had argued that the Commission's market definition had been fundamentally flawed by distinguishing the market for independent productions from in-house productions of the public broadcasters.[633] Endemol submitted that public broadcasters would equally produce low-budget game shows, talk shows and 'infotainment'. However, the CFI stressed the Commission's discretion when assessing according to provisions of an economic nature. There was no direct competition between in-house production and independent producers, because public broadcasters would for their substantial investment in in-house production facilities not be in a position to choose between their own and independent productions. By holding a market share of more than 50 per cent on the relevant market calculated by reference to the program's value, not the number of hours

[630] *OJ* 1994, L 364/1.

[631] *OJ* 1999, L 053/1.

[632] Appeal case of Commission Decision *RTL/Veronica/Endemol*, *OJ* 5.6.1996 L 134/32, [1999] ECR II-1299.

[633] Para 99 of the Judgment.

produced, Endemol would have obtained a dominant position. Particularly high market shares may in itself be evidence of a dominant position.[634] The Judgement fully upheld the Commission Decision.

Both the Commission and the CFI considered independent broadcasting productions to constitute a product market distinct from public broadcaster's productions. In-house productions used for captive use were defined as a different market than productions commissioned by a broadcaster or producer.[635] However, the CFI did not expressly refer to the applicant's argument that public broadcasting productions were of no better quality than independent productions but emphasised the different conditions of productions. It stated that even if some public broadcasters only run very modest production departments and thus had to obtain certain programs from independent producers,[636] would this not invalidate the Commission's argument. This is not entirely convincing and, in particular, the CFI did not take up the argument on product quality. It rather assumed that it would not be economically sensible for public broadcasters to resort to independent productions while maintaining production departments themselves.

Endemol is the leading case regarding the market definition for television broadcasting.[637] The Commission found that the relevant market had to be calculated on the basis of the value of programs not the number of hours produced, which was later upheld by the CFI.[638] Moreover, the CFI confirmed the established case law that, when assessing a dominant position, particular consideration must be given to the fact that the applicant held a very strong position with sports transmission rights and output-deals with major Hollywood studios.[639] However, the arguments concerning the comparability of independent productions and in-house production by public broadcasters is not entirely convincing, as the CFI confined itself to assuming different production conditions, without any detailed assessment.

6.2.2. *Decision 96/177/EC, Case IV/M.490 Nordic Satellite Distribution*

Nordic Satellite[640] concerned a proposed JV between Norsk Telecom (NT), Tele Danmark (TD) and Kinnevik of Sweden, to set up Nordic Satellite Distribution (NSD). The aim of the JV was to provide transponder capacity and transmit and distribute satellite TV in the Nordic market. NT was controlled by the Norwegian

---

634 *Hoffmann-La Roche,* [1979] ECR 461, *Akzo* [1991] ECR I-3359 and *Hilti* [1991] ECR II-1439.

635 This finding was confirmed in Cases IV./M.1574 *Kirch/Mediaset, OJ* C 255/3, 8.9.1999, at para 14 and IV./M.779 *Bertelsmann/CLT, OJ* C 364/3, 4.12.1996, at para 17.

636 Para 112 of the Judgment.

637 T. Jestaedt/J. Anweiler, 'Europaeische Fusionskontrolle im Medienbereich', 18 *EuZW* (1997), pp. 549-555, at p. 549.

638 [1999] ECR II-1299.

639 A. Bartosch, 'EuG:Fusion im Fernsehbereich', Case note to Case T-221/95 *Endemol*, 19 *EuZW* (1999) pp. 607, 608, at p. 608.

640 *OJ* L 53/20, 2.3.1996.

company Telenor, which was owned by the Norwegian State. TD, the Danish telecom operator, was 51 per cent owned by the Danish State and held certain exclusive rights, e.g., to provide public voice-telephony services. Finally, Kinnevik was a private Swedish group active, *inter alia*, in satellite and cable television, television distribution and conditional access systems. NSD would be 33.3 per cent owned by each of the parties, who would each appoint one director to the board; the fourth director was supposed to be independent. Thus, the Commission had no difficulty in establishing joint control and the turnover thresholds of the Merger Regulation were also met. As a full-function JV, the operation had to be assessed under the Merger Regulation.[641]

The Commission identified three relevant product markets: a market for the provision of transponder capacity (a), a market for the distribution of encrypted TV channels (b) and finally, a market for the operation of cable TV networks (c).[642] Moreover, the Commission distinguished between cable and satellite TV as separate markets, because there was only limited interchangeability between the two. Satellite dishes were, for aesthetic reasons, not permitted everywhere, and dispersed population and terrain difficulties in Scandinavia render cabling difficult in some areas.

On the market for transponder capacity (a), at the time of the Decision, 70 percent of Nordic households had their dishes directed to the Astra satellite. However, as NSD has carries popular national and international channels, such as TV3, Eurosport, CNN and MTV, broadcasters would stop transmitting the Nordic channels on Astra. Unlike Astra or Eutelsat, NSD would transmit in the national language, which, in the Commission's view, was a decisive advantage. As all transponder capacity on Astra and Eutelsat was occupied, they would not be able to successfully compete with NSD by offering attractive new programmes to viewers. Moreover, the Astra footprint did not cover the entire Scandinavian area, only southern parts of Sweden and Norway. Even if Astra planned to launch a new satellite to increase its transponder capacity, this would not put it into a position to offer an equally attractive bouquet as NSD. From a technical point of view, digitalisation could remedy the shortage of transponder capacity in the future, but this was not to be expected to occur in the short or medium term.

On the market of cable TV networks (b), TD held a legal monopoly and still retained the exclusive right to provide the infrastructure for transmission of radio and TV signals. Although the monopoly had been abolished, TD still held a strong position on the Danish cable TV market, which was reinforced by NSD. The other Nordic national cable markets were also found to be rather concentrated, although not to the same extent as the Danish market.

The market for distributing pay-TV and other encrypted TV-channels (c) was characterised by three major distributors, with Viaset enjoying a strong position in

[641] Para 48 of the Decision.
[642] Para 55 of the Decision.

the market. It also carried Kinnevik's channels, in particular the popular program TV3. These channels would be sold exclusively by Viaset, which would create a dominant position of Viaset on this market.[643]

The Commission left open the question whether the geographic market embraced all the Nordic countries (Denmark, Sweden, Norway and Finland) or was limited to national markets.[644] As TD and NT were important cable operators and Kinnevik held a strong position in providing television content, NSD would be in a position to foreclose the Nordic market to outside competition.

Although NSD did not use a closed encryption system, the JV was nonetheless held to restrict competition as it did not add any transponder capacity and led to an open[645] dominant position which denied third parties access. The participation of such a strong broadcaster as Kinnevik in NSD would necessarily lead to foreclosure effects. Undertakings offered by the parties were held to be too vague, limited in scope and difficult to monitor.

As a predecessor of the Decision in *Kirch/Bertelsmann/Premiere*,[646] *Nordic Satellite* already indicated which aspects of a JV would be critical in the assessment. First, it emphasises that a pooling of resources between powerful ex-monopolists in the telecom sector and a strong broadcasting content provider will raise the Commission's special attention. The Commission expressly referred to its Communication on the status and implementation of Directive 90/338/EEC on competition in the markets for telecommunications services.[647] Former dominant positions enjoyed by legal monopolists should not be replaced by dominant positions held by private companies.

Later in *Bertelsmann/Kirch/Premiere,* the Commission refrained from permitting the merger as it would lead to a potentially not only short-term dominant position. The barriers to entry erected by a strong network and premium content would be simply too high for future competitors. Moreover, this applies to an open system, such as the envisaged Nordic Satellite, which allows the use of different smart cards with one decoder. Thus, it was not surprising that the Commission showed even more reluctance towards a closed (proprietary) encryption system as was to be used later by *Bertelsmann/Kirch/Premiere*.

[643] Para 136 of the Decision.

[644] Para 72 of the Decision.

[645] In an 'open' encrypten system, decoders are available from many sources and different smart card can by used, whereas in 'closed' system, only broadcasters signing an agreement with the owner of the system are allowed to encrypt in it. Most European channels, such as Canal plus and BSkyB used closed systems. In contrast, NSD opted for an open encryption system.

[646] *OJ* L 053/1, 27.2.1999.

[647] *COM* (95) 113 final 4 April 1995.

6.2.3. *Decision 94/922/EC, IV./M.469 MSG Media Service*

MSG Media Service[648] concerned a proposed joint venture involving Bertelsmann, the parent company of the leading German media group primarily active in book and magazine publishing; Taurus, a holding company belonging to the German Kirch group; and Deutsche Telekom, the public Telecommunications operator. The parties proposed to create a JV called MSG, which would offer technical, business and administrative handling of mainly Pay-TV and which would be jointly controlled by the parties.[649] It would require the installation of a decoder which would, in most cases, be rented by the viewer, and a digital-analogue converter, because most viewers will for years only be equipped with analogue TV sets and a conditional access system. There were two basic options for a conditional access system. First, a proprietary encryption technology, such as used by BSkyB and Canal plus, and secondly, a common-interface system, where the decoder is technically designed to 'understand' different access systems. Potential Pay-TV operators preferred the latter system because it facilitates their access to the decoder. MSG would offer decoder, conditional access and subscriber management from a single body.

At the time of the Decision, Premiere, owned by Bertelsmann, Kirch and Canal plus, was the only supplier of Pay-TV in Germany and, at that time, itself provided the necessary technical services and the subscription management. Similar services as MSG's were only offered by Selco, a JV between PRO 7, a German private television company, and News Corporation, which belonged to the British Murdoch group. The German Telekom operated a cable network that is predominant on the German market, holding a monopoly for the German telephone network and covering over 90 percent of the German cable television network.[650]

At the time of the Decision, the Merger Regulation had not yet been subject to amendment and the distinction between cooperative and concentrative JVs was still relevant.[651] However, the Commission found that the JV performed 'on a permanent basis all the functions of an autonomous economic entity'[652] and that MSG had neither the object nor the effect of coordinating the competitive behaviour of undertakings, which remained independent.[653] There was no indication that the parties of MSG would coordinate their behaviour on the free-TV market.[654] Consequently, the JV was qualified as concentrative in the sense of Article 3 of the Merger Regulation. As the Merger satisfied the threshold criteria in Article 1, it had a Community dimension, and the Commission proceeded to assess whether the concen-

648 *OJ* 31.12.1994, L 364/1.

649 Every party would appoint 2 members of the supervisory board.

650 Para 56 of the Decision.

651 See *supra* at 5.2.2.

652 Para 9 of the Decision.

653 Para 14 of the Decision.

654 Two large German private TV-operators, RTL and SAT 1 where owned by Bertelsmann and Kirch respectively.

tration would create or strengthen a dominant position. The Commission distinguished between several different markets, where the effect of the Merger has to be appraised.

First, it identified a separate market for administrative and technical services for Pay-TV. As MSG would be the first supplier of technical and administrative services, it would necessarily enjoy a first-mover advantage and hold a monopoly in the beginning. Because of the involvement of the most likely potential competitor in this market, Deutsche Telekom, this strong position would not only be temporal.[655] It hardly appeared possible that a new supplier could establish itself against the combined competitive advantages of Telekom, on the one hand, and Bertelsmann/Kirch on the other. The latter, had via Premiere, established a strong subscriber base and, due to their activities in commercial free-TV, had preferential access to program software, such as transmission rights for Hollywood productions. Even if MSG would decide for a 'common interface', the average Pay-TV subscriber would prefer to deal only with one supply body, and whichever supplier can provide the widest choice and the most attractive programmes would occupy a favoured position.[656]

Secondly, the market for Pay-TV constituted a product market separate from commercial advertised-financed television and public television ('free-TV'). There is a direct trade relationship between the programme supplier and the viewer (subscriber), but the distinction could become blurred if Pay-TV was financed from a mixture of sources. In any event, there was some relationship between free-TV and Pay-TV, because growth of the latter was slower in a market with large and varied supply of free-TV, such as Germany.[657] As Kirch and Bertelsmann enjoyed preferential access to program software, had widespread activities in free-access commercial television and connections to print media, a new programme supplier would entail too great an economic risk to compete against MSG and virtually be forced to use MSG's technology.[658]

Thirdly, there is a separate market for cable television networks. Unlike satellite dishes, which consumers pay for only once, it is financed by a regular cable fee. Households that have opted for either cable or satellite are 'locked-in' and unable to easily switch.[659] The concentration would also adversely affect competition on the market for cable networks, because it prevents Deutsche Telekom from being available as a potential partner for other future cable network operators.[660]

---

[655] Para 56 of the Decision. The Commission also emphasised that Telekom held a 16.6 stake in SES, the main European satellite operator, which would enable it to influence the allocation of channels on the Astra satellite.

[656] Para 71 of the Decision.

[657] Para 32 of the Decision.

[658] This is to be expected against the background of new program suppliers in the UK and France depending on BskyB and Canal plus respectively. Para 82 of the Decision.

[659] Para 41 of the Decision.

[660] Para 92 of the Decision.

Fourthly, the relevant geographical market was limited to Germany, on language grounds and because of regulatory differences. However, the Commission left open if the geographical market could also comprise Austria, which would not entail any material change for the analysis.

The parties had proposed various undertakings to the JV, including, operating a transparent price policy, choosing a decoder on the basis of a common interface, and making the Telekom network available also for further digital program transmission and not disclosing any information of subscriber data to its parent companies.[661] But because these undertakings where subject to several conditions, the Commission found them to be merely declarations, being insufficient to remedy the restriction of competition. Thus, the JV was declared incompatible with the Common market, since it led to a sealing-off involving the main actors on the German Pay-TV market. It created a dominant position on the market for technical and administrative services in Germany that was not merely temporal.

MSG was the first Decision concerning the German Pay-TV market and it decisively shaped the Commission's approach on the matter. In particular, the Commission found Pay-TV to constitute a market different from commercial and public service television financed by advertising and/or fees.[662] As a result of this narrow market definition, and against the background of a market structure that made entry of potential competitors highly unlikely, it held that the concentration was incompatible with the Common market, even if MSG succeeded in developing a common interface solution. Regarding the only competitor on the market for technical services, Selco, the Commission determined that it merely operated in a niche market of providing foreign-language programmes in Germany.[663] It also considered that PRO 7, which was 47.7 percent controlled by Thomas Kirch, the son of the Kirch group's owner, somehow fell into the sphere of influence of the Kirch group, which is contestable in the light of the definition of 'control' as defined in Article 3(1)(b)('possibility of exercising decisive influence') of the Merger Regulation.[664]

It is also noteworthy that, in this Decision, the Commission appears to move towards a more permissive approach in its assessment of JVs. It stated that 'co-operation within a joint venture within the framework of the business object is a characteristic of every joint venture and cannot be used as evidence of its co-operative nature'. This can be read as altering the Commission's widely-criticised view, to almost *eo ipso* find a JV as restricting competition.[665] However, the Commission was ultimately not convinced by the parties' submission that they could assume the risk of investing jointly in digital infrastructure.[666] At the time of the Decision, the

---

[661] Para 94 of the Decision.

[662] See T. Jestaedt/J. Anweiler, op. cit. n. 637, p. 550.

[663] Para 65 of the Decision.

[664] See *supra* at 6.1.1. However, the approach appears justified in the light of the later integration of Pro 7 into the Kirch group. *Der Spiegel*, No. 41, 11.10.1999, pp.162-164; 'Alles unter einem Dach'.

[665] See e.g., R. Whish, op. cit. n. 480, p. 430 and *supra* at 5.3.5.3.

[666] Para 58 of the Decision.

Commission appeared to be less keen than in other Decisions to support the development of a new service. If we contrast this Decision with *BIB/Open*,[667] the Commission seems less prepared to consider the positive effect of the JV.

No express reference was made in *MSG* to public interest considerations. Yet, at least implicitly, the 'general good' does seem relevant, if defined it in a broader sense. Competition safeguards consumer welfare, and the Commission is determined to guarantee a level playing field and prevent barriers to entry, which would render it more difficult for other traders to enter the market. It prohibited the JV because the joined strength of two major private broadcasters, together with Telekom's expertise, would make further market entry almost impossible and deprive consumers of the benefits of competition between different Pay-TV suppliers.

6.2.4. *Decision 1999/53/EC, IV./M.993 Bertelsmann/Kirch/Premiere*

Bertelsmann/Kirch/Premiere,[668] can, generally speaking, be considered as an extension or 'second try' of the previously discussed *MSG* Decision.[669] The parties, Bertelsmann, CLT-UFA (a JV between Bertelsmann and Audiofina) and Taurus of the Kirch group proposed to change the shareholdings in Premiere, a German Pay-TV supplier as follows. Premiere was at that time 37.5 percent each controlled by CLT-UFA and Canal plus, Kirch held the remaining 25 percent. Canal plus should divest itself of its shareholding and CLT-UFA and Kirch should both increase their share in Premiere to 50 percent each. Simultaneously, Kirch planned to close down its Pay-TV channel DF 1 and transfer its assets to Premiere.

The subject matter of proceeding IV/M.1027 Deutsche Telekom/Beta Research was joined with this case, because the two projects, although constituting separate concentrations, were factually closely linked. CLT-UFA was to acquire a 50 percent interest in Beta Research, a wholly owned Kirch subsidiary. BetaResearch was active in the development of decoder software and worked on the encryption and operating software for the d-box technology. Moreover, Deutsche Telekom also intended to acquire a stake in BetaResearch, to ensure that it has the necessary rights in the technology on which the d-box was based.

Both Premiere and BetaResearch would perform on a permanent basis all the functions of an autonomous economic entity and should not lead to coordination of the parent companies. Both operations therefore constituted concentrations in the sense of Article 3(1)(b).[670] Relevant product markets were the markets for Pay-

---

[667] See *supra* at 5.3.5.

[668] *OJ* L 053/1, 27.2.1999.

[669] U. Immenga, 'Europäische Kommission: Marktbeherrschende Digital-Allianz', Case note for Case IV/M. 1027, (1999) *Computer & Recht*, pp. 424-431, at p. 430.

[670] Paras 13, 14 of the Decision. It is noteworthy to mention that, although with the entering into force on 30 June 1997 of Regulation 1310/97 amending the Merger Regulation the distinction between co-operative and concentrative JVs was abolished, the Commission still refers to the JV as 'concentrative'.

TV[671] and its technical services. The relevant geographical market was, as with *MSG*, limited to Germany, Luxembourg and possibly Austria and the German-speaking parts of Belgium and Switzerland. Still, the Commission left a definitive decision on the geographic market for Pay-TV open. Concerning technical services for Pay-TV, the Commission established a geographical market encompassing the entire German-speaking area, without, however, deciding if there was an overall market for satellite and cable transmission or two separate markets respectively.[672] After the concentration, Premiere would be the only program and marketing platform in Germany with the decoder technology part of the technical platform.

Thus, the Commission considered Premiere to be dominant on the relevant market. CLT-UFA and Kirch would account for about 90 percent of all advertising revenue (and approximately 50 percent of all viewers) in the German broadcasting market, with SAT 1 controlled by Kirch, RTL by Bertelsmann and PRO 7 owned by Mr. Kirch's son and likewise heavily depending on Kirch's program content.[673] The Commission expected, referring to a press report citing an internal Bertelsmann document, that this would give rise to a serious risk of coordination between free-TV and Pay-TV, whereby the program quality of the former was lowered in order to induce viewers to subscribe to the latter. Although Pay-TV and free-TV belonged to different markets, the Commission found some connection between them. Indeed, it would only be economically sensible to complement Pay-TV and Free-TV, for example, by showing a football final on Pay-TV and smaller events on Free-TV. It would also make sense to obtain television rights for sports events and Hollywood productions jointly, to recoup the expected tremendous losses of the start-up phase. Decreasing the attractiveness of Free-TV would not lead to advertisers moving to public service broadcasters, because the latter faced tight restrictions on advertising time (20 minutes per day) and accounted for less than 10 percent of advertising revenue.[674] Therefore, commercial private television could offer a less varied program without having to fear adverse effects on its advertising revenue.

On the market for technical services for Pay-TV, BetaDigital would occupy a monopoly on a lasting basis, and via its stake in BetaResearch, Telekom will secure a monopoly in the operation of conditional access for cable. The d-box would thus become virtually the digital standard in the German-speaking area and it would hardly be possible for a second Pay-TV operator to set up in Germany. The simulcrypt system used in the d-box also made access for third parties more difficult. Unlike a common interface, where another party could, generally speaking, plug in the d-box, simulcrypt requires an agreement with the installer of the decoder base and

---

[671] The Commission confirms the distinction between free-TV and Pay-TV made in *MSG*, see *supra* at 6.2.3. However, it also indicates that in the future a certain convergence between the two might occur. See para 18 of the Decision.

[672] Para 25 of the Decision.

[673] Para 80 of the Decision.

[674] Para 84 of the Decision.

some interference with the software.[675] Due to Deutsche Telekom's virtual monopoly for the supply of cable TV, the parallel concentration between Deutsche Telekom and BetaResearch would result in a 'dominant duopoly',[676] considering there was one market for technical services of satellite and cable TV.[677]

The parties failed to take into account the leasing costs for the d-box and miscalculated the costs for the decoder base. The Commission thus found it unconvincing that only Bertelsmann and Kirch together were capable of supplying the attractive programming necessary to establish Pay-TV in Germany. The criterion of technical and economic progress contained in Article 2(1)(b) of the Merger Regulation is subject to the condition that it is no obstacle to competition[678] and could not assist the parties' argument here.

The parties had proposed various undertakings. They suggested making 25 percent of Kirch's and CLT-UFA's Pay-TV rights for Hollywood productions available for third parties and Premiere would open up its bouquet structure. Moreover, Premiere would itself acquire its Pay-TV rights and no Free-TV rights. The Commission found that insufficient. It was unlikely that another Pay-TV operator could establish itself on the basis of 25 percent of the Pay-TV rights, excluding sports rights and the technological development, which would be controlled by Bertelsmann, Kirch and Telekom. Further undertakings were suggested, mainly regarding access to Premiere's bouquet, but the statements were found to be too vague and, because of Telekom's strong position, private cable operators would not be allowed to supply Pay-TV themselves. Hence, the concentration(s) were held to be incompatible with the common market. If we assess the findings of the Commission, it should, first, be mentioned that during the proceedings leading to this Decision, a lively discussion on the applicability of the so-called 'failing company defence' developed. The concept stems from US antitrust law[679] and, generally speaking, covers cases where an acquisition is justified on the grounds that otherwise the target undertaking could not survive. Although the concept is not explicitly referred to in the Merger Regulation and the Commission was reluctant to accept its relevance in *Aérospatial-Alena/de Haviland*,[680], the Commission in *Kali und Salz*[681] established that the 'failing company defence' could be taken into account 'pursuant to Art. 2(2)'. To satisfy the test, the notifying parties must demonstrate that, first, that the target company will not survive, secondly, in that event that the acquiring company will inherit its market share and thirdly, there is no alternative

[675] 'Other persons wishing to use their own independent application through the d-box would have to have it inserted into the operating system's source code by BetaResearch', Para 113 of the Decision.

[676] Collective dominance by two undertakings.

[677] Para 118 of the Decision.

[678] Para 122 of the Decision.

[679] Cook/Kerse, op. cit. n. 484, p. 178.

[680] *OJ* 1991, L 334/42.

[681] *OJ* 1994, L 186/38, paras 71 et seq.

solution which would be less anti-competitive.[682] The 'failing company defence' argues that there is no causal link between the merger and the creation or strengthening of a dominant position. In the present case, this was relevant because the parties argued that DF 1, the Pay-TV channel run by Kirch, would in any event not survive on the market. Later, this expectation proofed correct. DF 1 had to be closed down and Kirch sold a 25 percent stake in Premiere to Rupert Murdoch.[683] However, the parties in *Bertelsmann/Kirch/Premiere* did not successfully argue the 'failing company defence'. The Commission considered that the closing down of a certain business activity was a usual management decision and that this 'failing division defence' did not indicate that the causal link between the concentration and the emergence or strengthening of a dominant position was missing.[684]

One could agree with the Commission that if it had let the parties go ahead with the concentrations, a permanent dominant position of the Pay-TV market, the market for technical services and the cable market had been implemented. Yet, the Commission's argument does not appear entirely watertight. While it did not contest the assumption that the investment required to establish Pay-TV on the German market was indeed substantial and at present there was no competitor able to offer an alternative platform,[685] it was unable to answer the question how Pay-TV could be established on the German market in accordance with the Merger Regulation at all. During the proceeding, the parties emphasised that if their concentration was prevented, German Pay-TV would most probably be introduced on the basis of an already established foreign Pay-TV operator. Against this background, the Commission essentially took the view that it was better not to have Pay-TV in Germany at all than accepting the Bertelsmann/Kirch/Telekom-dominance. However, even if one accepts this argument, the Commission failed to explain how each of the parties would have been able to establish Pay-TV on its own.[686]

Again, this Merger Decision did not expressly refer to any kind of public interest, apart from the Commission's apprehension about the quality of Free-TV in the light of broader concerns about program diversity and pluralism.[687]

6.3. **Non-Opposition Procedures**

Since the early 1990s, the Commission cleared a substantial number of JVs under the Merger Regulation, since they did not result in the addition of market shares on

---

[682] Cook/Kerse, op. cit. n. 484, p. 179

[683] See e.g., *The Guardian Online*, 4.11.1999 'Murdoch master plan for Europe'; *Süddeutsche Zeitung Online*, 30.11.1999, "Milliarden für das Pay-TV".

[684] D. Buschle, 'Pay-TV in der Fusionskontrolle: Entscheidung Bertelsmann/Kirch veröffentlicht', 5 *ELR* (1999) pp. 218-221, at p. 220.

[685] See para 149 of the Decision.

[686] U. Immenga, op. cit. n. 669, p. 431.

[687] D. Buschle, op. cit. n. 684, p. 221.

the same product and geographical market.[688] In 1991, ESPN, controlled by ABC, Generale des Eaux and Canal plus and, in turn, wholly owned by Walt Disney, acquired most of the television interests of W.H. Smith. The Commission concluded that the French parties, in acquiring channels like Kindernet and Cable Jukebox, entered into a different linguistic and cultural market than the one which they had previously been active on. As these channels where moreover free access and not Pay-TV programs, and only held market shares of less than one percent respectively, the Commission found no reason to prohibit the operation.[689]

In 1996, ESPN entered into a JV with Star, which was controlled by a diversified media company. Each of the parties would hold a 50 percent stake in the JV NEWCO. Its main business was the distribution of sports programs on the Asian market. As the operation mainly concerned a market outside the EU/EEC area and would not make any significant sales in Europe, the JV was permitted.[690]

Less straightforward was a concentration between Canal plus, BankAmerica and DCPQ (a Canadian portfolio-management company) to change control in NCH, a French cable television operator previously under the sole control of Canal plus. As, on the Spanish broadcasting market, BankAmerica and CDPQ held controlling interests in Cableuropa and Canal plus, *inter alia*, controlled Sogecable, the Commission expected adverse effects on the markets for Spanish Pay-TV and the wholesale supply of films.[691] The number of subscribers indicated that Sogecable might have a dominant position. The JV taking place on the French market could have repercussions in Spain, as it might discourage Sogecable and Cableurope from competing. A content distribution agreement between Sogecable and Cableurope indicated, in the Commission's view, the strong incentive for Canal plus to favour Cableurope. As Canal plus, controlling Sogecable in Spain, would enter into a JV in France with BankAmerica and CDPQ, controlling Cableurope in Spain, the parties to the JV might coordinate their subsidiaries' behaviour on the Spanish market. The parties suggested an undertaking which the Commission found sufficient to remedy the threat to competition. Canal plus and Sogecable undertook to promise non-discriminatory access to their distribution rights to any Spanish cable operator. The Commission found this commitment sufficient to remove its serious doubts about the compatibility of the JV with the common market.

---

[688] From 1. September 2000 the Commission Notice on a simplified procedure for treatment of certain concentrations under Council Regulation (EEC) No 4064/89, *OJ* 2000 C217/32, became applicable. The Notice is *inter alia* applicable to concentrations where the parties are active on different product and geographical markets. When the conditions set out in the Notice are met, the Commission will adopt a short-form clearance decision within one month. Thus, JV taking place on different product and geographical markets could in the future benefit from this simplified procedure.

[689] Commission Decision of 10.0.1991, Case IV.M.110 *ABC/GENERAL DES EAUX/CANAL PLUS/ W.H. SMITH TV, OJ* C 244, 19.9.1991.

[690] Commission Decision of 11.11.1996, Case IV.M826 *ESPN/STAR, OJ* C 368/8, 6.12.1996 .

[691] Commission Decision of 3.12.1998, Case IV/M.1327 *NC/CANAL PLUS/CDPQ/BANKAMERICA, OJ* C 233/21, 14.8.1999.

Walt Disney and Sony via subsidiaries joined forces to set up the Pay-TV channel Movieco, which would operate in the Netherlands and Flemish-speaking Belgium. In its Decision,[692] the Commission identified the markets for the acquisition of broadcasting rights and wholesales supply of film and sport channels as potentially relevant product markets. As to the existence of competition on the market, the Commission was not entirely clear. Canal plus was also active on the upstream market for the acquisition of broadcasting rights but operated in a different geographical market. Still, the Commission found that Movieco was not dominant because, although Canal plus was strictly speaking not in the same market, it could not be ignored. Finally, the Commission did not oppose the JV, since it would be free to purchase film rights from any source.[693]

6.3.1. *The Kirch Group*

With regard to Pay-TV, Kirch had already in 1994 acquired a stake in the Italian TV operator Telepiù. In the Decision of 2 August 1994, the Commission declared compatible with the common market the acquisition of joint control of Telepiù by the Kirch group and the Swiss-based holding company Richemont,[694] which was mainly active in tobacco production and distribution but also held an interest in FilmNet. As the relevant market, the commission identified the Pay-TV market in Italy, because broadcasting markets for language reasons still remained national. Similarly, the markets for acquiring Hollywood rights were restricted to a national or language area, since the same film was released in different countries at different times. Although Kirch had access to a substantial movie library, this was only the case for the German versions of these films. Thus, a dominant position was neither created nor strengthened. One year later, control in Telepiù changed again and it was now to be jointly controlled by Kirch, Richemont and Multichoice, a South-African-based media and communications company. The features of the Decision remained essentially the same. As there was no addition of market shares in this altered situation, the Commission declared the concentration compatible with the Common Market.[695]

These Decisions, in accordance with the Commission's sustained practice, distinguished a separate market for Pay-TV, different from Free-TV. However, against this background, it is remarkable that the information given by the Commission on market shares in the Italian broadcasting sector did not distinguish between Free- and Pay-TV,[696] and made no reference to Telepiù's position on the Italian Pay-TV market.

---

[692] Case COMP/JV.30 *BVI Television (Europe)/SPE Euromovies Investments/Europe Movieco Partners*, available on CELEX 300J0030, nyr.

[693] An exclusive-supply-clause included into the JV agreement was not covered by the Decision.

[694] Case IV/M.410 *Kirch/Richemont/Telpiù, OJ* C 225/3, 13.8.1994.

[695] Case IV/M.584 *Kirch/Richemont/Multichoice/Telpiù, OJ* C 129/6, 25.5.1995.

[696] Case IV/M.410 *Kirch/Richemont/Telpiù, OJ* C 225/3, 13.8.1994, para 18; Case IV/M.584 *Kirch/Richemont/Multichoice/Telpiù, OJ* C 129/6, 25.5.1995, para 18.

Recently, the Kirch group again became involved in the Italian Media market by setting up a JV together with the Mediaset group controlled by Finninvest. The holding company 'Eureka' was to control various subsidiaries active in the markets for TV-broadcasting, TV-advertising, TV-production acquisition and distribution of TV content. The Commission did not block the merger, considering the parent companies' activities as having taken place on different geographical markets, and that there was not overlap in businesses, and market shares remained rather small.[697]

6.3.2. *The Bertelsmann Group*

In 1996, Bertelsmann merged its subsidiary UFA with CLT (Compagnie Luxembourgeoise de Télédiffusion).[698] CLT had previously been approximately 97 percent controlled by the Luxembourg-based holding company, Audiofina. CLTUFA intended to become active on the markets for Free-TV, Pay-TV, TV productions, TV rights/licences and free access radio. The Commission found that the JV would to a great extent be complementary, with the only significant overlap in the German TV market being the parties' already existing JV in RTL. Market shares of the channels linked to CLT/UFA remained well below the dominance-threshold,[699] and CLT/UFA was faced with a strong competitor on the German broadcasting market. Channels of the Kirch group together accounted for almost 50 percent market share in terms of advertising revenue. In the Pay-TV market, the JV would not add any market share, since CLT was not active on the German Pay-TV market.[700] As in *Kirch/Richemont/Telepiù*, the Commission found that the markets for the acquisition of TV-rights remained national.

Recently, the Commission approved the change in control in the Spanish corporation BOL Spain, which was mainly active in printing, publishing and other media, such as broadcasting and electronic publishing. It had previously been under the sole control of Bertelsmann, and after the transaction, the other party to the JV, Planeta, was to hold a 50 percent stake. As the market for various chains of publishing in Spain was very diverse (mail order, Internet), there was significant competition on the relevant product market. Thus, the JV did not raise any competition concerns.

Besides its main business areas publishing and broadcasting, Bertelsmann has also moved towards new media areas. In 1999, it entered into a JV together with Cegetal, Canal plus and AOL, AOL/CIS, which the Commission declared compatible with the Common Market.[701] The JV was mainly active in providing various

---

[697] Case IV.M.1574, *Kirch/Mediaset, OJ* C 255/3, 8.9.1999.

[698] Case IV/M.799 *Berteslmann/CLT, OJ* C 364/3, 4.12.1996.

[699] Generally, market shares from about 40/45 per cent indicate a dominant position. See e.g., Case *United Brands* [1978] ECR 207, *ECS/AKZO, OJ* 1983 L 252/13, upheld on appeal, Case C-62/86.

[700] At the time of the Decision, UFA held a 37.5 per cent market share in Premiere.

[701] Case IV/M.5, available as CELEX document 31999J0005, nyr.

services linked to the use of the Internet. Although the market for dial-up Internet access was found to be national, the other markets were very competitive, for instance, advertising on the Internet. Hence, there was no appreciable restriction of competition.

6.4. **Specific Regulation of Media Concentration**

6.4.1. *The Community Level*

As mentioned before, there is currently no Community secondary legislation specifically aiming to prevent concentrated media markets, especially on the market supplying television broadcasting. Yet, there has been protracted discussion in the past on the potential need for such a directive, starting with the Green Paper on Pluralism and Media Concentration in the Internal Market,[702] which can be considered as the first coherent Commission contribution on the subject matter. Therein, the Commission identified three potential options, first, to take no specific action. Secondly, to take action limited to increase transparency, and thirdly, harmonising, either by way of a Council directive or a Council regulation, whereby the Commission itself favoured the third option indicating that a Council directive could be based on Article 57(2)[703] (now Article 47(2)).

Subsequently, we witnessed several initiatives during the 1990s. In 1994, the Commission issued a Notice to the Council and the Parliament,[704] but the Commission's intention to pass a draft directive before the end of the year was frustrated by the fact that neither within the Commission nor amongst Member States agreement could be reached.[705] Commissioner Mario Monti, in 1996[706] and 1997,[707] submitted two more draft directives but, again, these initiatives were not supported by all commissioners.[708] It has, especially by German writers,[709] been suggested that the Community simply lacks competence to introduce legislation concerning the control of media concentration. Yet, the Commission clarified that it understood its initiative as a corollary to the 'Television Without Frontiers' Directive focusing on the freedom of establishment, and intended to achieve a balance

---

[702] *COM* (92) 480 final.

[703] Ibid., p. 116.

[704] *COM* (94) 353 final.

[705] H. Kresse,. 'Marktöffnung und Pluralitätssicherung. Eckpunkte zur effektiven Vielfaltsgestaltung im privaten Rundfunk' in H. Kresse, ed., *Pluralismus, Markt und Medienkonzentration: Positione* (Berlin, Vistas, 1995) p. 86.

[706] *COM* (96) 396 final.

[707] *COM* (97) 86 final.

[708] D. Kraus, 'Neuer EU-Anlauf gegen die Medienkonzentration.' *Die Presse online*, http://www.diepresse.at/aktuell/kultur-1.html., visited 11.3.1997.

[709] H. Kresse/M. Heinze 'Der Rundfunk: Das "jedenfalls auch kulturelle Phänomen"', 6 *ZUM* (1995) pp. 394-397.

with the freedom to provide services.[710] Moreover, it would not interfere with situations covered by national legislation but only remedy deficiencies 'due to circumstances outside the national authorities' control'.[711]

Lacking any specific control of media concentration, Article 21(3) of the Merger Regulation[712] remains the only Community law provision expressly protecting the 'plurality of the media'. Member States may take action against a merger that is compatible with the common market but incompatible with the national laws safeguarding pluralism. However, this measure must be appropriate and comply with the general principles of Community law. Member States cannot take advantage of Article 21(3) to authorise transactions the Commission has declared incompatible with the common market.[713]

6.4.2. *The National Level: The Example of Germany*

The former Treaty of 1991, concluded between the Länder in the unified Germany (*Rundfunkstaatsvertrag, RStV)*, in its Article 21 provided that a broadcaster was restricted to two national programmes, one general and one special interest program. By contrast, the current *Rundfunkstaatsvertrag*, in its Article 26 no longer does not restricts the number of channels per broadcaster. The decisive criterion is now the 'opinion power' (*Meinungsmacht)* enjoyed by a single broadcaster. Such a position is to be assumed if a program reaches 30 percent audience share, and can also be established at a slightly smaller audience share.

In Addition to the general anti-trust control exercised by the Federal Cartel Office (*Bundeskartellamt)*, an independent regulatory body, the Commission for the Establishment of Concentration in the Media (*Kommission zur Ermittlung der Konzentration im Medienbereich, KEK)* was set up in 1997.[714] Its main task is to assess if a merger would result in building 'opinion power'. The KEK consists of six member, all of whom are renowned scholars and experts in the field of competition law and the media. The *KEK* acts on behalf of the media authorities of the respective *Land* (*Landesmedienanstalten)* and its decisions are binding. Only if all the media authorities in Germany reach agreement is possible to deviate from the *KEK's* decision.[715] So far, the *KEK* has never vetoed a merger, and it is interesting to note that, for example, in the *Bertelsmann/Kirch/Premiere* case, which was also subject to the *KEK's* assessment, the commission concluded that no restriction of competition was to be expected. Unlike the EC Commission, which confined the

---

[710] *COM* (92) 480 final, p. 114.
[711] Ibid., p. 63.
[712] See *supra* at 6.1.2.
[713] *COM* (92) 480 final, p. 79.
[714] Information available on http://www.kek-online.de
[715] Ibid.

relevant market to pay-TV,[716] the *KEK* concluded that there was enough competition from free-TV and concluded that overall competition was sufficient.[717] Thus, so far, the *KEK's* impact on the German media landscape has been somewhat limited.

6.5. **Conclusion**

Since the introduction of the Merger Regulation, a large number of concentrations scrutinised by the Commission concerned the field of broadcasting. In the last decade, throughout Europe more and more broadcasters decided to enter JVs to penetrate new markets and ensure a sufficient financial basis for the considerable investment necessary to introduce new technologies. As these mergers took place on an inhomogeneous product market and on various geographical markets, a coherent pattern of analysis cannot be easily identified from the case law. However, some cornerstones in the assessment have become apparent.

First, the Commission is very reluctant to accept arguments of technical progress justifying some restriction of competition, if it expects that a concentration will lead to a protracted dominant position. When a new technology or service is first introduced to the market, a certain first-mover advantage renders some degree of dominance in an initial phase almost indispensable. However, if high barriers to entry on the relevant market make it difficult for potential competitors to enter the market later, in particular if the consumers are 'locked-in' a certain technical standard introduced by the first-mover, the Commission will rather acknowledge that certain services cannot be offered at all, instead of accepting a dominant position that is not only temporal in nature. As became apparent in *Kirch/Bertelsmann/Premiere*, 'the development of technical and economic progress' (Article 2(1)(b) of the Merger Regulation) must not form an obstacle to competition.

Secondly, public interest considerations are not discussed in any detail in merger proceedings. Although Article 21(3) of the Merger Regulation states that Member States 'may take appropriate measures to protect legitimate interests other than those taken into consideration by this Regulation[718] and compatible with the general principles and other provisions of Community law', in practice, Member States did not resort to such measures or, at least, did not rely on this provision. As the concentrations under scrutiny predominantly involved private broadcasters, and, at the most, a former public service telecom operator, as in *NSD* and *Kirch/Bertelsmann/Premiere*, aspects of balanced information and pluralism of the media was simply not an issue. However, the Commission in *HMG, Kirch/Mediaset* and *Bertelsmann/*

[716] *Bertelsmann/Kirch/Premiere, OJ* L 053/1, 27.2.1999.

[717] Premiere Medien GmbH & Co. KG, KEK026, available on http://www.kek-online.de or in 5 *ZUM-RD* (1999), pp. 241 et seq.

[718] Also Rec. 12 of the Merger Regulation clarifies that it was without prejudice to Art. 90(2) (now Art. 86(2)) of the Treaty.

CLT did distinguish between product markets for (mostly public-service) in-house productions as opposed by commissioned productions. In *HMG*, the parties had argued that there was no material difference between the programs offered by public and private broadcasters, which failed to convince the Commission.

It may seem striking that cross-border mergers could benefit from the non-opposition procedure much more easily than concentrations involving parties operating within one and the same geographical market. This simply follows from the fact that broadcasting markets remained largely national and the Commission consistently limited the relevant geographical market to one Member State. Sometimes it left the ultimate decision open if it also extended to a certain single language areas within the Common Market.[719] It appears that mergers predominantly effecting one national market pose a more serious threat to competition than if the parties have previously been active on different geographical markets. Only in the former case one can expect the addition of potentially substantial market shares. Thus, the market definition employed by the Commission does not have regard to the danger for pluralism by a large media company extending its business to another Member State. Such a case will normally concern different geographical markets and thus not lead to a dominant position. Nonetheless, it may be desirable, in order to ensure pluralism, to also monitor concentrations, whereby a media undertaking extends its business to another Member State and a geographical market where it had previously not been active.

Several Commission initiatives to introduce specific Community media anti-concentration legislation have remained fruitless and it is doubtful if the Commission will take up the issue again. This is due to lack of agreement between the different actors, if such legislation must be based on the freedom of establishment, Article 47 (ex-Article 57) or if it were a harmonisation measure in the cultural field, which, according to Article 151(4) (ex-Article 138(4)), is prohibited. The need for such Community legislation may currently not be a pressing problem; however, this could change over time. For the time being, television broadcasting remains largely national but converging media markets may produce a different situation. Media companies are becoming increasingly active across borders, and it would be desirable in merger proceedings to assess their position regarding market shares held in different geographical markets.

[719] For example the German market embracing Germany, Austria, the German-speaking areas of Switzerland, Luxembourg and Belgium or the French market covering France and the French-speaking areas of Belgium and or the Dutch market including the Netherlands and Flemish-speaking Belgium.

Chapter 7
PUBLIC SERVICE BROADCASTING AND PROBLEMS OF STATE AID

Public Service Broadcasting has for decades dominated most Member State's television landscapes, and it wasn't until the 1950s[720] – and in some countries as late as the 1980s[721] – that private commercial television was introduced and, for example, Austria still maintains a public service terrestrial broadcasting[722] monopoly.[723]

The financing of public service broadcasting differs across Member States.[724] Against this background, one has to highlight that the European legal framework has remained comparatively stable, although the Treaty of Amsterdam also introduced some relevant changes.[725] From the viewpoint of European law, the field of public service broadcasting touches upon various Treaty provisions. Articles 31 (ex-Article 37) deals with state monopolies, 86 (ex-Article 90) relates to public undertakings, 87 (ex-Article 92) regulates state aid and the new Article 16 (ex-Article 7b) moves 'services of general economic interest' to the 'principles' of the Treaty. These shall be analysed and discussed with regard to public service broadcasting.

But the shape and financing of public service broadcasting is also characterised by highly political implications. Member States consider it a prerogative to define and outline public service broadcasting as part of their cultural policy. In particular,

[720] In the United Kingdom the private broadcasters Independent Television (ITV) was introduced in 1954. See I. Freis, 'Das Recht der Finanzierung des öffentlich-rechtlichen Rundfunks in Deutschland, Frankreich, Großbritannien und Österreich im Vergleich', 1 *ZEuS* (1999) pp. 109-136, at p. 125.

[721] For instance in France and Germany, see I. Freis, op. cit. n. 720, pp. 112, 122.

[722] Since 1.1.1994, local private radio is allowed. See Regionalradiogesetz (RRG), *BGBl.* 1993, 506. See also W. Dillenz, 'Österreich. Vom Medien-Albanien zum Medien-Kalifornien', 10 *ZUM* (1994) pp. 544-551.

[723] This was not yet an issue under Community law, but it resulted in a judgement of the European Court of Human Rights condemning Austria for infringing the freedom of opinion embodied in Art. 10 of the European Convention of Human Rights (ECHR). See ECHR Series A Nr. 276, *Informationsverein Lentia u.a.,* Judgment of 24.11.1993. In November 1998 the Austrian Government suggested an amendment of the Austrian legislation to bring it in line with Directive 97/36/EC, amending the 'Television without Frontiers'-Directive. The draft law also included the introduction of commercial national broadcasting. However, the draft law was never adopted because parliament in a hearing on 13 July 1999 found that there was not yet enough information to introduce private terrestrial broadcasting. See information at http://www.austria.gv.at/regierung/VD/ksrginfo.htm, visited 28.5.2000.

[724] Eleven Member States charge fees for television and radio broadcasting, in Greece and Portugal an additional fee is levied on electricity to finance public service broadcasting. Source: *Media Perspektiven*, (1995) p. 458.

[725] This is particularly the case with the added Protocol on public service television which will be dealt with later.

continental European jurisdictions based on Roman law, such as the German or French legal systems have defined state monopolies rather broadly and often left it to them to decide on the content of the 'public interest'.[726] This fundamentally differs from the public utility regulation of the Anglo-Saxon world, in particular, the US, which focuses on efficiency and consumer welfare.[727] In the European context, the EC has undertaken to oblige dominant undertakings to charge prices that are in line with their costs incurred. Structure and conduct of monopolists have become subject to close scrutiny and they must justify their privileged position on the market by public interest considerations.[728]

Apart from these political and economic implications, serious legal difficulties arise. The problem of delimitation between national and community competence is highly contentious[729] and the European institutions are aware of the issue's sensitive nature. The Commission's reluctance to rule on the legality of the funding for Spanish public service broadcasting in the *Gestevision*[730] case, may serves an example. In 1992, a private Spanish broadcaster brought a complaint. The Commission took four years to reach a decision, indicating the sensitive nature of the subject matter. Member States have been very critical about the Commission intruding into what they consider to be their internal matters. Finally, the applicant brought an action before the Court of First Instance (CFI) in 1996, and the CFI upheld the applicant's claim that the Commission had failed to fulfil its obligations under the Treaty by failing to adopt a decision.[731] Under the influence of this Judgement, the Commission, in October 1998, presented an internal working document to the Member States, indicating that it was preparing general guidelines on the evaluation of the financing of public broadcasting under EC state aid law.[732] Finally, the Commission decided not to draft any general guidelines but to follow a case-by-case approach.[733]

An analysis of the legal writings shows that starting from necessarily the same legal provisions in the Treaty, different authors arrive at not only dissimilar but also even contrary conclusions, as will be demonstrated below. However, this is also the result of inconsistent case law and deliberate ambiguity in the Court's Judgements,

---

726 E.-J. Mestmäcker in U. Immenga/E.-J. Mestmäcker, eds., *Wettbewerbsrecht*, (München, C.H. Beck, 1997), p. 1574.

727 Ibid.

728 Ibid., p. 1575.

729 This is especially emphasised by several German authors. See e.g., S. Astheimer/K. Moosmayer 'Europäische Rundfunkordnung – Chance oder Risiko?', 7 *ZUM* (1994) pp. 395-404; D. Dörr, 'Konzentrationstendenzen im Bereich des Rundfunks und ihre Rechtsprobleme', 1 *ZUM* (1993) pp. 10-17, at p. 14.

730 Case T-95/96 *Gestevision Telecinco SA* v. *Commission* [1998] ECR II-3407.

731 Ibid., See detailed M. Núñes Müller./H.-G. Kamann, (1999) *Europäisches Wirtschafts- und Steuerrecht*, pp. 332-338; P.J. Slot, (1999) *CMLRev.* pp. 1335-1344.

732 *Süddeutsche Zeitung* 22 October 1998, 'Aber Van Miert gibt nicht auf'.

733 A. Bartosch, 'The Financing of Public Broadcasting and E.C. State Aid Law: An Interim Balance', 4 *ECLR* (1999) pp. 197-204, at p. 198.

also due to varying economic circumstances. Finally, an effort shall be made to trace the most recent developments and establish a coherent approach to public service broadcasting under EC law, by giving special regard to the Court of Justice's rulings on the subject.

7.1.1. *State Monopolies*

The relevant provision for the assessment of state monopolies is Article 31 (ex-Article 37), which provides in its paragraph 1 that

> Member States shall adjust any State monopolies of a commercial character so as to ensure that no discrimination regarding the conditions under which goods are procured and marketed exists between Member States ...

This provision complements the rules on the free movement of goods insofar as it obliges Member States to adjust their state monopolies in a way that excludes discrimination between nationals of the Member States after the expiry of the transitional period.[734] Article 31 is connected to Article 86 (ex-Article 90), as both can be understood as fleshing out the general principle of Article 10 (ex-Article 5) that Member States shall abstain from measures which could jeopardise the attainment of the objectives of the Treaty.[735] However, Article 31 is only applicable to goods and hence services are not covered. This was made clear by the Court of Justice, *inter alia*, in the television cases *Sacchi*,[736] and *ERT*,[737] whereas Advocate General Lenz in his Opinion had taken the view that Article 37 (now Article 31) should also be applied to service monopolies.[738] The Court did not take up this argument. Only if a service monopoly acts as a 'measure having equivalent effect' can Article 30 (now Article 28) become applicable.[739] Thus, Article 31 is not applicable to broadcasting monopolies.

---

[734] E.-J. Mestmäcker in U. Immenga/E.-J. Mestmäcker, op. cit. n. 726, p. 1491.

[735] E.-J. Mestmäcker, 'Staat und Unternehmen im europäischen Gemeinschaftsreht. Zur Bedeutung vom Art. 90 EWGV', (1988) *Rabels Zeitschrift*, pp. 526-586.

[736] Case 155/73 [1993] ECR 408, para 10. 'It follows both from the place of this provision in the Chapter on the elimination of quantitative restrictions and from the use of the words "imports" and "exports" in the second indent of Article 37(1) and of the word "product" in Article 37(3) and (4) that it refers to trade in goods and cannot relate to a monopoly in the provision of services. Thus televised commercial advertising, by reason of its character as a service, does not come under these provisions'.

[737] Case C-260/89 [1991] ECR I-2925.

[738] Opinion Case C-260/89 [1991] ECR I-2925, 2942.

[739] Confirmed in Case C-158/94, [1997] ECR I-5789, para 19.

7.1.2. *Public Undertakings, Undertakings enjoying Special or Exclusive Rights and Services of General Economic Interest*

Some 30 years ago, the discussion about the interpretation of (then) Article 90 (now Article 86) and its relation to the EC Competition rules centred around the question of what extent Member States were prevented from taking measures that contradicted EC Competition law.[740] Generally speaking, the rules on competition are addressed to private undertakings doing business within the Internal Market. However, as Member States, via public undertakings, also engage in economic activities and entrust certain undertakings with specific preferential rights, the founders of the Treaty inserted a provision that was aimed to safeguard that competition was not distorted by Member State's anti-competitive conduct, which would be illegal under the competition rules if the same measure had been taken by a private undertaking. Article 86 (ex-Article 90) reads as follows:

> 1. In the case of public undertakings and undertakings to which Member States grant special or exclusive rights, Member States shall neither enact nor maintain in force any measure contrary to the rules contained in this Treaty, in particular to those rules provided for in Article 12 and Articles 81 to 89.
> 2. Undertakings entrusted with the operation of services of general economic interest or having the character of a revenue producing monopoly shall be subject to the rules contained in this Treaty, in particular to the rules on competition; insofar as the application of such rules does not obstruct the performance, in law or in fact, of the particular tasks assigned to them. The development of trade must not be affected to such an extent as would be contrary to the interests of the Community.
> 3. The Commission shall ensure the application of the provisions of this Article and shall, where necessary, address appropriate decisions to Member States.'

The traditional interpretation understood this provision as outlawing Member State's measures that forced undertakings to engage in conduct contrary to Articles 81 and 82 (ex-Articles 85 and 86). Public undertakings and undertakings enjoying special or exclusive rights should not be put in a position as to distort competition to the detriment of their private competitors.[741] However, another interpretation of Article 86 went much further and considered that also states' measures that did *not* result in a particular conduct by an undertaking on the market but was, as such, in contradiction with, in particular, the Competition rules, were covered.[742] Initially, this was a

[740] See e.g., G. Marenco, 'Le Traité CEE interdit-il aux Etats membres de restreindre la concurrence?', 3/4 *Cahiers de droit europeén* (1986), pp. 285, Y. Galmot/J. Binacarelli 'Les réglementations nationales en matière de prix au regard du droit communautaire' (1985) *RTDE* pp. 269 et seq.

[741] A. Pappalardo, 'Der Europäische Gerichtshof auf der Suche nach einem Kriterium für die Anwendung der Wettbewerbsregeln auf staatliche Maßnahmen' in E.-J. Mestmäcker, ed., *Festschrift Hans van der Groeben* (Nomos, Baden-Baden, 1997) pp. 303-314, at p. 304.

[742] E.-J. Mestmäcker, 'Offene Märkte im System unverfälschten Wettbewerbs in der Europäischen Wirtschaftsgemeinschaft' in *Festschrift Böhm* (1965), pp. 345 et seq. *Contra*: D. Edward/M. Hoskins

merely academic dispute, but starting with the *Sugar*[743] case, the question arose how cases should be dealt with if state measures matched supply and demand in a way that left virtually no room for competition, and consequently, a restriction of competition could not be found. The Judgement in the *Sugar* case and subsequent case law[744] only excluded the undertakings' responsibility and did not indicate expressly if Member States were accountable.[745] In the *Inno case*,[746] the Court of Justice arrived at the conclusion that it follows in particular from Article 5(2) (now Article 10(2)) that 'Member States may not enact measure enabling private undertakings to escape from the constraints imposed by Articles 85 to 94 of the Treaty'.[747] But neither in this case did the Court of Justice expressly rule on the legality of the state measure itself. It confined the assessment to their effect.[748]

Hence, part of the literature understands Article 86(1) as only applying if there was an infringement of Article 82 by an undertaking in the first place.[749] Yet other authors[750] interpret this provision as also applying in cases where merely the exclusive right *itself* restricts competition, without resulting in a specific illegal conduct by the entrusted undertaking. *Mestmäcker*[751] reads the Court's ruling in *Höfner*[752] as proof of the second interpretation and that a system that excluded competition on a market where it is not active itself is also caught by Article 86(1). The Court found that 'a statutory provision that creates a situation in which a public employment agency cannot avoid infringing Article 86 is incompatible with the rules of the Treaty.'[753] Further, in *Porto do Genoa*,[754] the Court held that if a monopolist is induced to infringe Article 82 (ex-Article 86), this also amounts to an infringement of Article 86 (ex-Article 90), though the monopolist only *could* and not necessarily would engage in an abuse.[755] *Van der Woude* has criticised this application of Articles 86 and 90 (now Articles 82 and 86) by the Court as amounting to automatic

'Article 90: Deregulation and EC Law, Reflections arising from the XVI FIDE Conference', 32 *CMLRev.* (1995) pp. 157-186, at p. 162.

743 Cases 40-48, 50, 54-56, 111, 113, 114/73 *Suiker Unie* et al. [1975] ECR 1663.

744 Cases 209-215, 218/78 *Fedetab* [1980] ECR 3125.

745 *Pappalardo,* op. cit. n. 741, p. 307.

746 Case 13/77, *GB-INNO-BM/ATAB,* [1977] ECR 2115.

747 Ibid., para 33.

748 *Pappalardo,* op. cit. n. 741, p. 310.

749 See D.Edward/M.Hoskins, op. cit. n. 742, at p. 162.

750 E.-J. Mestmäcker in U. Immenga/E.-J. Mestmäcker, op. cit. n. 726, p. 1559.

751 Ibid.

752 Case C-41/90 [1991] ECR I-1979. Confirmed in Case C-55/96 *Job Centre coop* [1997] ECR I-7119.

753 *Höfner,* para 28.

754 Case C-179/90 [1991] ECR I-5889. Confirmed in Case C-163/96 *Silviano Raso* [1998] ECR I-533.

755 M. Hughes, 'Article 86 of the E.C. Treaty – State Monopolies and Competition', 8 /1,2 *Irish Journal of European Law* (1999) pp. 18-36, at p. 19.

abuse.[756] The granting of exclusive rights becomes almost impossible if the exercise of the exclusive right necessarily leads to an abuse.[757] This comes, indeed, very close to outlawing a Member State's option to grant exclusive rights, if these rights are found in themselves to be anti-competitive.

7.1.2.1. Public Undertakings and Special Rights (Art. 86(1))

Article 86(1) is of a 'dual legal nature'[758] insofar as it produces – in conjunction with the Treaty rules addressed to the Member States[759] – two different legal effects. First, it reminds Member States of their duty to consider this rule when it is a question of measures which concern or whose beneficiaries are public or privileged undertakings.[760] Secondly, it impedes Member States from evading their obligations by shielding behind the apparently independent behaviour of their public role privileged undertakings.[761]

In most systems, broadcasting is at least partly shed from market forces and financed by fees or directly by the state. Against this background, it was suggested, in particular by German authors, that, because of the Community's economic character, it lacks any competence to regulate broadcasting. As a 'cultural good' it could not simply come under the heading of a service in the sense of the Treaty.[762] However, this interpretation was clearly rejected by the Court of Justice in *Sacchi*[763] For the application of Competition law to public broadcasters, the Court in *Sacchi* highlighted that it needs, first, to be assessed if the undertaking in question engages in an economic or commercial activity.[764]

> If certain Member States treat undertakings entrusted with the operation of television, even as regards their commercial activities, in particular advertising, as undertakings entrusted with services of general economic interest, the same prohibitions apply, as regards their behaviour within the market, by reason of Art. 90(2) [now Art. 86(2)] , so

[756] M. Van der Woude, 'Art. 90: Competing for Competence', 17 *ELRev* (1992) Competition Checklist 1991, pp. 60-80.

[757] Ibid., p. 73.

[758] J.L. Buendia Sierra, *Exclusive Rights and State Monopolies under EC Law* (Oxford, Oxford University Press, 1999) p. 192.

[759] Art. 10 (ex-Art. 5) provides that 'Member States shall take all appropriate measures, whether general or particular, to ensure fulfilment of the obligations arising out of this Treaty or resulting form action taken by the institutions of the Community. They shall facilitate the achievement of the Community's tasks. They shall abstain from any measure which could jeopardise the attainment of the objectives of this Treaty'.

[760] J. Temple Lang, *Community Anti-trust Law and Government Measures relating to Public and Privileged Enterprises: Art. 90 EEC Treaty* (1984) Fordham Corporate Law Institute, p. 550.

[761] J.L. Buendia Sierra, op. cit. n. 758, p. 192.

[762] See the overview over the discussion by E.-J. Mestmäcker in E.-J. Mestmäcker, ed., *Kommunikation ohne Monopole II,* (1990) p. 162 et seq.

[763] Case 155/73, [1974] ECR 409.

[764] See also C. Bellamy/G.D. Child, *Common Market Law of Competition*, First Supplement to the 4th ed., p. 13, 2-004.

> long as it is not shown that the said prohibitions are incompatible with the performance of their tasks.[765]

Thus, the Court was not willing to exclude public service broadcasting from the application of EC law. It is not the legal nature of the undertaking but its activity that is decisive. If a public service broadcaster engages in an economic activity, it will only escape the Treaty rules if their application is irreconcilable with its public service tasks.

The term 'public undertaking' is used in Article 86(1) without giving a definition. Nonetheless it is clear that it has a Community law definition.[766] In this context, it is also worth mentioning that the Commission, in its 1996 Communication for the term 'universal service', clarified that this service had a 'European' definition:

> The basic concept of universal service is to ensure the provision of high-quality services to all at prices everyone can afford. Universal service is defined in terms of principles: equality, universality, continuity and adaptability; and in terms of sound practices: openness in management, price setting and funding and scrutiny by bodies independent of those operating the services. These criteria are not always all met at [the] national level, but where they have been introduced using the concept of *European universal service*, there have been positive effects for the development of general interest services.[767] (italics added)

A functional and Community-based concept of 'public service' can also be derived from the case law on Article 48(4) which established an exception to the principle of free movement of workers.[768] However, although the Court of First Instance uses the terminology of 'universal services', 'services of general economic interest' and 'public services' indistinctly, they may not be identical.[769]

As for the substantive elements of the definition of a public undertaking, decisive elements under Article 86(1) are the state's influence on the business and a lack of real autonomy, although some authors cast doubt over the requirement of the second aspect. Arguably, there is always some room for independent decisions and business conduct, which is then subject to the competition rules.[770]

Member States may, according to Article 86(1) also assign certain undertakings with 'special rights.'[771] This term has not been defined by the Court of Justice,

---

[765] *Sacchi,* para 15.

[766] E.-J. Mestmäcker in U. Immenga/E.-J. Mestmäcker, op. cit. n. 726, p. 1544.

[767] *OJ* 1996, C 281/3, para 28.

[768] C.-D. Ehlermann, 'Managing Monopolies: The Role of the State in Controlling Market Dominance in the European Community', 2 *ECLR* (1993) pp. 61-69, at p. 66.

[769] For a thorough discussion see V. Kronenberger, *Le monopole des alcools en Finland: exemple de la mutation des monopoles publices en droit communautaire*, (Toulouse, Septentrion, 1999) pp. 376-384.

[770] E.-J. Mestmäcker in U. Immenga/E.-J. Mestmäcker, op. cit. n. 726, p. 1544.

[771] The undertakings entrusted could be both public or private.

although it had opportunity to do so in *FFAD*,[772] but a definition is included in Directive 94/46/EC[773] on satellite communications. In rec. 6 it stipulates that

> ... special rights are in practice rights that are granted by a Member State to a limited number of undertakings, through any legislative, regulatory or administrative instrument which, within a given geographical area,
> – limits to two or more the number of such undertakings, otherwise than according to objective, proportional and non-discriminatory criteria, or
> – designates, otherwise than according to such criteria, several competing undertakings, or legal or regulatory advantages which substantially affect the ability of any other undertaking to engage in any of the above-mentioned activities in the same geographical area under substantially equivalent conditions.

In any event, Member States face certain limitations when granting special rights. In *Sacchi*, the Court of Justice ruled that, for *non-economic reasons*, television broadcasting, including cable transmission, could be removed from free market competition and that one or more entities may be assigned exclusive broadcasting rights.[774] Special (or exclusive) rights attributed for non-economic grounds do not in themselves constitute a violation of Article 86(1),[775] whereas an economic motivation, for example, to protect a national broadcaster from competition, will fall foul of the Treaty rules.[776] But even if the undertakings have been entrusted for non-economic reasons, they remain subject to Article 82, which outlaws the abuse of a dominant position. In *Telemarketing*,[777] the Court held that entrusting an undertakings with exclusive rights does not in itself amount to granting a dominant position. However, a careful analysis under Article 82 (ex-Art. 86) must be carried out. Additionally, Member States, when granting special or exclusive rights, must consider the other Treaty provisions.[778] They must not, in particular, contradict the free movement of services and the competition rules.[779] Whether the special or exclusive rights are compatible with the Treaty must be established on a case-by-case basis.

With regard to entrusted undertakings, the Member States are also under certain supervisory duties. The Court has held that Article 86, read in conjunction with

---

[772] C-209/98 *FFAD* v. *Københavns Kommune*, nyr.

[773] *OJ* L 268/15.

[774] E.-J. Mestmäcker in U. Immenga/E.-J. Mestmäcker, op. cit. n. 726, p. 1548.

[775] Cases C-323/93, *Artificial bovine insemination* [1994] ECR I-5077; C-387/93 *Banchero* [1995] ECR I-4663. Yet, in several cases the Court has come close to assume automatic abuse with the granting of the exclusive right. See *supra* at 7.1.2.

[776] As an example may serve the *Gouda* case were the Court found that Dutch law unduly favoured the STER. See *supra* at 4.2.3. Although the case was decided on the basis of Art. 59 (now Art. 49) and the Court did not refer to Art. 90 (now Art. 86), the underlying argument is the same.

[777] Case 311/84 [1985] ECR 3261.

[778] Case C-353/89 *Commission* v. *Netherlands* [1991] ECR I-4069.

[779] Case C-260/89 *ERT* [1991] ECR I-2925.

Article 82, is infringed if a Member State has created a situation where undertakings are, due to their exclusive rights, able to abuse their dominant position.[780] Similarly, the Court in *ERT* decided that the cumulation of exclusive rights for transmitting national and re-transmitting foreign broadcasts violated Article 90 (now Article 86) because the entrusted undertaking is in a position to favour its own program. Still, this consequence is subject to the national Court's finding whether the cumulating of exclusive rights in fact results in a discriminatory programming policy.[781]

7.1.2.2. Services of General Economic Interest (Art. 86(2))

Article 86(2) provides for an exemption from a fundamental Treaty provision and is thus to be interpreted narrowly. This provision does not relate to certain categories of undertakings defined by national law. Article 86(2) refers to the role of the undertakings in question and not to their public or private nature.[782] It includes a safeguard clause in the second sentence,[783] which is similar to Article 81(3)(b). Accordingly, the state measure must not exclude competition on a significant part of the Common Market. Most importantly, it is a Community and not a national law concept, i.e., it has to be defined in all Member States according to the same set of criteria.[784]

Legal writers have qualified Article 86(2) as difficult to apply or even superfluous.[785] The case law on Article 86(2) has been characterised as complex and obtuse.[786] Its underlying principle that public interest considerations or the general good justify diversion from the free movement rules was already familiar from other areas of Community law.[787] In the context of Article 86(2), the Court emphasised this principal first in its *Sacchi* Judgement.[788]

---

[780] E.-J. Mestmäcker in U. Immenga/E.-J. Mestmäcker, op. cit. n. 726, p. 1559.

[781] E.-J. Mestmäcker in U. Immenga/E.-J. Mestmäcker, op. cit. n. 726, p. 1560, referring to para 38 of the *ERT* Judgement. Mestmäcker emphasises that it is in any case for the national Court to establish, if the undertaking had in fact engaged in discriminatory programming. However, the wording of para 38 of *ERT* is indeed very precise. The Court held that 'The reply to the national court must therefore be that Article 90(1) [now Art. 86] of the Treaty prohibits the granting of an exclusive right to transmit and an exclusive right to retransmit television broadcasts to a single undertaking, where those rights are liable to create a situation in which that undertaking is led to infringe Article 86 by virtue of a discriminatory broadcasting policy which favours its own programmes ...'. This can be read as leaving the national Court hardly any room for deciding that the undertaking did not abuse its dominant position in this case.

[782] J.L. Buendia Sierra, op. cit. n. 758, p. 276.

[783] 'The development of trade must not be affected to such an extent as would be contrary to the interests of the Community.'

[784] J.L. Buendia Sierra, op. cit. n. 758, p. 279, sec. 8.32, E.-J. Mestmäcker in U. Immenga/E.-J. Mestmäcker, op. cit. n. 726, p. 1592.

[785] See e.g., V. Emmerich, *Kartellrecht*, (1994) 7th ed., p. 586, *contra*: C.D. Ehlermann, op. cit. n. 768.

[786] M. Ross, 'Article 16 E.C. and services of general interest: from derogation to obligation?', 25 ELRev (2000) pp. 22-38, at p. 23.

[787] See Chapter 4.

[788] See *supra* at 7.1.2.1.

However, it was still contentious how a 'service of general economic interest' should be specifically defined. The concept of services as used in Article 86(2) is not the same as in Article 50 (ex-Article 60). It is wider and also embraces the provision of certain goods, like electricity or gas.[789] The Court frequently omitted the requirement of an 'economic' interest is its judgements, which appears to indicate that the adjective is redundant.[790] The Commission initially took the view that only economic interests would justify the application of Article 86(2).[791] In the light of the Court's case law, it changes its interpretation in the *EBU* Decision[792] and also applied Article 86(2) to non-economic general interests. More recently, the Commission distinguished between 'services of general interest' and 'services of general economic interest'.[793] The former category is wider and also comprises the latter. The Competition rules would only apply to the narrower category of 'services of general economic interest'.

Furthermore, it is suggested that the stress should be rather on the activity in context than in defining the interest.[794] From the Court of Justice's case law and Commission practice, it appears that the underlying doctrine emerging from *Sacchi*[795] and *Screensport*[796] requires the achievement of a *non-economic objective*, to benefit from the protection offered by Article 86(2).[797] Recently, the Court of First Instance has confirmed that a cultural policy and the maintenance of pluralism in the press constitute legitimate objectives compatible with the Treaty.[798] Moreover, the service must be of a 'general' nature. In several copyright cases,[799] the Court established that copyright management does not qualify as a task of general economic interest because it merely concerns private interests. Regional development limited to certain geographical areas[800] and action directed at certain disadvantaged groups of people are of a general nature.[801]

---

[789] Case C-393/92 *Almelo* [1994] ECR I-1477. The wide application of Art. 86(2) is also advocated by *Franck, P.A.,* 'Les entreprises visée aux articles 90 et 37 du Traité CEE' in *Various*, L'entreprise publique et la concurrence. Les articles 90 et 37 du Traité CEE et leurs relation avec la concurrence. Semaine de Bruges 1968, (1969) Bruges: De Temple, p. 41.

[790] J.L. Buendia Sierra, op. cit. n. 758, p. 277.

[791] Commission Decision *GEMA, OJ* 1971, L134/15, see also 'Television Without Frontiers: Green Paper on the establishment of the common market for broadcasting, especially by satellite and cable', *COM* (84)300.

[792] *OJ* 1993, L 179/23.

[793] Commission Communication, Services of general interest, *COM* (96) 443.

[794] A.C. Page, 'Member States, Public Undertakings and Article 90', 7 *ELRev.* (1982) p. 28.

[795] C-155/73, [1974] ECR 409.

[796] *OJ* 1991 L63/32.

[797] J.L. Buendia Sierra, op. cit. n. 758, p. 278.

[798] Case T-266/97, *VTM* v. *Commission,* [1999] ECR II-2329, para 108.

[799] Case 127/73 *BRT II* [1974] ECR 318, Commission Decision *GEMA OJ* 1971, L 134/15, Comission Decision *GVL OJ* 1981 L 370/58.

[800] Case 66/86 *Ahmed Sahed* [1989] ECR 853, Case T-260/94 *Air Inter* [1997] ECR II-997.

[801] J.L. Buendia Sierra, op. cit. n. 758, p. 279.

With particular regard to broadcasting, it has already been pointed out that the Court of Justice in *Sacchi* held that public service broadcasters can be entrusted with services of a general economic interest in the sense of Article 86(2). [802] Whether, in a certain case, the exemption of Article 86(2) is available, must be established on the facts of the case.

7.1.3. *Commission Powers under Art. 86(3)(ex-Art. 90(3))*

To ensure the efficient application of Art.icle86(1) and (2), the Commission was given the competence to address directives or decisions to Member States. It was claimed that this amounts to discriminating against public undertakings. However, as *Mestmäcker*[803] correctly points out, the situation of public and private undertakings is not comparable. Without supervision, Member States could, via the public sector, introduce measures that would otherwise be prohibited by Treaty rules.

Article 86(3) allows the Commission itself to establish, through a binding decision, the non-compliance by a Member State with its obligations.[804] If the addressed Member State disagrees, it must bring an action for annulment of the decision before the Court within the time limit of two months.[805] More extraordinary is the Commission power to adopt directives under Article 86(3), which gives rise to difficult problems of a legal but also political nature.[806]

7.1.4. *Sacchi, ERT and some lessons from the case law on Article 86*

Cases on (public service) broadcasting have played an important role for developing the Court of Justice's analysis under Article 90 [now Article 86]. In particular, the famous *Sacchi* judgement can be considered as a 'leading' case.[807] It concerned criminal proceedings in Italy against Guiseppe Sacchi, who operated a private television-relay station. He also possessed premises open to the public, where television sets were used for the reception of cable television, without there having been paid the licence fee prescribed by Italian law. The Judgement is material for mainly two reasons. First, it states that television broadcasting 'by its nature' qualifies as a service in the sense of the Treaty.[808] Secondly, it emphasises that although Member States may confer exclusive rights on broadcasters and thus remove them from competition, they remain subject to the Treaty provisions referred to in Article 90 [now Article 86] as regards their behaviour on the market.[809] In other words, al-

[802] *Sacchi,* at paras 14, 15; Commission Decision *Screensport/EBU, OJ* 1991 L 63/43.

[803] In U. Immenga/E.-J. Mestmäcker, op. cit. n. 726, at p. 1606.

[804] J.L. Buendia Sierra, op. cit. n. 758, p. 384.

[805] Ibid.

[806] For a detailed discussion see J.L. Buendia Sierra, op. cit. n. 758, pp. 402-430.

[807] See N. March-Hunnings, 'Cable Television in Italy' (1975) *Journal of Business Law* pp. 72-74.

[808] *Sacchi,* para 6.

[809] Ibid., para 14, 15.

though exclusivity is not illegal in itself, the undertaking benefiting from the exclusive right still had to comply with the Treaty rules.

In the subsequent *ERT*,[810] case, the Thessaloniki Regional Court applied for a preliminary ruling in a case involving the Greek radio and television undertaking ERT ('Elliniki Radiophonia Tileorassi Anonimi Etairia'), which had been granted exclusive rights, and the DEP ('Dimotiki Etairia Pliroforissis'), a municipal information company. ERT's right also comprised the right to receive and retransmit programmes from other Member States ('double-monopoly'). DEP and the Mayor of Thessaloniki had, notwithstanding the exclusive rights of ERT, started to broadcast television programs. The Court of Justice held that 'Article 90(1) (now Article 86(1)) of the Treaty prohibits the granting of an exclusive right to transmit and an exclusive right to retransmit television broadcasts to a single undertaking, where those rights are liable to create a situation in which that undertaking is led to infringe Article 86 (now Article 82) by virtue of a discriminatory broadcasting policy which favours its own programmes, unless the application of Article 86 obstructs the performance of the particular tasks entrusted to it'. It has already been pointed out[811] that this interpretation leaves the Member State not much room. Only if it could be demonstrated that the application of the competition rules *obstructed*[812] the performance of the assigned task, the public broadcaster would be exempt from their application. It appears that such a case could not be easily argued.

Generally, the Court of Justice has applied Article 86 to public service broadcasters in a way that suggests that in all but the most exceptional cases the burden of proof will rest heavily on a Member State to demonstrate that the particular task assigned to the public broadcaster excludes the application of the competition rules to it. The Court has consistently held that, as far as public broadcasters engage in economic activities, they come within the Community definition of an undertaking. Moreover, the distinction between the *existence* and *exercise* of rights has been transcended to a distinction between *structure* and *exercise* of a monopoly.[813] This results in the Court of Justice respecting general concepts of law, such as a statutory monopoly but ultimately striking it down on the particular facts of the case. In other words, the question, if a Member State is uninhibited to create a monopoly, must be in answered: in theory yes, but in practice no.[814] The argument used in *ERT* of 'inevitable abuse'[815] because of structural reasons can also be found in the *Höfner*[816]

---

[810] Case C-260/89 [1991] ECR I-2925, see C. Degenhart, (1992) Juristenzeitung pp. 685-687; D. Chalmers, 'Competition and Industrial Property. Television and the Court of Justice', 17 *ELRev* (1992) pp. 248-257; P.J. Slot, Case note on *inter alia* C-260/89 *ERT*, 28 *CMLRev* (1991) pp. 964-988.

[811] See *supra* 7.1.2.1.

[812] D. Chalmers, op. cit. n. 810, p. 250.

[813] Ibid., p. 251, taking the terminology from *Marenco/Banks* 'Intellectual Property and Community Rules on Free Movement: Discrimination unearthed', (1990) 15 *ELRev* 224.

[814] M. Hughes, op. cit. n. 755, p. 19.

[815] C.D. Ehlermann, op. cit. n. 768, pp. 61-69, at p. 62.

[816] C-41/90 *Höfner and Elser* v. *Macrotron* [1991] ECR I-2925.

and *Porto do Genoa*[817] cases, recently confirmed in *Silviano Raso*.[818] In *Höfner*, the Court held that a Member State violated its duties under the Treaty if it creates a situation in which the provision of services is limited because the undertaking entrusted with exclusive rights is not in a position to satisfy demand, and in *Porto do Genoa*, it was sufficient that the undertaking was induced to abusive conduct. Moreover, the Court in *Corbeau*[819] found that specific services which can be dissociated from the service of general interest traditionally not offered from the public undertakings do not justify the exclusion of competition. Thus, Member States are not free to extend a monopoly to areas which are not strictly connected to the 'general interest'.

7.1.5. *Article 16 (ex-Article 7(d))*

The Treaty of Amsterdam also introduced in its Article 16 (ex-Article 7d) a rather opaque provision. It governs the legal principle, which refers to what are variously described as services of general interest, public services or universal service obligations.[820] Article 16 reads as follows:

> Without prejudice to Articles 73, 86 and 87, and given the place occupied by services of general economic interest in the shared values of the Union as well as their role in promoting social and territorial cohesion, the Community and the Member States, each within their respective powers and within the scope of application of this Treaty, shall take care that such services operate on the basis of principles and conditions which enable them to fulfil their mission.

This provision introduces a new dimension in the already contentious interpretation of the public service and the delimitation between Community and national competence under the Treaty. Declaration 13 annexed to the Treaty of Amsterdam states that Article 16 'shall be implemented with full respect for the jurisprudence of the Court of Justice, inter alia as regards the principles of equality of treatment, quality and continuity of such services'. For example, *Hancher*[821] appears to interpret this as bestowing hardly any meaning on Article 16. This provision could only be understood along the lines of the *acquis* on public services and the competition rules, without adding anything to the established case law.[822]

Another view, strongly argued by France, interprets Article 16 as enhancing national powers. It is suggested that this provision, together with the Amsterdam

---

[817] C-179/90 [1991] ECR I-5889.

[818] Case C-163/96 [1998] ECR I-533.

[819] Case C-320/91 [1993] ECR I-2533, at para 19.

[820] M. Ross, op. cit. 786, p. 22.

[821] 'Community, State and Market' in Craig, P./De Burca, G., eds., *The Evolution of EU Law* (Oxford, Oxford University Press, 1999) Chapter 20.

[822] Ross calls this the 'no-change view', p. 29.

Protocol on public service broadcasting,[823] the Declaration on public credit institutions in Germany and a similar Declaration added by Austria and Luxembourg must be understood as guaranteeing the status of the public service and protecting it from the full application of competition law. However, this claim is somewhat difficult to sustain. The wording of Article 16 suggests that there is a borderline between Community and the Member State's competence, yet it does not explain where the line is to be drawn.[824] Even if Article 16 was a derogation authorised by EC law, it would still be subject to the principles of proportionality and necessity.[825]

On a teleological construction, the meaning of Article 16 remains difficult to grasp and no uniform picture emerges. As *Ross* points out, the reconciliation between the public interest and the competition rules remains difficult. In any event, it should not be more difficult for public undertakings to escape the competition rules than pre-Amsterdam. But the retention of Articles 73, 86 and 87 ensure that it is not misused for outright protectionism.[826]

7.1.6. *Broadcasting and State Aid*

The EC state aid regime until fairly recently has been a much neglected body of law[827] and it was only with growing economic interdependence that it has become subject to more detailed research.[828] In other words, 'EC state aid law finally comes of age'.[829] In a truly integrated Internal Market, in which all physical, technical and fiscal obstacles are eliminated, state aids remain virtually the only possible instrument to favour and protect national industries.[830] Given highly political and socio-economic implications of the subject matter, it does not come as a surprise that the Commission enjoys substantial discretionary powers. It takes into consideration a large set of factors and is capable of arriving at somewhat different conclusions in cases appearing similar at first sight. Yet, one cannot blame the Commission for a lack of consistency or strict analysis, as the Member States have played a key role in blocking the development of meaningful guidelines in sensitive areas such as public broadcasting.[831]

---

[823] See *infra* at 7.1.7.

[824] M. Ross, op. cit. n. 786, p. 30.

[825] T. Tridimas, *The General Principles of EC Law* (1999) Oxford.

[826] M. Ross, op. cit. n. 786, p. 33.

[827] Speech by Manfred Caspari at the 1989 Fordham Corporate Law Institute conference, cited in F.Y. Jenny, 'Competition and State Aid Policy in the European Union', 18-I *Fordham Int. LJ.* (1994/95) pp. 525-554, at p. 552.

[828] Most importantly, the Council of Ministers finally adopted a Regulation on procedures; Council Regulation 659/99 of March 1999, *OJ* 1999, L 83/1.

[829] L. Hancher/T. Ottervenger/P.J. Slot *E.C. State Aids* (London, Sweet & Maxwell, 1999) p. 3, See also M. Ross, State Aids: Maturing into a Constitutional Problem, (1995) *YEL*, p. 79.

[830] C.D. Ehlermann, op. cit. n. 768, p. 65.

[831] L. Hancher/T. Ottervenger/P.J. Slot, op. cit. n. 829, p. 12, sec. 1-022. In 1995 the Commission had commenced working on guidelines in 1995 but appears to have given it up since.

As a general principle, state aids which affect trade between Member States are forbidden.

> Save otherwise provided in this Treaty, any aid granted by a Member State through State resources in any form whatsoever which distorts or threatens to distort competition by favouring certain undertakings or the production of certain goods, shall, in so far as it affects trade between Member States, be incompatible with the common market.[832]

7.1.6.1. Definition of 'State Aid'

As a preliminary remark one should highlight that 'existing aid', i.e., old aid schemes in operation before the entry into force of the EEC Treaty[833] are not subject to the requirement of prior notification and authorisation as 'new aid'. However, the Commission shall keep these aid schemes under constant review (Article 88, ex-Article 93). Regulation 569/1999[834] laid down detailed procedural rules for the notification of both new and existing aid.

The term 'aid' as used in Article 87 (ex-Article 92) is not defined in the Treaty, but the case law indicates that it related to the *effect* of a state measure rather than their causes or aims.[835] However, in the absence of a definition given by the Treaty, there remains some uncertainty about how broad or narrow 'aid' shall be interpreted. It is well established that the concept of aid is broader than that of a subsidy.[836] Traditionally, the Commission has endured a wide notion of state aid in its enforcement practice.[837] It had consistently pleaded that state aid would not necessarily involve a 'charge on the public account'.[838] Yet, the Court of Justice, first in *Van Tiggele*,[839] decided that measures which do not emanate from state resources do not fall under Article 92 (now Article 87). The ruling was later confirmed in *Sloman Neptun*.[840] However, in light of what was said before on the lack of coherence and consistency in the case law, this is by no means a conclusive interpreta-

---

[832] Article 87(1), ex-Art. 92(1).

[833] January 1, 1958. In the case of Member States which joined the Community later the date of accession.

[834] *OJ* 1999, L83/1

[835] Case 173/73 *Italy* v. *Commission* [1974] ECR 709, repeated in Case 310/86 *Deufil* [1987] ECR 901.

[836] Cases 187 and 188/85, *Fediol,* [1989] ECR 4155; see also L. Hancher/T. Ottervenger/P.J. Slot, op, cit. n. 829, p. 20, sec. 2-003; R.G. Otten, 'Die Gebührenfinanzierung der öffentlich-rechlichen Rundfunkanstalten im Rahmen des Art. 92 EGV', 11 *ZUM* (1997) pp. 790-800, at p. 792; *contra* D. Dörr/ W. Cloß, 'Die Vereinbarkeit der Gebührenfinanzierung des Österreichischen Rundfunks mit dem EG-Beihilferecht', 2 *ZUM* (1996) pp. 105-118, at p. 110, who do not distinguish between aid and subsidy.

[837] M.M. Slotboom, 'State Aid in Community Law: A Broad or Narrow Definition?', 20 *ELRev* (1995) pp. 289-301, at p. 290.

[838] Ibid., p. 291, quoting Case C-72 and 73/91, *Sloman Neptun* [1993] ECR I-887.

[839] Case 82/77 [1978] ECR 25.

[840] [1993] ECR I-887.

tion.[841] The Court has subsequently, e.g., in *Banco Exterior*,[842] recalled its broad effect-based approach.[843] Moreover, also the wording of Article 87 does not suggest a narrow definition of Article 87. It refers to 'aid granted ... in any form whatsoever'. It has been suggested that three different categories of aid are covered by this definition. First, aid granted by the state through state resources, secondly, aid granted by the state but not through state resources and, thirdly, aid granted not by the state but through state resources. None of these categories requires that the aid involves a charge on the public account.[844]

If we apply this concept to the financing of public service television, it is apparent that direct state funding, i.e., the state grants resources to a public broadcaster, is covered. In such a case, the funds will most probably emanate from tax revenue. The case appears to be slightly different with public service broadcasting financed by fees. These fees are levied on the viewer/owner of a television set *directly* by the public broadcaster. The state is only involved insofar as it provides a legal framework whereby it authorises the fee. The question how the Commission and Court of Justice dealt with these problem in their case law shall be assessed below at 7.1.6.6.

7.1.6.2. Distortion of Competition

Originally, the Commission took the view that an aid always adversely effects competition and thus it was not necessary to assess its effect in any detail.[845] This interpretation did not succeed before the Court of Justice. Although the Commission is not under the same duty as under Articles 81 and 82 to conduct a thorough market analysis, a mere statement that competition has been or may be distorted will not suffice. Yet, a qualitative rather than a quantitative assessment is sufficient;[846] failure to give adequate reasoning will usually lead to the annulment of the Commission's decision.[847]

As an additional requirement, state aid must also 'affect trade between Member States'. Hence, it appears that, where a broadcast was limited to one Member State, this condition was not fulfilled. In the light of cable transmission and the emergence of a Community broadcasting market, this will, however, be extremely difficult to prove.

---

[841] See illustrative Case T-358/94 *Air France* v. *Commission* [1996] ECR II-2109.

[842] Case C-387/92, [1994] ECR I-877.

[843] L. Hancher/T. Ottervenger/P.J. Slot, op, cit. n. 829, p. 26, sec. 2-018.

[844] W. Rodriguez-Curiel, 'Chronique de jurisprudence: quelques réflexions sur la jurisprudence de la Cour de justice en matière d'aides d'Etat', 3 *RIDE* (1993) pp. 433-460.

[845] *11th Report on Competition Policy*, 1981, p. 176.

[846] L. Hancher/T. Ottervenger/P.J. Slot, op. cit. n. 829, pp. 36, 37, sec. 2-045, 2-046.

[847] See joined cases C-324/90 and 342/90 *Germany and Pleuger Worthington* [1994] I-1173 and joined Cases C-329/93, C-62/95 and C-63/95 *Bremer Vulkan* [1996] ECR I-5151.

7.1.6.3. Illegal Aid

As a general 'rule of thumb', to identify illegal aid may serve the so-called 'market-investor-test' following the Court of Justice's case law.[848] The Commission, in its Guidelines of 1984,[849] which were further expanded in 1993,[850] stated that state funds that provided going beyond the normal role of a proprietor qualified as state aid. In situations where, for example, the financial position of the company, and particularly, the structure and volume of its debt, is such that a normal return cannot be expected within reasonable time, the provision of funds by the state would qualify as state aid.[851] The Commission's approach was upheld by the Court of Justice, which ruled that capital provided in circumstances where no ordinary investor would be prepared to invest constituted state aid.[852] This principle has been further refined in two Judgements involving aid by the Italian government.[853]

7.1.6.4. Exemptions and Cultural Aid

Article 87(2) provides for a list of activities which, although constituting state aid, are automatically exempt from the prohibition in Article 87(1).

> The following shall be compatible with the common market.
> (a) aid having a social character, granted to individual consumers, provided that such aid is granted without discrimination related to the origin of the products concerned;
> (b) aid to make good the damage caused by natural disaster of exceptional occurrences;
> (c) aid granted to the economy of certain areas of the Federal Republic of Germany affected by the division of Germany, insofar as such aid is required in order to compensate for the economic disadvantages caused by that division.

Article 87(3) is of a different nature. It covers aid that *may* be compatible with the common market but which requires formal Commission approval to determine that status. Of specific interest for public service broadcasting is Article 87(3)(d). It has been inserted by the Treaty of Maastricht, together with the new Article 128 (now Article 151), and reads as follows.

> The following may be considered to be compatible with the common market:
> aid to promote culture and heritage conservation where such aid does not affect trading conditions and competition in the Community to an extent that is contrary to the common interest;

---

848 This institution has been confirmed and widened in Case C-305/89, *Alfa Romeo,* [1991] ECR I-1603, especially para 20.

849 EC Bulletin, no. 9; *14th Report on Competition Policy*, p. 198.

850 *OJ* 1993, C 307/3.

851 L. Hancher/T. Ottervenger/P.J. Slot, op. cit. n. 829, p. 143, sec. 7.024.

852 Cases 234/84 *Belgium* v. *Commission* [1986] ECR 2263, 40/85 *Belgium* v. *Commission* [1986] ECR 2321, C-329/93, C-62/95 and C-63/95 *Bremer Vulkan* [1996] ECR I-5151.

853 Cases C-303/88 *ENI-Lanerossi* [1991] ECR 1470, C-305/89 *Alfa Romeo* [1991] ECR 1635.

It is accepted that under Article 87(3), the Commission enjoys considerable discretion to evaluate an aid scheme. In *Philip Morris*,[854] the Court established certain criteria upon which the Commission must base its decision. It implies an assessment of economic, technical and policy considerations and that Commission should also take into account social objectives. The Commission has identified three factors that it will consider when assessing the compatibility of an aid with the Common Market. First, the aid must be in the Community interest as a whole, secondly, it must be necessary for achieving that aim and it must, thirdly, be proportionate.[855] Apparently, this is just another application of the necessity- and proportionality-test we are already familiar with from other areas of Community law.[856]

As regards Article 87(3)(d), *Loman et Al,* interpreted this insertion as confirming the practice of the Commission.[857] Before the Treaty of Maastricht, Article 92(3)(c) (than Article 92) contained a similar provision but did non expressly refer to an adverse effect on competition. If the changed terminology has any specific legal significance, it is difficult to establish.[858] *Loman et al.*[859] distinguishes between 'economic' and 'purely cultural' activities. Only the latter would be subject to Article 87(3)(d) inserted by the Treaty of Maastricht. If one took up this distinction, it would result in rendering Article 92(3)(d) inapplicable to public service broadcasting, because it can, in the light of *Sacchi* and subsequent case law, not be interpreted as a solely cultural activity.

7.1.6.5. Public Service Broadcasting and Article 87: The Examples of Austria and Germany

As a preliminary question, the relationship between Article 86(2) and Article 87 needs to be assessed, but no clear picture emerges and various arguments are suggested by legal authors. One part of the literature understands that, first, an analysis under Article 87 has to be carried out, before an exemption under Article 86(2) can be considered.[860] For example, *Otten*[861] maintains that only after an assessment under Article 87 (ex-Art. 92) can it be established if the application of state aid law interferes with the public service obligation. Yet, others emphasise that if the condi-

---

[854] Case 730/79 [1980] ECR 2671.

[855] *12th Report on Competition Policy*, p. 160.

[856] See detailed Chapter 4.

[857] *Culture and Community Law. Before and after Maastricht* (1992) Kluwer, p. 191. See also A. Ewans, *European Community Law of State Aid* (Clarendon Press, Cambridge, 1997), p. 17.

[858] On the interpretation of Art. 92(3)(c) see e.g., H. van der Groeben/J. Thiesing/C.D. Ehlermann, *Kommentar zum EWG-Vertrag*, (Baden-Baden, 1991) p. 2688.

[859] *Culture and Community Law. Before and after Maastricht,* op. cit. n. 857, pp. 191, 192.

[860] See e.g., I. Pernice in E. Grabitz/M. Hilf, *Kommentar zur Europäischen Union* (1994), commentary on Art. 90, para 53 and 'Die Gebührenfinanzierung der öffentlich-rechlichen Rundfunkanstalten im Rahmen des Art. 92 EGV', 11 *ZUM* (1997) pp. 790-800.

[861] Op. cit. n. 836. Yet Otten erroneously refers to D. Dörr/W. Cloß, op. cit. n. 836, to substantiate his view.

tions of Article 86(2) are fulfilled, other Treaty provisions (including Article 87) are not applied.[862] In the *SIC* judgement,[863] the Court of First Instance clarifies that

> ... the case-law shows, the fact that a financial advantage is granted to an undertaking by the public authorities in order to *offset* the cost of public service obligations which that undertaking is claimed to have assumed has *no bearing on the classification* of that measure *as aid* witching the meaning of Art. 92(1) [now Art. 87(1)] of the Treaty ...[864] (italics added)

However, the CFI goes on to stress that the compensatory character can result in considering the measure compatible with the common market under Article 90(2) (now Article 86(2)). Thus, it appears that Article 87(1) is *lex specialis* with regard to Article 86(2).

Whether a particular system of broadcasting financing violates Article 87 must be assessed according to these criteria developed by the Court of First Instance. Therefore, it must be established on the facts of the financing system in question. First, is the public broadcaster 'favoured' in the sense of Article 87(1), i.e., is it granted an advantage other companies do not obtain. Secondly, is this benefit provided by 'a Member State or through State resources' and thirdly, does Article 87(3)(d) exempting cultural aid apply or is the aid compatible with the common market according to Article 86(2). As this cannot be assessed in the abstract, the examples of Austria and Germany shall serve as examples and will be dealt with briefly.

In Austria, the public broadcaster ORF ('Österreichischer Rundfunk Fernsehen') is financed partly by a fee levied by the Austrian post and partly from advertising revenue. *Dörr* and *Cloß*[865] prepared a legal opinion for the ORF on the compatibility of this financing scheme with (then) Article 92 (now Article 87). The authors explain that only if the funds available to the ORF overcompensated it for its costs, would a favour in the sense of Article 92 (now Article 87) exist. As the legal basis for financing the ORF provides for an 'economical administration',[866] and the additional income from advertising is also considered when determining the television fee, an overcompensation was not to be expected.[867] Moreover, the body which

[862] D. Dörr/W. Cloß, op. cit. n. 836, p. 109.

[863] Compare already Case T-106/95 *FFSA* [1997] ECR II-229, para 167, 168.

[864] Case T-46/97, Judgment of 10 May 2000, nyr., para 84. The Court namely refers to Case T-106/95 *FFSA* et al. v. *Commission* [1997] ECR II-229, where the CFI held that a tax concession that merely offset costs constituted state aid.

[865] 'Die Vereinbarkeit der Gebührenfinanzierung des Österreichischen Rundfunks mit dem EG-Beihilfenrecht. Kurzgutachterliche Stellungnahme des Instituts für Europäisches Medienrecht e.V. – erstattet im Auftrag des Österreichischen Rundfunks', (1996) 2 *ZUM*, pp. 105-118.

[866] My translation. The Austrian Broadcasting Law ('Rundfunkgesetz', BGBl. 1984, 379, as amended by in 1993, BGBl. 1993, 505.) provides in its § 20(1) 2nd sentence that the level of the television fee has to be established *unter Zugrundelegung einer sparsamen Verwaltung.*

[867] D. Dörr/W. Cloß, op. cit. n. 836, p. 114.

decided on the television fee ('Kuratorium') was independent from governmental influence. Although the Court of Justice has not yet decided such a case, the authors of the study conclude that this was sufficient to remove the levy from the ambit of a state aid 'from state resources'.[868] Hence, the financing of the Austrian public service broadcasting was found not to qualify as state aid in the sense of Article 92 (now Article 87).[869]

It appears that this view is contestable, in particular against the background of the *SIC* and *FFSA* cases, where the Court of First Instance found that direct state contributions and privileges qualify as a favour in the sense of Article 87. Moreover, it is relevant if the aid is to be qualified as 'existing aid' as opposed to new aid, because it will then benefit from a different notification procedure under Regulation 659/1999.[870] As to substance, it must be assessed if the fees merely offset the costs for the duties specifically linked to the public service obligation. There may be some doubt if the public broadcasters will be able to demonstrate exactly where these funds go and what they are used for. This is linked to the issue of cross-subsidisation and whether the aid is meant to finance other activities not covered by the public service obligation.

Germany[871] had also decided for a 'mixed' system of financing through fees and advertising (*duales Rundfunksystem*). Yet, there are also fundamental differences from the Austrian approach. In Germany, anyone *owning* a TV-set is obliged to pay the television fee,[872] regardless if it is even capable of *receiving* the public service program. The most important duty of the public service broadcasters is to provide for a balanced and varied 'basic supply' (*Grundversorgung)* of programs, which follows from Article 5(1) of the German Basic law (*Grundgesetz)*. The German broadcasting system does not aim for a level playing field of public service and private competitors.[873] Private broadcasting is merely tolerated, as long as it does not threaten the overall balance of the system. The German Constitutional Court *(Bundesverfassungsgericht*; *'BVerfG')* has held that public broadcasters must be sufficiently funded to be in a position to fulfil their duties as conferred by law.[874] The level of the fee is determined on the basis of a recommendation by an independent body *(Kommission zur Ermittlung des Finanzbedarfs der Rundfunkanstalten; 'KEF')*. The KEF determines the financial requirements of the public service broad-

[868] Ibid., p. 116. It should be emphasised that the authors apply a narrow concept of state aid, without, however, discussing the problem of defining this concept before. See also *supra* at 7.1.6.1.

[869] Consequently, there was not need to consider if the aid qualified for exemption as cultural aid under (now) Art. 87(3)(d).

[870] Austria acceded to the EEA on 1.1.1994. All aid existing at this date is thus to be considered 'old aid'.

[871] On the broadcasting system in general see *supra* at 3.4.3.

[872] N. Holzer, 'Deutsche Rundfunkgebühr als unzulässige Beihilfe im Sinne des europäischen Rechts?', 4 *ZUM* (1996) pp. 274-285, at p. 277.

[873] I. Freis, op. cit. n. 720, p. 114.

[874] BVerfGE 87, 181, 204.

casters' based on the broadcasters' own suggestions and guided by the principles of efficiency and economy. Finally, the KEF's decision also requires consent of all *Länder* parliaments.[875]

Against this background, *Eberle*[876] found that the public broadcaster is not 'favoured' in the sense required by Article 92 (now Article 87) and that fixing the level of the television fee does not qualify as a state measure. In any event, public broadcasters would benefit from the exemption in Article 92(3)(d) (now Article 87(3)(d)). *Holzer*[877], by contrast, emphasises that even if for the time being the television fee did not infringe Article 92 (now Article 87), this could change if the public broadcasters moved towards a more 'market-sensitive' approach and neglected their specific legal and constitutional duties. Another line of argument considers that the fee does fall within the ambit of Article 87 (ex-Article 92) but ultimately benefits from the cultural exemption in Article 87(3)(d).[878]

7.1.6.6. Financing of Public Service Broadcasting: Commission and Court Practice

In the 1990s, the Commission was faced with several complaints from private television stations.[879] For instance, in Spain, France and Portugal, private broadcasters argued that public broadcasters received preferential treatment which resulted in unfair competition.[880] In the UK, competitors challenged the free advertising on BBC television to BBC Enterprises magazine titles, but the Commission in December 1992 closed the investigation.[881] In Germany a complaint of private broadcasters about a special children's and a news channels run by public broadcasters was rejected by the Commission as unfounded.[882] In 1999, it decided that the public funding of *Kinderkanal and Phoenix*[883] was compatible with the common market. Also in France, the private broadcaster TF 1 launched a complaint on the allegedly illegal financing of the public service broadcaster France 2 and France 3.[884]

The Commission, in its Decision of 14 December 1999,[885] held with regard to the publicly funded 24-hour news channel BBC News 24, that the funding consti-

---

[875] I. Freis, op. cit. 720, p. 116.

[876] 'Aktivitäten der Europäischen Union auf dem Gebiet der Medien und ihre Auswirkungen auf den öffentlich-rechtlichen Rundfunk', 11 *ZUM* (1995) pp. 763-769.

[877] Op. cit. n. 872, p. 285.

[878] A. Damm, *Gebührenprivileg und Beihilfenrecht. Zur Vereinbarung der Finazierung des öffentlich-rechtlichen Rundfunks in Deutschland mitArt. 92 EGV* (1998); R.G. Otten, op. cit. n. 836, 11 *ZUM* (1997) pp. 790-800.

[879] R.M. D'Sa, *European Community Law on State Aid* (London, Sweet & Maxwell, 1998) p. 151.

[880] Report on Competition Policy 1993, para 546.

[881] Report on Competition Policy 1992, para 445.

[882] I. Freis, op. cit. n. 720, p. 132, footnote 107.

[883] Commission Decision in case NN 70/98, *OJ* 1999 C238/3. See also XXIX. Report on Competition Policy, footnote 7. Unfortunately, the full text of the Decision has not been published in the *OJ*, nor is it available on the Commission's homepage.

[884] S. Astheimer/K. Moosmayer, op. cit. n. 729, p. 398. The Commission's failure to act was dealt with in Case T-17/96, *TF1* v. *Commission* [1999] ECR II-1757.

[885] *BBC News 24,* NN 88/98, available on http://europa.en.int/comm/sg/sgb/state_aids .

tuted state aid, simply by conferring a benefit and regardless of its aim or motivation. BSkyB had challenged the new service arguing that it constituted state aid within the meaning of Article 87, of which the applicant had not been notified, and was unlawful and incompatible with the common market. The Commission held that the measure constituted a favour in the sense of Article 87 and thus qualified as state aid. Moreover, Article 87(3)(d) was not available, because the news programme was 'aimed more at fulfilling the information needs of UK citizens than at promoting culture or national heritage.'[886] Proceeding under Article 86(2), the Commission pursued three main arguments. First, news was important for a democratic society and could qualify as a service of general economic interest; secondly, a news service free of charge and without advertising was a useful addition to commercial news programmes; and thirdly, the financing system ensured that the BBC was merely compensated for its costs. No new fees where levied and News 24 had to be financed from internal BBC sources, by way of rationalisation and re-structuring. The Commission acknowledged that the lack of notification of the state aid was contrary to Article 88(3), but considered the aid compatible with the common market.

Still, this considerable number of complaints cannot be said to have produced any coherent Commission practice on the subject matter nor any significant case law of the Court of First Instance. In the *Gestevision* case, the Court of First Instance exclusively dealt with procedural issues. A Spanish commercial broadcaster had lodged a complaint with the Commission about public service broadcasters receiving state funds and the Commission failed to deliver a decision. During the proceedings, the Commission emphasised both the legal and political complexity of the issue as well as the lack of accounting transparency.[887] The Commission had entrusted an external consultant firm to carry out a study on the funding of public television companies in the Community and indicated that it awaited the outcome of that study.[888] These arguments failed to convince the Court of First Instance. It found that the Commission had violated its obligations under the Treaty by failing to adopt a decision.[889]

Of more interest is the recent Judgement of the Court of First Instance in the *SIC*[890] case, where the Court, for the first time in substantive law terms, decided on the application of the EC state aid rules to the financing of a public service broadcaster. The Sociedade Independendente De Comunicação (SIC), a commercial broadcaster of Portugal, had challenged the direct contributions[891] to public service broad-

[886] Ibid., para 36.
[887] *Gestevision,* para 44.
[888] Ibid., para 9.
[889] See already Case T-17/96, *TF1* v. *Commission* [1999] ECR II-1757, where the Commission also failed to act within the time limit of Art. 175 (now Art. 232).
[890] T-46/97, *SIC* v. *Commission*, nyr., available at http://curia.eu.int/en/jurisp/index.htm.
[891] Direct state contributions amounted to 15-18 per cent of RTP's budget.

caster Radiotelevisão Portugesa (RTP), preferential cable rates, tax benefits and the granting of a certain delay in social security payments with the Commission as illegal state aid. The Commission, after issuing various letters, finally in January 1997 delivered a Decision. Therein, it essentially found that none of these measures constituted state aid because the direct contributions amounted to mere *compensation* for the public service obligation conferred upon RTP and thus did not qualify as state aid. It concluded that it 'has no doubt as to the transparency of the system for financing expenses inherent in public service obligations ...'.[892] Neither would the preferential cable rates, tax benefits etc. qualify as state aid. This Decision is inconsistent with the Commission's findings in *BBC News 24* and the Court of First Instance's judgement in *FFSA*. Thus, these arguments failed to succeed before the Court of First Instance which clarified that the correct test required asking whether the recipient undertaking received an economic advantage which it would not have obtained under normal market conditions.[893]

> The fact that, according to the Decision the grants where merely intended to offset the additional cost of the public service tasks assumed by RTP cannot prevent them from being classified as aid within the meaning of Article 92 [now Art. 87] of the Treaty.[894]

Referring to *Belgium* v. *Commission*[895] the Court of First Instance emphasised that the concept of aid related to the effect of a state measure. As already held in *Ladbroke Racing*,[896] it was an *objective concept* focusing on the financial advantage of a certain state measure. The innovation of the Judgement lies in the Court explicitly stating that the compensatory character of the measure does not remove it from the ambit of Article 92 (now Article 87). In other words, the Court of First Instance rejected the interpretation pleaded for by various legal writers[897] and opted for a more strict application of Article 87. The Commission had failed to initiate a procedure under Article 92(3) (now Article 87(3)) and the Court of First Instance annulled its Decision. It held that the aspect of mere compensation can only be taken into account when considering whether the aid is compatible with the common market under Article 90(2).

Thus, it appears that correct application of Article 87 to public service broadcasting will, first, qualify as state aid, if the public broadcaster is in any way 'favoured' in the sense of Article 87, provided that it affects trade between Member States. In *BBC News 24*, the Commission considered this condition already fulfilled by the

---

[892] T-46/97, para 24.

[893] Case C-342/96 *Spain* v. *Commission* [1999] ECR I-2459, para 41; Case C-256/97 *DM Transport* [1999] ECR I-3913, para 22.

[894] T-46/97, para 82.

[895] Case C-56/93 [1996] ECR I-723.

[896] Case T-67/94 [1998] ECR II-1.

[897] See *supra* 7.1.6.5.

fact that the favoured broadcaster faced inter-Community competition.[898] This will usually be the case, as public service broadcasters generally receive some kind of reward, be it direct state contributions or the permission to levy fees. Secondly, an assessment of the funding must be carried out, and the aid will be compatible with the Treaty only if is does not overcompensate the broadcaster for its duty under the public service obligation. It appears that in the second part of the analysis, the Member State will enjoy a certain degree of discretion because it is competent to define the public service remit, as the Commission made clear in *BBC News 24*.

7.1.7. *The Amsterdam Protocol on Public Broadcasting*

Member States have for some time been aware of the potential 'danger' that EC state aid law poses to their national public service broadcasters. Resulting from doubts about the compatibility of state aid law and the funding of public broadcasting, Germany has initiated a Protocol annexed to the EC Treaty by the Treaty of Amsterdam. Protocol 9 on the System of Public Broadcasting in the Member States states that:

> The provisions of the Treaty establishing the European Community shall be without prejudice to the competence of Member States to provide for the funding of public service broadcasting insofar as such funding is granted to broadcasting organisations for the fulfilment of the public service remit as conferred, defined and organised by each Member State, and insofar as such funding does not affect trading conditions and competition in the Community to an extent which would be contrary to the common interest, while the realisation of the remit of that public service shall be taken into account.[899]

The political intention behind the Protocol is clear, whereas its legal significance is less straightforward. In a way, one is faced with similar problems as under Article 16.[900] The German government was seeking clarification that it was exclusively for the Member State to define the public service mission of the national broadcaster and thus also its funding.[901] Its 'success' if unclear, remains doubtful. The Protocol certainly did not remove public service broadcasting from the application of the state aid rules. The Court of First Instance did not rule on the subject matter, because in *Gestevision*, the Protocol was not yet applicable; it was only adopted 19 months after the application[902] and no express reference was made to it in *SIC* either. Only the Commission in *BBC News 24* expressly acknowledged that the

---

[898] Case 730/79 *Philip Morris* v. *Commission* [1980] ECR 2671.
[899] *OJ* 1997, C340/109.
[900] See *supra* at 7.1.5.
[901] 'Denkschrift der Bundesregierung', BR-Drucksache 784/97, p. 163, quoted in I. Freis, op. cit. n. 720, p. 111, footnote 4.
[902] Ibid., para 83.

Member States' competence to define public service remit in any economic sector was confirmed by the Protocol.

Nevertheless, the Protocol is important for interpreting the Treaty rules. Although it does not have the same status as a 'new provision',[903] it is binding and under Article 311 (ex-Article 239) forms an integral part of the Treaty. Arguably, it reduces the Commission's margin of discretion to the extent that only funding which clearly is not connected to the public service mission is illegal under the state aid rules.[904]

7.1.8. *Conclusion*

Public service broadcasting and its affinity to state aid is a fairly 'young' topic of Community law. As in other areas, the founders of the Treaty would hardly have considered that it would one day become relevant. It must be stressed that what changed was not so much the legal framework but the technical and socio-economic environment. State aid rules have long been considered as not applicable to public service broadcasting because of a presumed prerogative of the Member States to shape their national television systems. However, with the increased commercialisation of public service broadcasting, we are currently witnessing a shift towards the application of state aid rules.

These are to be interpreted as an 'objective concept' and, accordingly, a general exemption because of the public service obligation does not apply. To establish if the financing of public service broadcasting constitutes state aid, under Article 87(1), it is necessary to, first, assess if it is granted by the state or through state resources. In most cases, public service broadcasters will receive funds, be it directly or via the authorisation to levy fees. The latter will come under the definition of being granted by state resources, because the state authorises certain broadcasters to levy fees. Secondly, the measure must amount to the favouring of certain undertakings, i.e., the recipient undertaking receives an economic advantage which it would not have obtained under normal market conditions. Again, any kind of funding is capable of putting an undertaking in a more favourable position, be it by direct funding or the authorisation to levy fees. As the judgement in *SIC* and Commission Decision *BBC News 24* clarified, the merely compensatory character of the funding will not alter the fact that the public service broadcaster receives a favour. Thirdly, the measure must have an effect on community trade. This condition is already fulfilled, if the public broadcasters and their competitors are active on the international broadcasting market. A direct impact on actual trade between Member States is not required. If these three conditions are met, the state measure will qualify as state aid in the sense of the Treaty.

---

903 R. Streinz, 'Der Vertrag von Amsterdam', 5/6 *EuZW* (1998) pp. 137-147, at p. 145.

904 Ibid., p. 145.

It is then necessary to assess if the aid is compatible with the common market. In *SIC,* the Court of First Instance held that Article 86(2) is to be considered *lex generali vis-à-vis* Article 87. Thus, we must first appraise if any of the exemptions in Article 87 applies. According to Article 87(3)(d), the aid 'may be considered compatible with the common market' if it is intended to promote cultural or national heritage. In *BBC New 24*, the Commission considered that a programme predominantly intended for a Member State's own nationals did not fulfil this condition and thus could not benefit from the exemption in Article 87(3)(d). Assuming such a narrow understanding of Article 87(3)(d), most national financing systems, that are predominantly designed to ensure pluralism within one Member State and not to promote (national) culture across borders, would fall foul of this exemption. Although several authors have suggested Article 87(3)(d) is the correct legal basis for justifying the public financing of public service television, it has never been invoked successfully before the Commission or Court of First Instance. But even if this provision is available and Article 87(3)(d) is interpreted less restrictively, the compatibility of the aid is still subject to the condition that 'it does not affect trading conditions and competition (...) to an extent contrary to the common interest'.

If Article 87(3)(d) is not available, we need to pursue the analysis under the *lex generali*, Article 86. From the case law on Article 86 (ex-Article 90) it follows that public service broadcasting must pursue a non-economic objective, such as offering a pluralism of opinions and/or a cultural valuable program for which no market exists large enough to recoup the costs. Article 86(2) aims to strike a balance between, on the one hand, specific public service duties and rights emanating from it these duties and, on the other hand, the Treaty rules aiming to establish a common market and to ensure competition. As with most balancing tests, there are no hard-and-fast solutions, but the case law indicated that Article 86(1) is concerned with the *activity* of the public or entrusted undertaking and not with its legal status. Thus, an *ex ante* guarantee (*Bestandsgarantie)* that a certain activity is not illegal, as known for example by German constitutional law, is problematic under Community law. A direct causal link must be established between the funding and the public service obligation.

The 'general' nature of a measure required by Article 86(2) should not cause any problems, because public service broadcasters are usually required to cover the whole national territory. Yet, the conditions of Article 86(2) are not easily met. The national court will have to consider, if (a) the service in question qualifies as a service of general economic interest, (b) the undertaking in question is officially entrusted by the Member State, (c) the application of the competition rules obstruct the performance of the public service task and (d) the exemption does not affect the development of trade to an extent contrary to the interests of the Community. In particular, the requirement that the application of the Treaty rules *obstruct* the performance of the assigned tasks will be difficult to meet. The Court never explicitly ruled that this was the case, which also results from the limits of a request for a preliminary ruling. For example, in *Sacchi*, the Court did not elaborate on Article

86(2) (then Article 90(2)) in any detail, but in paragraph 15 merely stated that 'the same prohibitions apply (...) so long as it is not shown that the said prohibitions are incompatible with the performance of their task'. Thus, ultimately it will be for the national Court to decide on the questions raised by Article 86(2).

Within this context, it appears that the legal significance of both Article 16 and Protocol 9 is limited. As with many policy-inspired Treaty provisions,[905] it is first of all unclear if and where they fit into the analysis and secondly, how much weight will be attached to them. In general, we must conclude that the case law on public service broadcasting and EC state aid law is just beginning to evolve. But it promises to touch upon interesting questions of competence delimitation between the Community and the Member States and, in a broader context, has the potential to turn into another test case on Community interest versus Member States' sovereignty.

[905] Art. 151 (ex-Art. 128) may serve as another example.

Chapter 8
BROADCASTING, SPORT AND COMPETITION LAW

8.1. Sport and EC law: The '*Bosman* Revolution'

> In terms of the economic activity that it generates, the sporting sector is subject to the rules of the EC Treaty, like other sectors of the economy. This does not mean that sporting activity in the strict sense, that performs a social, integrating and cultural function, should not be preserved.[906]

Under Community law, sport as an economic activity fairly and squarely falls into the ambit of EC law and the Court of Justice in the *Walrave*[907] case has rejected to grant it a general exemption.[908] Still, sporting activities have not been treated as 'normal business', and the Court in *Walrave* also stressed that EC law would not interfere with the internal regulation of sports as far as it is based entirely on grounds specifically necessary to maintain the particular type of sport.[909] Generally, EC law prohibits restrictions of the 'four freedoms' or anti-competitive measures to the extent that they are not strictly necessary for sustaining the sporting activity but are merely a by-product of specific sporting rules, which adversely affects the common market.

The Court further developed its approach towards sport in the famous *Bosman*[910] ruling, where a player for the first time had been qualified as a 'worker' in the sense of Article 39[911] (ex-Article 48) of the Treaty. The transfer rules under consideration

[906] Competition Commissioner Mario Monti in a speech given at a conference on sports, 17 April 2000, Brussels, available over RAPID, SPEECH/00/152.

[907] Case C-36/74, [1974] ECR 1405.

[908] D. Brinkman/E. Vollebregt, 'The Marketing of Sport and its Relation to E.C. Competition Law' (1998) 5 *ECLR* pp. 281-288.

[909] It should be mentioned that a similar approach was taken by the European Commission on Human Rights in Case No. 35722/97, Decision of 15 October 1987.

[910] Case C-415/93 [1995] ECR I-4921; see J. Wertenbruch ,'EuGH: Freizügigkeit von Berufsfußballspielern', 3 *EuZW* (1996) pp. 82-92; M. Hilf/E. Pache 'Das Bosman-Urteil des EuGH. Zur Geltung der EG-Grundfreiheiten für den Berufsfußball', 18 *NJW* (1996) pp. 1169-1177.

[911] '1. Freedom of movement for workers shall be secured within the Community.
2. Such freedom of movement shall entail the abolition of any discrimination based on nationality between workers of the Member States as regards employment, remuneration and other conditions of work and employment.
3. it shall entail the right, subject to limitations justified on grounds of public policy, public security or public health:
(a) to accept offers of employment actually made;
(b) to move freely within the territory of a Member State after having been employed in that State, subject to conditions which shall be embodied in implementing regulations to be drawn up by the Commission.

required the acquiring club to pay a transfer fee to the club, where the player had previously worked. Mr. Bosman had worked for several years for the RC Liège and his contract had expired in 1990. He contacted with the French club US Dunkereque and eventually entered into contract with it. Additionally, his new club was required to pay a transfer fee to his former employer. The rational behind this requirement established by UEFA and FIFA rules was to compensate the former club for the investment undertaken, especially for training the player. In *Bosman*, RC Liège failed to pay the fee because of the doubtful solvency of the acquiring club. This resulted in Mr. Bosman being unable to play for *any* club. His old contract had expired and was not renewed and he could not work for his new employer without the transfer fee being paid by his former club.

The Court found that these professional rules regarding the transfer fee restricted the free movement of professional sportsmen. Neither could they be justified as necessary for the sports associations. The legal autonomy of sports associations could not take precedence over the free movement rules; nor could the internal rules of the sports association be justified under one of the exceptions contained in Article 39(3), i.e., public policy, public security or public health.

The Court in *Bosman* for the first time comprehensively ruled on the relationship between the rules of sports organisations and the Treaty. It found that EC law and specifically, the four freedoms, also apply to the internal regulation of sports organisations if they regulate an economic activity in the sense of the Treaty. The Court decided that a transfer system that required a transfer fee being paid by the acquiring club violated the free movement of workers, and has thus liberated professional footballers from their peculiar status as employees not entitled to sell their labour to the highest bidder once their contract of employment expires.[912] It emphasised the individual's right to choose the most appropriate employment, i.e., the club he or she wants to play for.

Additionally, the Judgement also ruled on the nationality-based discrimination applying to European club competition. The so-called 'three plus two' rules permitted three foreign players plus two foreign players who have played in the respective country for five years. The Court found that this quota-system, applied to EU-nationals, violated the non-discrimination-principle in Article 12 (ex-Article 6) of the EC-Treaty.

In sharp contrast to this case law, football associations such as UEFA have argued that, in principle, sport was not an economic activity and should be excluded

---

(c) to stay in a Member State for the purpose of employment in accordance with the provisions governing the employment of nationals of that State laid down by law, regulation or administrative action;
(d) to remain in the territory of a Member State after having been employed in that State, subject to conditions, which shall be embodied in implementing regulations to be drawn up by the Commission.
4. The provisions of this Article shall not apply to employment in the public service'.

[912] S. Weatherill, 'After Bosman: tracking a sporting revolution'. A lightly amended version of a paper delivered under the auspices of the Sports Law Centre of Anglia Polytechnic University as the First Bosman lecture in the Middle Temple, London 5 May 1999.

from the application of the Treaty provisions. The German government in the proceedings of *Bosman* maintained that the subsidiarity principle enshrined in Article 5 (ex-Article 3b) dictated that public authorities' intervention in private commercial affairs should be limited to what is strictly necessary.[913] This argument failed to succeed before the Court. Generally, the subsidiarity principle only applies if there is concurrent competence of the Community and the Member State. This is not the case within the ambit of the basic freedoms, which fall into the exclusive competence of the Community. Thus, the notion of subsidiarity cannot be of any assistance to sports clubs' arguments.

In sum, *Bosman* left the sporting world irritated by the consequent application of EC law and it was considered that this ruling endangered the entire football financing system. Following *Bosman*, there has been intense discussion on the relationship between sport and EC law, which ultimately resulted in the Declaration on Sport attached to the Treaty of Amsterdam, which expressly recognises the special characteristics of sports:

> The Conference emphasises the social significance of sport, in particular its role in forging identity and bringing people together. The Conference therefore calls on the bodies of the European Union to listen to sports associations when important questions affecting sport are at issue. In this connection, special considerations should be given to the particular characteristics of amateur sport.

However, this Declaration does not in any way derogate from the four freedoms or abolish the dichotomy between sporting activities that are at the same time economic activities under the Treaty and those that are not. This 'hybrid' role of sport as an economic *and* at the same time cultural activity fostering national identity also follows from Article 3(a) of the 'Television Without Frontiers' Directive, which stresses sports' significance for national identity and restricts the possibility to grant exclusive rights:[914]

> 1. Each Member State may take measures in accordance with community law to ensure that broadcasters under its jurisdiction do not broadcast on an exclusive basis events which are regarded by that Member State as being of major importance for society in such a way as to deprive a substantial proportion of the public in that Member State of the possibility of following such events via live coverage or deferred coverage on free television. If it does so, the Member State concerned shall draw up a list of designated events, national or non-national, which it considers to be of major importance for society. ...

Essentially, this leaves one with the difficult task of delimiting between the sporting activity strictly speaking and the economic activity. Only the latter is subject to the Treaty provisions, in particular, the free movement of workers but also the applica-

---

913 Ibid.

914 See *infra* at 8.3.3.

tion of competition law, as will be demonstrated below. In particular the problems arising from exclusive television rights and collective marketing of sport's broadcasting rights shall be discussed in more detail.[915]

Finally, the exercise of certain professions *related* to sports, such as, for example, working as a coach,[916] need to be distinguished from cases concerning sportsmen and women *performing* sports. The former is part of the extensive case law on the mutual recognition of diplomas and special certificates that Member States considered necessary to work in a certain profession, be it as a lawyer[917] or a ski instructor.[918] The extent to which the Member States are successful in maintaining their specific legal systems largely depends on whether they are able to convince the Court that the specific requirements were justified, necessary to exercise the profession, and did not act as an indirect discrimination against other Member States' citizens. According to Council Directive 92/51/EEC on mutual recognition of diplomas, Member States have the right to require fully qualified migrants from other Member States whose training is substantially different from that available in the host Member State to take an aptitude test or undergo a training period. This also applies to sports-related professions.

8.2. **Sport and the Free Movement of Persons: After *Bosman***

As has already become apparent from the case law in *Walrave* and *Bosman*, sport is not as such exempt from the Treaty provisions and, in particular, the free movement of persons also applies to sportsmen and women who want to change clubs within Europe. Subsequently, the Court further fleshed out this principle in the case law of *Lehtonen*[919] and *Deliège*.[920]

In *Lehtonen*, the Belgian transfer system for basketball was under scrutiny, which provided for different time limits for national, European and international players during which they were allowed to change clubs. Mr. Lehtonen, a Finnish basketball player, entered into a contract with the Belgian club Castors Braine two days after – according to the internal rules of the basketball league – the period for European players to change clubs had been exhausted. The matches he took part in were subsequently declared lost for his club. The national court applied for a preliminary ruling to determine if the system of transfer rules was compatible with EC-law.

The Advocate General had in his Opinion stated that, on the one hand, rules simply organising the sporting activity ('*bloße Ausübungsregeln*', paragraph 70 of the Opinion) did not contradict the free movement of persons as enshrined in the

[915] See *infra* at 8.3.
[916] See e.g., Case 222/86, *Heylens*, [1987] ECR 4097.
[917] See e.g., Case 340/89, *Vlassopoulou*, [1991] ECR 2357.
[918] See IP/99/499.
[919] Case C-176/96, Judgment of 13 April 200, nyr.
[920] Joined Cases C-51/96 and C-191/97, Judgment of 11 April 2000, nyr.

Treaty. On the other hand, rules impeding access to an economic activity ('*Zugangsschranken*', id.) infringed the Treaty and needed to be justified by the special requirements of the sporting activity.[921] He concluded that, in principle, a system of transfer periods could be justified if it provided for the comparability of results and prevented distortions by one or several excellent players who first finish off one season in a particular league and then change to another league. In other words, if team A, consisting of a certain team, plays B and subsequently acquires another player before it plays C, the conditions for B and C are not comparable. It is admissible to enact rules preventing such a situation. However, the system must be designed as to actually achieve this aim and must not inhibit players from changing clubs for other legitimate reasons. The Belgian system of different transfer periods for players from different 'zones', in the Advocate General's opinion, violated EC law, because there was no proof that the system of transfer periods fulfilled the conditions of necessity and proportionality. In particular, it did not safeguard that changing one's club is possible for reasons other than to distort the comparability of results.

The Court's judgement in this case is much less detailed than the opinion but it follows the Advocate General insofar as, 'at first sight, such a rule [meaning different transfer periods for players from different zones] must be regarded as going beyond what is necessary to achieve the aim pursued'.[922]

We can draw the conclusion that a system that differentiates transfer periods is not *per se* incompatible with the free movement of services but it will be very hard to argue such a case successfully. A causal link between the legitimate aim, for instance, preventing unfair playing conditions and the measure to achieve this aim, for example, different time-limits for changing clubs, must be established.[923]

In the recent *Deliège*,[924] Judgement, the Court had to deal with a complaint of a Belgian judo player, who challenged the decision taken by the national judo association not to select her for various international tournaments. Unlike the '*Bosman*-style' *Lehtonen* case, in this case, a sportswoman who felt discriminated by her national sports association raised the 'Eurodefense' to attack what appears at first sight to be an internal matter of this sporting body, namely, to select persons for participation in a tournament. The Belgian Tribunal de Première Instance (Namur) applied for a preliminary ruling asking if the selection criteria were contrary to Article 59 (now 49).[925] The Court of Justice held that it was for the national Court

[921] This distinction is a very common approach in analysing cases under the 'four freedoms' and reminds of the Court's ruling in *Keck,* Case C-267/91, [1993] ECR I-6097, were it excluded 'selling arrangements' from the ambit of Art. 28. The principle has subsequently also been extended to the free movement of persons.

[922] Para 58 of the Judgment.

[923] See detailed Chapter 4.

[924] Joined Cases C-51/96 and C-191/97, Judgment of 11 April 2000, nyr.

[925] The national Court also asked about the selection process being contrary to Articles 85 and 86 (now Articles 81 and 82), but the European Court of Justice maintained that it was not presented sufficient

to determine if the possible participation in tournaments abroad involved enough of a cross-border-element to render Article 59 (now Article 49) applicable. Assuming its applicability, the Court points out that 'selection rules (...) inevitably have the effect of limiting the number of participants'[926] which does not in itself constitute a restriction of the freedom to provide services. Moreover, these criteria have to take into account also 'considerations unconnected with the personal situation of any athlete'.[927] In sum, the Court did not find that employing certain selection criteria in itself violated Article 59 (now Article 49), and indicated that the sporting body has wide discretion to chose these criteria.

It should be pointed out that *Deliège* contains a remarkable reminiscence on the so-called 'Sunday trading' cases,[928] and equally draws a line between issues regulated by EC law and aspects that are left to the internal regulation of the sports associations. With 'Sunday trading' we associate the British food retailer's attempt in the 1980s to attack national shop-opening laws by arguing that they would also adversely affect the marketing of imported goods. After some confusion about 'Sunday trading', the Court finally drew the line between Community and national competence in the famous *Keck*[929] Judgement. There, it distinguished 'selling arrangements'[930] from restrictions adversely affecting trade between Member States and held that only the latter fell within the ambit of EC law.

Similarly, Ms Deliège had attacked the selection criteria of her national sports association with the argument that her non-selection restricted her from taking part in competitions abroad and thus prevented her from supplying a service in another Member State. In *Deliège,* the Court left open the question if Article 59 (now Article 49) applied to the case[931] but concluded that it 'naturally falls to the body concerned (...) to lay down appropriate rules'.[932] Hence, the Court avoided becoming involved with the internal decision of selecting athletes for tournaments. Sports organisations are not prevented from selecting sportsmen and women according to internal criteria, such as meeting certain benchmarks or targets. The Court's ruling even allows for the conclusion that criteria not strictly related to the athlete's performance may lawfully be employed.

information to rule on the interpretation of these provisions. Thus, it confined itself to assess the case with regard to Art. 59 (now 49). See para 38 of the Judgment.

926 *Deliège,* para 64.

927 *Deliège,* para 65.

928 C-145-88 *Torfaen Borough Council* [1989] ECR I-3851, C-312/89 *Conforama* [1991] ECR I-997; See further A. Arnull, 'What shall we do on Sunday?', 16 *ELRev* (1991) p. 112.

929 C-267/91, [1993] ECR I-6097.

930 Ibid., para 16.

931 The wording in para 48 leaves the decision to the national Court but appears to indicate that Art. 59 (now Art. 49) will probably apply.

932 *Deliège,* para 67.

8.3. Sport and EC Competition Law: The Marketing of Broadcasting Rights

8.3.1. *Commission Practise*

In a debate in February 1999,[933] the Commission distinguished between two levels of activity in the field of sport. First, 'the sporting activity strictly speaking, which fulfils a social integrating and cultural role that must be preserved and to which in theory the competition rules of the EC Treaty do not apply' and, second, 'a series of economic activities generated by the sporting activity, to which the competition rules of the EC Treaty apply, albeit taking into account the specific requirement of this sector.'[934] Thus, the Commission's applies the same approach as pursued by the Court of Justice, albeit in cases regarding sport and the free movement principle. As a general rule, the Treaty provisions on competition law apply to economic sporting activities in the first place, but non-economic interests may nonetheless take precedence. Certain agreements restricting competition may be allowed if they are indispensable to the functioning of the economic entity.[935] Unlike 'normal' competition, where competitors share 'a relationship of potential contention and rivalry'[936] and try to acquire monopoly status by driving competitors out of the market, sports organisations essentially need competitors and unpredictable outcomes to keep their audience interested. Therefore, unlike 'ordinary' market participants, they do have an interest in their competitor's survival.[937]

Moreover, the Commission identified four categories of sporting organisations' practices:

(1) Rules to which in principle, Article 85(1) (now Article 81 (1)) of the EC Treaty does not apply;

(2) Rules which are, in principle, prohibited if they have a significant effect on trade between Member States;

(3) Rules which are restrictive of competition but which, in principle, qualify for an exemption (for example, rules encouraging recruitment and training of young players) and

(4) Rules which are abusive of a dominant position under Article 86 (now Article 82) of the EC Treaty.[938]

These considerations make no express reference to the issue of the relevant market. However, it is an indispensable part of every EC Competition law analysis, as

---

[933] IP/99/133 of 24.2.1999

[934] The same distinction was made by K. Van Miert in a speech at the European Sport's Forum in Luxembourg on 27.11.1997, http://www.europa.eu.int/com/dg04/speech/seven/fr/sp97069.htm, visited 21.09.1999

[935] D. Brinkman/E. Vollebregt, op. cit. n. 908, p. 283; see also Mario Monti, SPEECH/00/152.

[936] DG. Goyder, 'EC Competition Law' (1998), p. 9.

[937] I. Nitsche 'Collective Marketing of Broadcasting Rights by Sports Associations in Europe' (2000) 4 *ECLR* pp. 208-214, at pp. 208, 209.

[938] http://www.europa.eu.int/com/dg04/speech/seven/fr/sp97069.htm, visited 21.09.1999.

has been emphasised by *Wachtmeister*.[939] First, there may already exist different product markets for specific sports because, for the viewer, Formula One and football are not readily interchangeable with other types of sport.[940] Second, when defining the relevant market, it is necessary to take into consideration which kind of service is provided, i.e., *how* the broadcasting rights are sold: possible options are exclusive or non-exclusive selling, for live transmission or broadcasting of highlights and subcontracting. Third, the conditions of competition also vary between types of broadcasters and free-access TV is different from pay-TV.[941]

This can serve as a framework within which the question whether a measure infringes EC Competition law can be assessed. However, the Commission also acknowledges that its decisions and administrative practice in the field of sport and competition law is not yet sufficiently developed to answer all the important issues on the agenda. Moreover, there are – at least in the understanding of DG X – limits to the pursuit of specific non-economic aims, as Competition law is neutral with respect to different types of broadcasting and does not provide a legal base for favouring one category of broadcaster over others, e.g., free-TV over pay-TV. The extent to which it may guarantee protection of specific public interest is limited, as it predominantly seeks to prevent the distortion of competition. The first would require positive action rather than the 'defensive and reactive' tool of competition rules.[942]

8.3.2. *Relevant Market*

Sport coverage on television exhibits certain particular characteristics different from other programs. It is an ephemeral product, particular sports events can hardly be subsidised and rights holders are in a very strong position, especially if the rights are concentrated in the hands of national or international sports federations.

The Commission in *Bertelsmann/CLT*[943] made it clear that television broadcasting rights constitute a market in themselves, because 'sports programs covering widely popular sports or major international events are often able to achieve high audience ratings and are generally considered to be particularly suited for carrying advertisements ...'.

---

[939] 'Broadcasting of Sports Events and Competition Law', 2 *Competition Policy Newsletter* (1998) pp. 18-28. Wachtmeister is Chef d'Unité in DG IV, Unit C2 and the Article is called an 'orientation document'. Therefore, it can to some extent count as the Commission's point of view.

[940] J. Temple Lang, *Media, Multimedia and European Community Antitrust Law*, (1997) Fordham Corporate Law Institute, p. 20.

[941] Ibid.

[942] Communication from Mr. Oreja to the Commission: Exclusive Rights for TV Broadcasting of major (Sports) Events. Brussels, 3.2.1997, http://www.europa.eu.int/en/record/other/tven.html visited on 22.9.1999.

[943] Case IV/M.799 *Berteslmann/CLT, OJ* C 364/3, 4.12.1996.

Generally, the relevant market for broadcasting rights to sports can be considered as a downstream market from the market for the organisation of sports. Moreover, specific sports have developed into markets in themselves and are only to a very limited extent interchangeable with other sports.[944] For example, in *Football World Cup 1998*,[945] the Commission held that the market only comprised a single football tournament.

Furthermore, pay-TV and free-TV have different structures of demand, the former being characterised by a direct trading relationship between the consumer and the broadcaster.[946] Pay-TV subscribers are also subject to a certain 'lock-in' effect because of the specific equipment and the subscription fee, which render it difficult for consumers to switch. Finally, the services offered by free- and pay-TV are not always interchangeable from a content point of view. For example, in the UK, live transmission frequently takes place on the pay-TV channel BskyB, whereas the BBC only acquired rights for deferred transmission or to show summaries.

In sum, the relevant market tends to be narrow, comprising only specific types of sport or even single events. Geographic markets for transmission rights remain largely national, because the audience is mainly interested in 'their' teams and most broadcasting rights are still sold by a territory or Member State.[947] Thus, the structure of the market for the selling of TV rights tends to be oligopolistic. Similar considerations apply to the purchasers, i.e., the broadcasting companies. Broadcasters prefer to acquire exclusive rights, which enable them to achieve high audience shares. In turn, this results in narrow markets for the acquisition of television rights because only few broadcasters have enough funds to successfully bid for these rights.

8.3.3. *Exclusive Transmission Rights*

8.3.3.1. Exclusive Transmission Rights and Community Law

The intensive discussion on where EC law draws the line between sporting activities strictly speaking and economic activities has become particularly pressing for problems arising from broadcasting transmission rights. Television stations are interested in acquiring exclusive rights especially for live but also for deferred transmission because this will guarantee them a considerable audience share. For the successful introduction of Pay-TV, an attractive sports program is almost indispensable.[948]

---

[944] D. Brinkman/E. Vollebregt, op. cit. n. 908, p. 286.

[945] Decision 2000/12/EG, Case IV/36.888, *OJ* L 5/55, 8.1.2000, case annotation by I. Nitsche 'Fussball-WM 1998: Missbrauch der marktbeherrschenden Stellung beim Kartenverkauf', 5 *ELR* (2000) pp. 175-177.

[946] D. Brinkman/E. Vollebregt, op. cit. n. 908, p. 286.

[947] Ibid., pp. 287, 288.

[948] See Commission Decision IV/M993-*Bertelsmann/Kirch/Premiere*, *OJ* L 364/1, 27.2.1999, Recitals 34 and 48 and Commission Decision IV/36.539 *BIB/Open*, *OJ* L 312/1, Rec. 28.

Against this background, it is accepted practice that under Community law exclusive rights are not illegal in themselves.[949] Yet it is also clear that there are certain limits to exclusive rights, most notably in Article 3(a) of the Television Without Frontiers Directive,[950] which states that exclusive rights must not interfere with the public's interest to view 'national or non-national events of major importance for society'.[951] According to Article 3(a), Member States have drawn specific lists, including all the major sports events they want to make accessible to the public on free-TV. It intended to strike a balance between the business interest of the broadcasters, who require exclusive rights to attract audiences and the viewing public, which should be able to view major sports events on free TV. For example, Italy has, *inter alia*, listed the summer and winter Olympic games, the football World Cup final, the European football Championship final, the final of the UEFA Cup and the Giro d'Italia.[952] Similarly, Denmark regards Olympic games, World and European football and handball championships and Denmark's respective qualifying matches as being of 'major importance of society'. [953]

Additionally, exclusive rights have to comply with the general competition law framework, especially with Article 81 (ex-Article 85). Although exclusivity is not illegal in itself, a certain restrictive effect is inherent. If exclusive rights are granted to one broadcaster, as a matter of logic, no on else can compete in showing this particular program, which is, as such, not a restriction of competition. However, it will be demonstrated that the Commission did not accept restrictions going beyond what it considered necessary and proportionate. Restrictions could be justified by the need to secure a certain audience share or attract subscribers to recoup substantial initial investment.

8.3.3.2. Commission and Court Practice

Apart from limits to exclusive broadcasting rights for public interest reasons as contained in Article 3(a) of the Television Without Frontiers Directive, specific

---

[949] See Resolution on the broadcasting of sports events by the European Parliament, *OJ* 10.6.1996, C166/109, at Rec. F.; 'The European model of sport. Consultation document of DG X', http://www.europa.eu.int/comm/dg10/sport/publication/docconsulten.html, visited 22 September 1999.

[950] Council Directive 89/552/EEC on the coordination of certain provisions laid down by law, regulation or administrative action in Member States concerning the pursuit of television broadcasting activities, as amended by Directive 97/36/EC of the European Parliament and of the Council, *OJ* C 227/3, 30.9.1999. *Supra* at 8.1.

[951] Rec. 18 of the 'Television Without Frontiers' Directive.

[952] Publication in accordance with Article 3(a)(2) of Council Directive 89/552/EEC on the coordination of certain provisions laid down by law, regulation or administrative action in Member States concerning the pursuit of television broadcasting activities, as amended by Directive 97/36/EC of the European Parliament and of the Council, *OJ* C 227/3, 30.9.1999.

[953] Publication in accordance with Article 3(a)(2) of Council Directive 89/552/EEC on the coordination of certain provisions laid down by law, regulation or administrative action in Member States concerning the pursuit of television broadcasting activities, as amended by Directive 97/36/EC of the European Parliament and of the Council, *OJ* C 209/3, 21.7.2000.

exclusive rights may constitute an infringement of Article 81 (ex-Article 85) on the particular circumstances of the case. In the assessment, specific consideration will be given to the duration of the contract, the number of seasons or events and the territory covered. For example in the *Sport 7*[954] case, concerning an agreement between the Koninklijke Nederlandsche Voetbal Bond (KNVB) and a new Dutch broadcasting channel (Sport 7), the Commission indicated that it deemed seven years of exclusivity too long. Yet, the Commission did not carry out a full assessment in this case but instead awaited the outcome of the national investigation. Sport 7 ceased broadcasting in December 1997, so the case never reached the stage of formal decision by the Commission.[955] However, Karel Van Miert, the former Competition Commissioner, voiced his concern about the long duration and the renewal clause in the agreement envisaged[956] and, more recently, Commissioner Marion Monti stressed that only exclusive contracts for one season would not lead to market foreclosure.[957]

In the *Football Association* case,[958] the English Football Association (FA) concluded agreements with BSB (now BSkyB) and the BBC, granting them exclusive rights to the live broadcasting of English football matches organised by the FA and some international matches involving the English national team from 1988 to 1993. The Commission decided that these agreements violated Article 85(1) (now Article 81 (1)), because of their long duration. However, individual exemption was granted, as BSB was found to require a long-term contract in order to develop its new service of direct broadcasting by satellite.[959]

8.3.3.3. Conclusion

With expanding broadcasting markets, competition among broadcasters for exclusive rights will increase[960] which will result in soaring prices[961] for exclusive broadcasting rights. Thus, more cases before the Commission on the subject matter can be expected to provide further clarification. This would be helpful to further de-

---

[954] Notification of a licensing agreement for the broadcasting of Dutch football matches, Case IV/36.033 *KNVB/Sport* 7, *OJ* 7.8.1996, C 228/4; see also European Competition Policy Report 1997, p. 122.

[955] H. Fleming, 'Exclusive Rights to Broadcast Sporting Events in Europe', 3 *ECLR* (1999) pp. 143-148, at p. 146.

[956] '*Mon principal souci concernant cet accord a été, d'une part, la durée de l'accord sept année me paraissait un laps de temps beaucoup trop long et, d'autre part, la clause de renouvellement, qui favorisait Sport 7 dans la procédure d'appel d'offres prévue à l'exporation de la licence que lui accordait la KNVB.*' Speech held at the European Sport's Forum in Luxembourg on 27.11.1997.

[957] RAPID, SPEECH/00/152.

[958] Draft notice pursuant to Article 19(3) of Council Regulation No. 17 concerning a notification in Cases IV/33.145 *ITVA/Football Authorities* and IV/33.245 *BBC, BSB and Football Association OJ* C 94/6 , 3.4. 1993. See H. Fleming, op. cit. n. 955, at pp. 143, 145 and IP93/614, 20.7.1993.

[959] H. Fleming, op. cit. n. 955, p. 145.

[960] Ibid.

[961] BSkyB paid £1.2bn for securing broadcasting rights for 66 Premiere League games over three years; *Financial Times online,* 14 June 2000.

velop a more coherent analysis because, for the time being, there remains an inherent contradiction in the Commission's approach. On the one hand, exclusivity as such is said not to contravene EC Competition law, on the other hand, all the cases required some kind of justification for obtaining exclusive rights, and it is unclear how narrow the exclusivity needed to be defined not to require justification. Thus, one is left with the impression that the Commission pays mere lip service to admissibility of exclusive rights while, in fact, assuming a breach of Article 81(1). In sum, the Commission mainly focused on the duration of the exclusive agreements. Recently, Competition Commissioner Mario Monti indicated that exclusive rights may cover one season and a longer duration could only be justified if the operator wishes to enter a new market or introduce a new technology requiring heavy investment.[962] One could read this as a statement that only exclusivity for one year falls outside Article 81(1) and that any longer duration must be justified by additional reasons under Article 81(3).

8.3.4. *Collective Marketing by Sports Associations*

8.3.4.1. General Remarks

As a preliminary remark, it should be emphasised that collective selling of broadcasting rights and its potentially anti-competitive effects must be distinguished from the competition problems deriving from the acquisition of exclusive rights.[963] Yet, they are also intertwined to a certain extent. On the one hand, sports associations prefer to sell broadcasting rights jointly as they will be able to extract higher profits than by individual sale. On the other hand, the broadcasting operators wish to acquire exclusive rights, especially for the live transmission of sports events, because this will guarantee a certain audience share. Both aspects tend to minimise the business risk of the parties involved and limit supply on the market of broadcasting rights.[964]

The Central marketing of television rights to sports events by sports associations rather than individual selling by the single clubs allows the sports bodies to extract considerable profits from the marketing of the event. By obliging the individual clubs to abstain from extracting the highest possible profit from *their* matches and, instead, cross-subsidising between more and less wealthy clubs, the funding of the training of the youth and the existence of smaller clubs is safeguarded. This is considered justified by the interest of the wealthier clubs in maintaining a competitive balance and funding the training of the youth, often called the 'grass roots' argument. As UEFA put it, joint selling enables it to 'redistribute income in a fair and balanced manner' and filter income back down to the 'grass roots' of foot-

---

[962] SPEECH/00/152, available on RAPID, http://www.europa.int/rapid/start.

[963] See *supra* at 8.3.3.

[964] I. Nitsche, op. cit. n. 937, p. 209.

ball.[965] Still, collective selling arguably restricts competition because it reduces the number of suppliers on the market as compared to individual marketing by the single clubs. The situation is thus comparable to joint ventures, where the Commission has repeatedly held that competition is restricted because the number of competitors on the market is reduced, which results in a loss of so-called 'potential competition'.[966]

Moreover, the outcome of the analysis also depends on who owns the rights. Potential owners are the individual clubs, the organiser of the sports event or the sports federation. According to Article 295 (ex-Article 222), the Treaty shall in no way prejudice the Member States rules governing property ownership.[967] The question of property ownership is also intertwined with internal rules. If the sports association owned the transmission rights, a restriction of competition contravening Article 81 (ex-Article 85) would not be easy to establish. By contrast, if we assumed that the individual clubs themselves owned 'their' broadcasting rights, central marketing would most probably fall into the ambit of Article 81 (ex-Article 85) and thus needed to be justified by special interests.[968] This preliminary question of who owns the broadcasting rights in the first place is not to be answered by Community but by national law.[969]

Another distinction can be drawn from basing the broadcasting rights either on the provision of an entertainment service or the so called 'arena right'. The latter refers to the civil law principle that the home club may allow or refuse admission to its premises where a tournament takes place. Under this hypothesis, it is more likely that the individual clubs will own the broadcasting rights because they have a closer connection to the premises than the sports association.[970] By contrast, if the rights are based on the entertainment service, the sporting federation organising the tournament will be in a stronger position.[971]

8.3.4.2. Collective Marketing in the Member States

In the UK, in the case of *BSkyB/BBC/Premiere League*,[972] the selling of the broadcasting rights of the English Football Premiere League (PL) for the 2000/01 season

---

[965] Memorandum by *UEFA* 'The European Union and Sport: Current Issues', Nyon, October 1998.

[966] See V. Korah, op. cit. n. 615, p. 284 and the case law quoted in I. Nitsche, op. cit. n. 937, footnote 18.

[967] D. Brinkman/E. Vollebregt, op. cit. n. 908, p. 284.

[968] Ibid.

[969] Ibid.; for a comprehensive analysis under German law see U. Haas/C. Reimann 'Das "Fernsehrecht" an Sportveranstaltungen als Abwehrrecht', 5 *SpuRT* (1999) pp. 182-187 and M. Stopper, 'Wer ist Veranstalter und Rechtsträger im Profi-Fußball?', 5 *SpuRt* (1999), pp. 188-192.

[970] This view was for instance taken by the Dutch authorities, see I. Nitsche, op. cit. n. 937, p. 212.

[971] D. Brinkman/E. Vollebregt, op. cit. n. 908, p. 284

[972] Judgment of the Restrictive Practices Court (in England and Wales), 28 July 1999, in the Matter of the restrictive Trade Practices Act 1976 and in the Matter of an Agreement between the Football Association Premier League Limited and the Football Association Limited and their respective Member

was under scrutiny. The PL agreement prevented the participating clubs from selling broadcasting rights individually. Instead, the PL collectively sold exclusive live transmission rights to the pay-TV operator BSkyB and exclusive rights to show recorded highlights to the BBC. The Restrictive Practices Court (RPC) had to decide on the legality of the collective selling agreement. It decided to discuss the issue with regard to the practicability of an alternative individual selling system. In the proceedings, the special characteristics of the broadcasting of sports events was emphasised and economic evidence before the RPC indicated that the PL was to be qualified as a 'differentiated product', i.e., a product fulfilling specific demand that is not interchangeable, resulted in very narrow markets.[973] Thus, competition was based not so much on price as on product quality. A strong position of a pay-TV provider did not give rise to any competition concern but merely indicated that the provider fulfilled consumer needs and competition was enhanced rather than diminished. In any event, there was found to be enough competitive pressure from free-TV, and the PRC held that the restrictions contained in the PL agreement did not violate the 1976 Competition Act.[974]

In Germany, the antitrust authority (*Bundeskartellamt*) in 1994 had decided on the incompatibility of the joint selling of broadcasting rights to home matches by the German Football Association (*Deutscher Fussballbund, DFB*)[975] and had also rejected an application for exemption as an efficiency enhancing cartel.[976] The competent court of appeal (*Bundesgerichtshof, BGH*) held that although sport federations such as the DFB and UEFA provided for an administrative framework, it was the individual clubs that offered the service.[977] They acted as 'natural market participants' and thus owned the broadcasting transmission rights of matches in which they took part. The argument that collective selling could help to redistribute revenue amongst the clubs was not successful before the Court. The restriction of competition was held to infringe the German Competition Act and its motivation or potentially beneficial effects were irrelevant. The institution of competition as such needed to be protected. However, the Court left open if UEFA participated in the ownership of broadcasting rights and if its organisational effort qualified it as a natural market participant besides the clubs.

Commentators found the order poorly reasoned,[978] and it resulted in an intense lobbying campaign by the DFB that feared losing important sources of income.

Clubs and in the Matter of an Agreement relating to the Supply of Services consisting in the Broadcasting on Television of such Matches, 1996 No. 1 (E&W).

[973] I. Nitsche, op. cit. n. 937, p. 210.

[974] Ibid.

[975] Order of September 2, 1994, B 6-747000-A105/92, WuW/BKartA 2682, see detailed P.W. Heermann, 'Kann der Ligasport die Fesseln des Kartellrechts sprengen?', 1 *SpuRt* (1999) pp. 11-15.

[976] Order of September 2, 1994, B 6-727000-J-60194, WuW/BKartA2696.

[977] Order of the BGH, 11 December 1997, KVR 7/96.

[978] H. Waldhauser, 'Anmerkung zum Beschluß der BGH vom 11. Dezember 1997 (KVR 7/96) zur Zentralvermarktung der Europacupspiele durch den DFB', 2 *ZUM* (1998) pp. 129-132, at p. 130.

Subsequently, the German Cartel Act was amended to exempt the central marketing of broadcasting rights from the application of competition law.[979] The DFB also applied to the EC Commission for negative clearance or an exemption under Article 81(3),[980] which is still pending.[981]

In France, the national football federation is designated as the sole authority for exploiting the broadcasting rights for tournaments organised by it, but the agreements between the national football federation and the broadcasters must not exceed five years. Compared to the other Member States, this is a unique solution.[982]

In the Netherlands, the competent court in the case of *Feyenord/KNVB*[983] decided that the transmission rights at least partly belonged to the individual clubs. Subsequently, the Dutch Ministry of Economic Affairs granted an exemption limited to 'a reasonable time', although the Ministry was not convinced that the aim of reducing financial inequality among the clubs could not also be met by creating a 'solidarity fund'.[984]

The Italian competition authority considered that the national football federation Lega Calcio did not bear any direct entrepreneurial risk and hence could not be considered the owner (or even co-owner) of the broadcasting rights. Nor did the Lega Calcio's functions of promoting financial equality and consumer interest justify the collective selling of broadcasting rights. Yet, an individual exemption for the collective selling of broadcasting rights for the Coppa Italia was granted because of the high transaction costs, the uncertainty broadcasters faced and the comparatively small market share of the event.[985]

8.3.4.3. The Commission's Approach

The Commission has preliminary concluded that collective selling agreements restrict competition; because they amount to a price fixing mechanism, they limit the availability of rights; and finally they strengthen the market position of the most important broadcasters.[986] Financial solidarity between stronger and weaker economic actors could, however, be taken into consideration if a link between these factors was established.[987] Yet, it should be emphasised that, again, the Commission itself considers its practice in this field to be not yet sufficiently developed.[988] No case has yet been decided, although several cases concerning collective selling are currently pending.

---

[979] § 31 of the *Gesetz gegen Wettbewerbsbeschränkungen (GWB)* was amended accordingly.

[980] Case IV/37.214, *OJ* C 6/10, 9.1.1999.

[981] See *infra* at 8.3.4.3.

[982] I. Nitsche, op. cit. n. 937, p. 211.

[983] Hof Amsterdam, 8 November 1996, RvdW/KG 1996, No. 448.

[984] *Lugard,* Markt & Mededingen (1998) 1, p. 28.

[985] Werner Rumphorst, Director of the European Broadcasting Union in a speech given at the IBC Conference on Sport and Competition Law in London, 12 October 1999.

[986] Mario Monti in a speech available on RAPID, SPEECH/00/152.

[987] Ibid.

[988] IP/99/133, 24 February 1999.

In Case IV./37.398 *UEFA*,[989] the Commission received a notification and application for negative clearance or exemption of the central marketing of the commercial rights to the UEFA Champions League. In its notification, UEFA argues that it must at least be viewed as the co-owner of the commercial broadcasting rights for the Champions League because it is responsible for the administration and regulation of the tournament and bears the financial risk.[990] Thus, it did not infringe Article 85(1) (ex-Article 81(1)). *In eventu*, the agreement should benefit from individual exemption as the distinctive UEFA Championship brand rationalises distribution of commercial rights and benefits consumers by providing for a great variety of competing football clubs.[991] On preliminary examination, the Commission finds that the agreement 'could fall within the scope of Regulation 17'[992].[993]

Following the German DFB Order,[994] the DFB also decided to notify its system of central marketing to the Commission.[995] This notification makes clear that home matches of German clubs in the UEFA Cup and the UEFA Cupwinners' Cup[996] are commercialised individually by the clubs but the matches sold collectively by UEFA, *inter alia*, the matches of the *Bundesliga* and the *DFB-Vereinspokal*, were not covered by the national court's decision and form the subject of this application.

Similar to the arguments in other applications for negative clearance/individual exemption, the DFB maintained that its organisational effort and the need to provide for a balance between financially stronger and weaker clubs justified collective marketing of the relevant matches. In particular, the DFB rejected the idea of a solidarity fund 'because of conflicting interests between the different clubs and (...) tax reasons'.[997]

Formula One reaches similarly high audience shares as football. The competent sports federation for 4-wheel motor sport, including Formula One, is the *Fédération Internationale de l'Automobile* (FIA). It has notified the Commission about its statutes and several of its regulations.[998] These rules also deal with broadcasting and, in particular, Article 27 of FIA's internal rules, the general prescriptions for events run on circuits provides that 'all filming and moving picture rights (...) shall be vested in the FIA'.[999] Thus, the notified agreements between the national organisation and

---

[989] Central marketing of the Commercial rights to the UEFA Champions League, *OJ* C 99/23, 10.4.1999.

[990] Ibid., para. 7.

[991] Ibid., para 8.

[992] Regulation 17, *OJ* 13/204, 21.2.1962, as amended by *OJ* 58/1655 of 10.7.1962, *OJ* 162/2696 of 7.11.1963 and *OJ* L 285/49 of 29.12.1971, contains the procedural rules on the application of Articles 81 (ex-Art. 85) and 82 (ex-Art. 86).

[993] *OJ* C 99/23, para 10.

[994] See *supra* at 8.3.4.2.

[995] Case IV/37.214 – *DFB*, *OJ* C 6/10, 9.1.1999.

[996] The Cupwinners' Cup has been abolished since.

[997] Case IV/37.214 – *DFB*, *OJ* C 6/10, 9.1.1999, para 7.

[998] Case IV./35.163/D3 – *FIA*, *OJ* C 361/5, 27.11.1997.

[999] Ibid., para 1.

FIA also contain a clause on collective marketing of broadcasting rights. Again, the Commission primarily concluded that the notified agreement could fall into the ambit of Regulation 17. On 30 June 1999, the Commission opened formal proceedings and indicated that the contracts might seriously infringe competition law and 'could result in substantial fines' (K. Van Miert). In particular, the FIA is accused of forcing competing series out of the market, abusively acquiring all the television rights to international motor sports events, blocking series competing to its own events and protecting Formula One from competition by tying up everything that is needed to stage a rival championship.[1000]

For the time being, one can only speculate how the Commission will decide these cases. Although there has not yet been a ruling on collective selling, the Commission has ruled on another aspect of UEFA's internal organisation: the UEFA rules and regulations providing for certain 'closed times', during which no football matches must be broadcast on television.[1001] The rational of these prohibitions is to protect the organisers of football matches from competition on TV as this could adversely affect ticket sales.

Article 14 UEFA Statute, which limited broadcasting times for football matches, was successfully challenged by various broadcasters, e.g., *TESN*, Case IV/33.742, *BSkyB*, Case IV/33.245 and *ITVA,* Case IV/33.145.[1002] Subsequently, this provision has been renamed Article 44.1., and currently provides that:

> UEFA and the Member Associations shall have the exclusive right to authorise audiovisual and sound broadcasting transmission, as well as any other use and dissemination by picture and sound, either live or recorded, in whole or as excerpts of matches which come within their jurisdiction.[1003]

This provision is implemented by Article 44.2, which still indicates particular 'closed hours' for each Member State's association.

8.3.4.4. Some Tentative Conclusions on Collective Selling

It appears that most standard collective selling agreements will violate Article 81(1) (ex-Article 85(1)) and will require individual exemption under Article 81(3) (ex-Article 85(3)). Therefore, it will be necessary to demonstrate a causal link between, on the one hand, the sporting activity's special characteristics, i.e., the requirement to maintain a sufficient number of clubs, and the collective selling agreement on the other hand. This will be more difficult for Formula One than for football, because the so-called 'grass roots' argument only applies to the latter.[1004] Moreover, the

---

1000 IP/99/434, 30.6.1999.

1001 I. Nitsche, op. cit. n. 937, p. 213.

1002 2/1 *Sports Law Bulletin*, (1999), p. 15.

1003 See http://www.uefa.com/UEFA/Regulations/Statues_Media_Article44.html, visited 5.10.1999.

1004 I. Nitsche, op. cit. n. 937, p. 214.

measure must be necessary and proportionate; there must not be any less restrictive means available to achieve the same aim. Alternatives such as setting up a solidarity fund amongst the clubs have been rejected by the sports federation as not appropriate. However, if the sporting associations wish to benefit from Article 81(3), the burden of proof will rest on them to convincingly explain why no other option is open to them.

8.4. **Summary and Results**

Sport, broadcasting and Competition law has developed into a major European law issue in the last decade. Yet, some Community law aspects of this topic are still to be developed in more detail. Nevertheless, the Commission practice provides some guidance on the subject matter.

First, the 'internal rules' of sporting organisation primarily remain to be regulated by sports bodies, as has been recently confirmed in *Deliège*. Yet, the Community institutions will interpret the notion of an 'internal rule' fairly narrowly and these internal rules must not contravene Treaty provisions, as was made clear in *Bosman* and has been confirmed in *Lehtonen*. In these cases, the Court of Justice decided that discrimination on grounds of nationality is, in any event, prohibited and in such cases, no justification by the public interest or the specific characteristics of sports is available.

With specific regard to the Competition law implications, it should be noted that neither in *Bosman* nor in *Deliège* or *Lehtonen* did the Court assess the implications of transfer rules on competition but confined itself to an analysis under the free movement rules.[1005] Only the marketing of sports events has been dealt with from a Competition law angle. It was held that exclusive broadcasting rights are not illegal in themselves but permitted only to a very limited degree. From what Commission officials said, it appears that a duration of one year will not violate Article 81(1), whereas contracts granting longer exclusivity will be subject to Article 81(3) and must fulfil the conditions for individual exemption thereof. Concerning collective selling of television rights, no clear-cut approach has yet emerged. Several factors, however, indicate that collective selling will in all but the most exceptional cases violate Article 81(1) and it will be for the parties of such an agreement to prove the necessity and proportionality of this measure under Article 81(3).

In a broader context, it is to be welcomed that the Commission and the Court of Justice have applied the same principles to sport as to other business activities, and thereby avoided discrimination between different types of businesses. In *Lehtonen* and *Deliège*, the Court recently confirmed what already is clear from *Walrave*, i.e., that the freedoms are inapplicable only to amateur sport in the strict sense of the

[1005] A. Röthel, 'EuGH: Dienstleistungsfreiheit für Judoka. Freizügigkeit von Basketballspielern', 12 *EuZW* (2000) pp. 371-380, at p. 380.

word, which does not embrace any economic activity. As a result of the increased commercialisation[1006] of sports, 'pure' amateur sport has almost disappeared. Consequently, these new commercial activities connected to sport are to be regulated by EC law. Some authors have suggested that the autonomy of sporting bodies should be recognised by the Court of Justice.[1007] However, they fail to take into account that Community law draws from the (economic) nature of an activity and cannot recognise certain types of organisation, for instance, sport bodies, as *eo ipso* exempt from Community law. This also applies to other areas of Community law. For instance, under competition and state aid rules, it is the qualification of the activity that determines the application of EC law and not the public or private nature of a certain entity.[1008]

[1006] U. Becker, 'Basketball-Transferregelungen und gemeinschaftliche Freizügigkeit – "Lehtonen"', 7 *RIW* (2000), pp. 552-555, at p. 554.

[1007] A. Röther, op. cit. n. 1005, p. 380.

[1008] See Chapter 7.

Chapter 9
RESULTS AND CONCLUSION

This Chapter draws on the results and conclusions found earlier in this book and aims to specifically highlight those aspects that play an important role in the discussion of the legal framework in which a European media policy is embedded. It argues that limits to harmonisation measures, as resulting from the shared competence between the Community and the Member States, must be interpreted in the light of Community law, whereas limits resulting from Member States' constitutional laws cannot be of any assistance. This already results from the general principle of supremacy of Community law.[1009]

Moreover, this Chapter will focus on the criteria that must be fulfilled for a Member State's measure to qualify for the public interest exception as developed by the Court in its case law on the free movement of services, state aid and competition cases. The Community concept of public interest has become especially relevant for broadcasting and does not necessarily correspond to Member States' definition of the public interest.

Some remarks shall also be made with regard to the ideas developed in Chapter 7 on state aid. Problems resulting from the application of Community state aid law to public service broadcasting in the Member States have so far not produced substantial case law and it appears that the Commission employed a different analysis than the Court of First Instance. Thus, the issue merits specific attention.

Finally, a summary on the specific shape and limits of a European media policy as determined by Treaty provisions and principles developed by the case law and its possible future evolution shall be given.

9.1. Community Competence in the Audio-Visual/Broadcasting Area

Some authors have argued that competition law is not an appropriate tool to deal with media pluralism[1010] and that economic and publicist competition are necessarily distinct concepts,[1011] whereby all aspects of media pluralism fall into the exclu-

[1009] Neither the Treaty of Rome nor its subsequent amendments explicitly established the supremacy of Community law over the Member States' laws. Yet, this principle was first laid down by the Court of Justice in the case *Costa* v. *ENEL,* C 6/64, [1964] ECR 585 and has been consistently confirmed in subsequent case law. For a detailed discussion and the Member States' reactions to this principle, see P. Beaumont/S. Weatherill, op. cit. n. 59, pp. 433-453.

[1010] D. Frey, op. cit. n. 225, p. 76.

[1011] W. Hoffmann-Riem, *Rundfunkrecht neben Wirtschaftsrecht. Zur Anwendbarkeit des GWB und des EWG-V auf das Wettbewerbsverhalten öffentlich-rechtlichen Rundfunks in der dualen Rundfunkordnung*, (1991) Baden-Baden.

sive competence of the Member State. These arguments have often been bolstered with reference to Member States' Constitutions, which allegedly define competencies in the Community field more clearly than the Treaty. In the light of Article 5(1) (ex-Article 3b(I)), this argument must be rejected. It prescribes that the 'Community shall act within the limits of the powers conferred upon it by this *Treaty* and of the *objectives* assigned to in therein' (emphasis added). In assessing the Community's activity in the broadcasting field, its competence must be delimited and appraised by the Treaty. This task must be distinguished from the question of how the Community competence resulting from the Treaty can be reconciled with Member States' Constitutions.

Generally, a concept of conclusive enumeration of competence, such as contained in some Member States' Constitutions, is alien to the Treaty. Articles 2 and 3 contain a wealth of vague objectives the Community shall achieve, ranging from the establishment of a common market and a common commercial policy to a high level of employment, the protection of the environment and equality between men and women, some of which seem difficult if not impossible to reconcile. These aims are matched by rather wide Community powers to attain them. In addition to more specific legislative powers in certain areas, Article 308 (ex-Article 235) contains a very broad lawmaking power[1012] to attain one of the objectives of the Community. So far, the definition of what qualifies as a Community objective has been fairly extensive.[1013] The Community's legislative powers under Article 308 are potentially unlimited in substantive law terms, but constrained by the requirement of unanimity in the Council.[1014]

Additionally, there are certain limits in the Treaty itself. The Treaty of Amsterdam has created an obligation that, for any proposed Community legislation, the reasons 'shall be stated with a view to justifying its compliance with the principles of subsidiarity and proportionality'.[1015] Hence, in cases of shared competence between the Community and the Member State, subsidiarity reasoning must be given. If, conversely, a measure concerns areas within the exclusive competence of the Community, the subsidiarity principle does not apply.[1016]

The Community competence in the field of broadcasting must be assessed against this background. Since the *Sacchi*[1017] case, the Court of Justice has consistently held that television broadcasting qualifies as a service in the sense of the Treaty. Insofar as a common market in broadcasting as a commercial activity is concerned, it falls into the exclusive competence of the Community. The Television Without

[1012] See J.A. Usher, 'The Development of Community Powers after the Single European Act' in R. White/B. Smythe, eds., *European and International Law* (1990) p. 3.

[1013] Ibid., p. 17.

[1014] P. Beaumont/S. Weatherill, op. cit. n. 59, p. 156.

[1015] *OJ* 1997, C 340/105, para 4.

[1016] See A.G. Léger's Opinion in Case C-233/94, *Germany* v. *European Parliament and Council* [1997] ECR I-2405, paras 87-90.

[1017] Case 155/73 [1974] ECR 409.

Frontiers Directive[1018] was based on (then) Articles 57(2) and 66, with the aim of achieving a common market in broadcasting services. Yet, in the Preamble it is also clarified that the Directive does not interfere with the Member States' responsibility to organise broadcasting.[1019] Thus, broadcasting is a service of a 'hybrid' nature and the question arises whether this affects the availability of the free movement of services as a legal basis for harmonisation.

In the discussion preceding the adoption of the Directive, it had been submitted that the free movement of services was not a sufficient legal basis because it would disregard the specific cultural nature of broadcasting.[1020] This argument is not convincing. Article 128 (now Article 151), inserted by the Treaty of Maastricht, expressly provides in paragraph 4 that 'the Community shall take cultural aspects into account under other provisions of this Treaty ...', and in paragraph 5 excludes harmonisation measures in the cultural field. These provisions read in conjunction can only mean that purely cultural aspects, which are not covered by any other Treaty provision, are excluded from harmonisation and remain in the Member State's competence, whereas cultural aspects of an economic activity must be considered as inherent part thereof and do not exclude the application of the free movement of services. Given that television broadcasting is not a purely cultural but a mixed activity according to settled case law, the Council correctly based the Television Without Frontiers Directive on the free movement of services.

Concerning the proposed anti-concentration directive, similar concerns as for the Television Without Frontiers Directive have been voiced.[1021] Some commentators contested that in its Green Paper on Pluralism and Media Concentration[1022] the Commission favoured harmonisation by a Council directive based on (then) Article 57(2). This was intended to achieve a balance with the free-movement-of-services-aspects of television, which had already been covered by the Television Without Frontiers Directive. Merger control specifically designed to prevent dominant positions on the media market would also touch upon pluralism of opinions, but not exclusively. An anti-concentration directive would first and foremost enable the Community to prohibit dominance of media undertakings, which increasingly operate on a trans-national basis. Since the proposed directive would have only cov-

[1018] Directive 88/552/EC, *OJ* 1989 L 298/23, as amended by Directive 97/36/EC, *OJ* 1997, L 202/60.

[1019] Rec. 13 to Council Directive 89/552/EEC.

[1020] See J. Delbrück, *Die Rundfunkhoheit der deutschen Bundesländer im Spannungsfeld zwischen Regelungsanspruch der Europäischen Gemeinschaft und nationalem Verfassungsrecht, Rechtgutachten erstattet im Auftrag der deutschen Bundesländer'* (1986), p. 46; F. Ossenbühl, *Rundfunk zwischen nationalem Verfassungsrecht und europäischem Gemeinschaftsrecht – Rechtgutachten erstattet der Regierung des Landes Nordrhein-Westfalen* (1986) p. 49; J. Rüggeberg, 'Rundfunk als Wirtschaftsgut – Die Europäische Wirtschaftsgemeinschaft im Zugriff auf den öffentlich-rechtlichen Rundfunk', 83 *Verwaltungsarchiv* (1992) p. 330, at p. 332 et. seq.

[1021] H.Kresse/M. Heinze 'Der Rundfunk: Das "jedenfalls auch kulturelle Phänomen"', 6 *ZUM* (1995) pp. 394-397.

[1022] *COM* (92) 480 final.

ered media concentrations *outside* the national authorities' control, it was not contrary to Article 151(5),because this provision only outlaws the harmonisation of issues relating to Member States' own cultural policy. Thus, objections to the proposed directive and the fact that it was never adopted ought to be explained with reference to political factors rather than to lack of a proper legal basis.

9.2. **The Significance of a General Interest**

The concept of mandatory requirements was first developed in the context of the free movement of goods, but was later extended to the free movement of services. With specific regard to broadcasting, the Court in *Debauve* recognised that restrictions on advertising could be justified by a general interest, as long as they were indistinctly applicable. While maintaining this approach in *Bond*, it considered the national measure to be disproportionate. It confirmed the view that the Dutch media law violated Article 59 (now Article 49) in *Gouda.* The latter judgement can be read partly as a deviation from the test first employed in *Debauve.* As the new Dutch media law, which had been enacted as a reaction to the judgement in *Bond,* no longer differentiated between domestic and foreign broadcasts, i.e., the national measure was indistinctly applicable, one could have expected that the measures would be justified in the general interest. But the Court, considering that the new legislation merely disguised a projectionist motive, held that it could not be justified by general interest concerns.

Moreover, in *VTM*, the Court of First Instance found that an exclusive right to broadcasting television commercials violated the freedom of establishment (now Article 43, read in conjunction with Article 86(1)) and could not be justified by a general interest. Whereas in several judgements the Community Courts did decide whether the national measure was appropriate and proportionate to the envisaged aim, it was more reluctant to do so in *De Agostini*, and left it for the national court to decide upon these questions. Thus, there is no coherent approach as to the use of the concept of a public or general interest. In most cases, however, the Courts undertook to assess itself, whether the national measure and the public interest goal were connected by a causal link.

Although the Courts will assess the effect of national measures and whether they in fact confer a benefit to the public, no harmonisation has taken place and Member States still retain their regulatory choice over aspects of media pluralism. The Court in *Commission* v. *Belgium* avoided a decision on whether the Television Without Frontiers Directive had already harmonised the maintenance of pluralism on a European level. Moreover, the principle of minimum harmonisation on which the Directive is based also indicates that no harmonisation has taken place with regard to aspects of media pluralism. As media pluralism is to be considered a cultural issue, this interpretation is also in conformity with Article 151(5) (ex-Article 128(5)), which excludes harmonisation in the cultural sphere.

Public interest considerations have not (yet) been an issue in merger proceedings, although the Merger Regulations contains in Article 21(3), a provision, which leaves Member States free to take appropriate measures to protect legitimate interests other than those taken into consideration by the Merger Regulation. This provision specifically recognises plurality of the media, whereas other public interest concerns not mentioned must be notified to the Commission. Thus, national rules on concentration, which are specifically intended to safeguard pluralism, may provide a basis for the national authorities to examine a merger that the Commission has cleared. Yet, Article 21(3) is not available to authorise a concentration the Commission has declared incompatible with the common market. Again, this indicates that the Community and Member States' competence are delimited fairly clearly and that Community law does not interfere with purely cultural issues.

Public service broadcasting according to Article 86 (ex-Article 90) must be designed in such a way that the Member State conferring exclusive or special rights to the broadcaster does not violate the Treaty rules. Article 86(2) intends to balance a certain degree of protection from market forces with the aim of establishing a common market and ensuring undistorted competition. Everything depends on the causal link between the activity of the public broadcaster and the aim of pluralism and a high-quality television program. A certain preferential status of a broadcaster, which exempts it from the application of the Treaty rules, is not recognised by Community law. The test employed in Article 86(2) is quite strict and requires that the application of the Treaty rules obstruct the performance of the public broadcaster. If, however, the Treaty rules do not hinder the realisation of the tasks assigned to the public broadcaster, they must be applied. Yet, the Court of Justice has not expressly ruled on the question whether Treaty rules obstructed the performance of the public broadcaster's tasks, but left it to the national Courts to decide.

Concerning the broadcasting of sports events, the Television Without Frontiers Directive, in Article 3(a) also recognises the interests of the viewing public. It authorises Member States to draw up lists of sports events which they consider being of major importance for society and must therefore not be broadcast on an exclusive basis. Collective marketing and exclusive transmission of tournaments both tend to restrict competition and limit consumer choice. Thus, the Commission will review these measures under Article 81(ex-Article 85), and if they are found to restrict competition under Article 81(1)(ex-Article 85(1)), the parties to such exclusivity or collective selling agreement will need to apply for individual exemption under Article 81(3)(ex-Article 85(3)). Generally, in cases assessed under Article 81 (ex-Article 85), the public interest is catered for indirectly, because the prevention of anti-competitive restrictions, such as cartels or price-fixing agreements, ultimately results in lower prices for consumers.

Moreover, sporting bodies are free to regulate their internal matters and may do so by considering specific requirements of sport, such as the need to maintain a competitive balance and redistribution of resources among clubs. Yet, as has been clarified in *Bosman* and recently confirmed in *Lehtonen*, internal organisational matters, which comprise an economic activity, are subject to the Treaty provision, and only indistinctly applicable measures can benefit from a public interest in maintaining the special characteristics of sports.

9.3. **State Aid**

Public service broadcasting has during the last years continuously moved into the limelight of Community state aid law. With Protocol 9 annexed to the Treaty of Amsterdam on the System of Public Broadcasting in the Member States, some governments intended to clarify that they did not desire any interference with their national systems of (public service) broadcasting financing. In addition, some legal authors have repeatedly argued that, only if a public service broadcaster was overcompensated through its financing, be it directly by state funds or by television fees, could one speak of state aid in the sense of the Treaty.

This interpretation cannot be sustained in the light of recent case law. The Court of First Instance clarified in *SIC* that state aid, also in the field of broadcasting, is an objective concept that focuses on the financial advantage ('favour') of a certain state measure. The merely compensatory character of the financial benefit does not remove it from the scope of Article 87 (ex-Article 92). Only under Article 87(3)(d) may cultural aid, such as the financing of a public broadcaster in order to ensure a high quality and pluralism of opinions, be considered compatible with the common market. Yet, such aid must be notified to the Commission to be exempted.

The Court of First Instance's case law on state aid has repercussions for the shaping of public service broadcasting in the Member States. Protocol 9 annexed to the Treaty of Amsterdam did not remove the financing of public service broadcasting from the ambit of EC state aid law. Both in purely fee- and mixed fee-and-advertising-financed systems, the public broadcaster is conferred a benefit, which is a favour not obtainable by other broadcasters.[1023] Funds stemming from licence fees are thus to be considered state aid. As for the justification of cultural aid under either Article 87(3) or Article 86(2), the Member State will have to demonstrate a causal link between the funds provided and the public service obligation. This indicates that public service broadcasting must remain distinguishable from its private competitors in terms of quality and plurality.

Against this background, it is problematic that public service broadcasters become increasingly concerned with audience shares, because commercial success is evidently not the key characteristic to distinguish themselves from their commercial counterparts. Also a system of 'basic supply', as in Germany, where the public

[1023] It is the very essence of public service broadcasting that it is not entirely financed by advertising but at least also partly from non-market sources. Whether this is done directly by state funds or indirectly by fees is irrelevant, because also the authorisation to levy compulsory fees is a benefit conferred by the state.

service broadcaster is obliged to cover *all* potential viewer interests, is potentially at odds with the Community framework. The latter has to safeguard that competition is not distorted within the Common market, whereas 'basic supply' can result in a situation where in a certain market segment, public and commercial broadcasters provide for an exchangeable program from the audience's point of view, with the fundamental difference that only the public service broadcaster is subsidised for it. This would distort competition within the internal market.

9.4. **A Television Broadcasting Policy for Europe?**

The EC's broadcasting television policy today merely is piecemeal and is characterised by divergent approaches pursued by different Directorate Generals. Important players in shaping the framework for television in Europe have been the European Courts through their Judgements.

Although no clear-cut picture has yet emerged, one can say that the emphasis in the Community broadcasting policy lies on a market integration approach. The Court had initially based its case law solely on the free movement of services and proceeded as follows; first, it had consistently held that to be compatible with the free movement of services, a Member State's measure must be applied in a *non-discriminatory* manner. Secondly, it must pursue a legitimate aim in the *general interest*, and the Court stated that cultural policy objectives could constitute such a legitimate aim. This line of reasoning has first been clarified for restrictions to the free movement of services, for example in *Debauve,* but has lately also been confirmed with regard to undertakings entrusted with services of general economic interest in *VTM.* Thirdly, the measure enacted by the Member State must be *suitable* to achieve the envisaged goal; i.e., causality must be demonstrated. Fourthly, the national measures must not go beyond what is necessary in order to attain the objective. The aim must not be achievable by less restrictive means to the common market to pass the *proportionality* test.

After the Television Without Frontiers Directive had partly harmonised broadcasting within the EC, there was no fundamental change in the Court of Justice's approach, probably because the Directive was also based on the free movement of services and its provisions merely followed the case law previously developed by the Court. Yet, it also comprised provisions on some public interest objectives, such as the need to restrict advertising time and to control its content and the protection of minors, but the issue of safeguarding media pluralism was left to be dealt with by the Member States.

Notwithstanding this focus on the internal market, the Commission also recognised public interest objectives and especially the need to safeguard plurality in broadcasting programs. In its Green Paper on the Regulatory Implications,[1024]

[1024] *COM* (97) 623.

the Commission stressed the need to clearly identify public interest objectives in the first place. Indeed, a definition of the envisaged aim is indispensable in order to assess whether the measures in question are suitable and proportionate to achieve it.

This ties in with the case law of the Court of Justice and the Court of First Instance, which have consistently used effect-based tests in Judgements concerning the free movement of services, public undertakings, exclusive rights and state aid. Their analysis focuses not on the specific legal status conferred by national law but on how Member States' measures affect the internal market. Public interest considerations concerning broadcasting are fitted into the analysis in much the same way as consumer's interests are taken into account under the free movement of goods. This approach is open to criticism for not offering a high degree of legal certainty, but it does nevertheless constitute a dynamic concept, which is adaptable to a changing environment. To the extent that the commercialisation of public service broadcasting continues and intensifies, the tension between Member States' broadcasting systems and Community law can be expected to heighten. Whether and how this tension will be resolved depends not only on the further development of the legal framework but also on the extent to which Member States maintain an approach that considers (public service) broadcasting as closely connected to their sovereignty.

BIBLIOGRAPHY

Altman, W. et al., 'TV: from monopoly to competition', 15 *Hobart Paper* (1962) Institute of Economic Affairs, London.

Arnull, A., 'What shall we do on Sunday?', 16 *ELRev* (1991) p. 112.

Astheimer, S./Moosmayer, K., 'Europäische Rundfunkordnung – Chance oder Risiko?', 7 *ZUM* (1994) pp. 395-404.

Baeren, B./Rauppi, J., eds., *Transnational Communication in Europe. Practice and Research* (Berlin, Vistas, 2000).

Bain, J., 'Relation of Profit Rate to Industry Concentration', 64 *Quarterly Journal of Economics* (1951) pp. 293-324.

Baldwin, R., *Rules and Government* (Oxford, Oxford Socio-Legal Studies, 1995).

Bartosch, A., 'The Financing of Public Broadcasting and E.C. State Aid Law: An Interim Balance', 4 *ECLR* (1999) pp. 197-204.

———, 'Öffentlichrechte Rundfunkfinanzierung und EG/Beihilfenrecht – eine Zwischenbilanz', 6 *EuZW* (1999) pp. 176-180.

———, 'EuG: Fusion im Fernsehbereich', Case note to Case T-221/95 *Endemol*, 19 *EuZW* (1999) pp. 607, 608.

Barzanti, R., 'Audiovisual Opportunities in the Single Market', in *MEDIA 92* Newsletter of the MEDIA 92 Programme, No. 9 (1990) Brussels, p. 1.

Baumann, H., *Die Dienstleistungsfreiheit auf dem Gebiet der audiovisuiellen Medien im Rahmen des GATS im Spannungsfeld von Marktfreiheit und kutureller Selbstbestimung der Staaten der Europaeischen Union* (Duncker und Humblot, Berlin, 1998).

Bausch, H., *Rundfunkpolitik nach 1995* Vol. 1 (Munich, dtv, 1980).

Beaumont, S./Weatherill, P., *EU Law* (London, Penguin Books, 1999).

Becker, U., 'Basketball-Transferregelungen und gemeinschaftliche Freizügigkeit – "Lehtonen"', 7 *RIW* (2000) pp. 552-555.

Begg, D./Fischer, S./Dornbusch, R., *Economics*, 4th ed. (London, McGraw-Hill, 1994).

Bellamy, C./Child, G.D., *Common Market Law of Competition.* First Supplement to the 4th ed. (London, Sweet & Maxwell, 1996).

Benett, T., 'The Debauve and Coditel Cases', 5 *ELRev.* (1980) pp. 224-232.

Bishop, S./Walker, M., *The Economics of EC Competition Law* (London, Sweet & Maxwell, 1999).

Blumler, J.G., ed., *Television and the Public Interest* (London, Sage Publications, 1992).

Bouterse, R.B., *Competition and Integration – What Goals Count? EEC Competition Law and Goals of Industrial Monetary and Cultural Policy* (Deventer/Boston, Kluwer Law and Taxation Publishers, 1994).

Braun, M.,/Parker, L., 'Trade in culture: Consumable Product or Cherished Articulation of a Nation's Soul', 22 *Denv. J. Int'l L & Pol'y* (1993) pp. 155-191.

Briggs, A., *The History of Broadcasting in the United Kingdom: The Birth of Broadcasting*, Vol. 1, (Oxford, Oxford University Press, 1961).

Brinkman, D./Vollebregt, E., 'The Marketing of Sport and its Relation to E.C. Competition Law', 5 *ECLR* (1998) pp. 281-288.

Bröhmer, J./Ukrow, J, *Self-Regulation of the Media in Europe. A Comparative Legal Study, prepared at the request of the Federal Government for Cultural Affairs and the Media* (Saarbrücken, University of Saarbrücken, 1999).

Brozen, Y., 'The Concentration-Collusion Doctrine', (1977) *Antitrust Law Journal* p. 826.

Buendia Sierra, J.L., *Exclusive Rights and State Monopolies under EC Law* (Oxford, Oxford University Press, 1999).

Burns, T., *The BBC: Public Institution and Private World* (London, Macmillan, 1977).
Buschle, D., 'Freistellung vom Kartellverbot für den Markteintritt ins Pay-TV', 7 *ELR* (1999) pp. 305-308.
———, 'Pay-TV in der Fusionskontrolle: Entscheidung Bertelsmann/Kirch veröffentlicht', 5 *ELR* (1999) pp. 218-221.
Caine, S., 'Paying for TV',, 43 *Hobart Paper* (1968) Institute of Economic Affairs, London.
Cavallin, J., 'European Policies and Regulation on Media Concentration', IJCLP online, http://www.digital-law.net/IJCLP/1_webdoc_3_1_1998.html.
Chalmers, D., 'Competition and Industrial Property. Television and the Court of Justice', 17 *ELRev* (1992) pp. 248-257.
Coing, H./Kronstein, H./Mestmäcker, E.-J., eds., *Festschrift Böhm* (Karlsruhe, C.F. Müller, 1965), p. 345.
Collins, R., *Broadcasting and Audio-Visual Policy in The European Single Market* (London, John Libbey & Comp., 1994).
———, *From Satellite to Single Market. New communication technology and European public service television* (London, LSE/Routledge, 1998).
Cook, C.J. & Kerse C.S., *E.C. Merger Control*, 3rd ed. (London, Sweet & Maxwell, 2000).
Clark, J.M., 'Toward a Concept of Workable Competition', 30 *A.E.R.* (1940) p. 241.
Craig, P./De Burca, G., eds., *The Evolution of EU Law* (Oxford, Oxford University Press, 1999).
Criscuolo, A., 'The "TV Without Frontiers" Directive and the Legal Regulation of Publicity in the European Community', 23 *ELRev* (1998) pp. 357-363.
Damm, A., *Gebührenprivileg und Beihilfenrecht. Zur Vereinbarung der Finanzierung des öffentlich-rechtlichen Rundfunks in Deutschland mit Art. 92 EGV* (Berlin, Springer, 1998).
De Blois, M., 'Case Note in Case 352/85 Bond van Adverteerders', 27 *CMLRev.* (1990) pp. 371-381.
De Burca, G., 'The Principle of Proportionality and its Application in EC Law', 13 *YEL* (1993) p. 113.
De Witte, 'The European content requirements in the EC Television Directive – Five years after', (1995) *Yearbook of Media and Entertainment Law* p. 101.
Degenhart, C., 'Rundfunkordnung im europäischen Rahmen', 8 *ZUM* (1992) p. 449-456.
———, Case note on Case C-260/89 (1992) *Juristenzeitung* pp. 685-687.
Delbrück, J., *Die Rundfunkhoheit der deutschen Bundesländer im Spannungsfeld zwischen Regelungsanspruch der Europäischen Gemeinschaft und nationalem Verfassungsrecht, Rechtgutachten erstattet im Auftrag der deutschen Bundesländer* (Frankfurt a.M., Metzner, 1986).
Dhooge, L.J., 'No Place for Melrose', 16 *New York Law School Journal of International and Comparative Law* (1996) pp. 279-336.
Di Piazza, G., *Vertical Integration in TV Broadcasting. Strategic positioning for the digital age* (London, An FT Management Report, 1997).
Dillenz, W., 'Österreich. Vom Medien-Albanien zum Medien-Kalifornien', 10 *ZUM* (1994) pp. 544-551.
Dörr, D., 'Europäische Medienordnung und –politik', in *Internationales Handbuch für Hörfunk und Fernsehen 1996/97* (Baden-Baden, Nomos, 1996) p. 36.
———, 'Konzentrationstendenzen im Bereich des Rundfunks und ihre Rechtsprobleme', 1 *ZUM* (1993) pp. 10-17.
———, 'Die Maastricht-Entscheidung des Bundesverfassungsgerichtes und ihre Auswirkungen auf die Medienpolitik', 1 *ZUM* (1995) pp. 14-20.
Dörr, D./Cloß, W., 'Die Vereinbarkeit der Gebührenfinanzierung des Österreichischen Rundfunks mit dem EG-Beihilferecht. Kurzgutachterliche Stellungnahme des Instituts für Europäisches Medienrecht e.V. – erstattet im Auftrag des Österreichischen Rundfunks', 2 *ZUM* (1996) pp. 105-118.
Donaldson, J.D., 'Television without Frontiers; The continuing Tension between liberal Free Trade and European Cultural Integration', 20 *Fordham International Law Journal* (1996) pp. 90-180.

Dondlinger, J., 'Europe's Media Future', 6 *Media Bulletin* (1989) p. 3 (Manchester, European Institute for the Media).

Downs, A./Ellison, J., *The Legal Control of Mergers in the European Communities* (London, Blackstone Press, 1990).

Drijber, B., 'The Revised Television without Frontiers Directive: Is It Fit For The Next Century?', 36 *CMLRev.* (1999) p. 87.

D'Sa, R.M., *European Community Law on State Aid* (London, Sweet & Maxwell, 1998).

Dyson, K. /Humphreys, P., *Broadcasting and New Media Policies in Western Europe* (London, Routledge, 1988).

———, *The Political Economy of Communications. International and European Dimensions* (London, Routledge, 1990).

Eberle, C.-E., 'Aktivitäten der Europäischen Union auf dem Gebiet der Medien und ihre Auswirkungen auf den öffentlich-rechtlichen Rundfunk', 11 *ZUM* (1995) pp. 763-769.

Edward, D./Hoskins, M., 'Article 90: Deregulation and EC Law, Reflections arising from the XVI FIDE Conference', 32 *CMLRev.* (1995) pp. 157-186.

Ehlermann, C.-D., 'Managing Monopolies: The Role of the State in Controlling Market Dominance in the European Community', 2 *ECLR* (1993) pp. 61-69.

Emmerich, V., *Kartellrecht* 7th ed. (München, C.H. Beck, 1994).

Van Empel, M., 'Merger Control in the EEC', 13 *World Competition Law and Economics Review* (1989) pp. 5-22.

Engel, C., *Kabelfernsehen, Law and Economics of International Telecommunications* (Baden-Baden, Nomos, 1996).

Eriksen, E.O. and Fossum, J.E., *Democracy in the European Union: Integration Through Deliberation?* (London, Routledge 2000) pp. 206-229.

Esser-Wellié, M., 'Das Verfassungs- und Wirtschaftsrecht der Breitbandkommunikation in den Vereinigten Staaten von Amerika. Zusammenhänge zwischen technischer Konvergenz und Wettbewerb', (Baden-Baden, Nomos 1995).

Ewans, A., *European Community Law of State Aid* (Cambridge, Clarendon Press, 1997).

Farda, C., 'Unerwünschte Kontrolle. Versuch einer Antikonzentrationsrichtlinie der Europäischen Union', in 2 *Medienjournal* (1997) p. 60.

Feenstra, J., 'Case Note on Cases C-288/89 Gouda and C-353/89 *Commission* v. *Netherlands*', 30 *CMLRev.* (1993) pp. 424-432.

Fejø, J., *Monopoly Law and Market. Studies of EC Competition Law with US American Antitrust Law as a frame of reference and supported by basic market economics* (London/Dordrecht/Boston, Kluwer, 1989).

Fidler, D.P., 'Competition Law and International Relations', 41 *ICLQ* (1992) pp. 563-589.

Filipek, J., 'Cultural Quotas: The Trade Controversy over the European Community's Broadcasting Directive', 28 *Stanford Journal of International Law* (1992) p. 324.

Fleming, H., 'Exclusive Rights to Broadcast Sporting Events in Europe', 3 *ECLR* (1999) pp. 143-148.

Font Galarza, A., 'The Commission's Assessment of the Eurovision System pursuant to Article 81 EC', 2 *CPN* (2000) pp. 28-33.

Francis, J.G., *The Politics of Regulation. A Comparative Perspective* (Oxford, Blackwell, 1993).

Franck, P.A., 'Les entreprises visée aux articles 90 et 37 du Traité CEE', in Various, *L'entreprise publique et la concurrence. Les articles 90 et 37 du Traité CEE et leur relation avec la concurrence.* Semaine de Bruges 1968 (Bruges, De Temple 1969).

Freis, I., 'Das Recht der Finanzierung des öffentlich-rechtlichen Rundfunks in Deutschland, Frankreich, Großbritannien und Österreich im Vergleich', 1 *ZEuS* (1999) pp. 109-136.

Frey, D., *Fernsehen und audiovisueller Pluralismus im Binnenmarkt der EG* (Baden-Baden, Nomos, 1999).

Friden, G., 'The "Bond van Adverteerders" case and recent legal developments in EEC "television law"', *Leiden Journal of International Law* (1990) pp. 231-238.

Galmot, Y./Binacarelli, J., 'Les réglementations nationales en matière de prix au regard du droit communautaire', (1985) *RTDE* pp. 269-311.

Garnhem, N., 'The media and the public sphere', in Calhoun, C., ed., *Habermas and the Public Sphere* (Cambridge, Cambridge MIT Press, 1992).
Garrett, L.L., 'Commerce versus Culture: The Battle Between the United States and the European Union Over Audiovisual Trade Policies', 19 *NCJ. Int'L & Com. Reg.* (1994) pp. 553-577.
Gellner, E., *Nations and Nationalism* (Oxford, Blackwell, 1983).
Gerber, 'Constitutionalising the Economy: German Neo-liberalism, Competition Law and the "New Europe"', 42 *American Journal of Comparative Law* (1994) p. 25.
Goyder, D.G., *EC Comptition Law*, 3rd ed. (Oxford, Clarendon Press, 1998).
Grabitz, E./Hilf, M., *Kommentar zur Europäischen Union*, Vol. I (Munich, C.H. Beck, 1994).
Groeben, H. von der/Thiesing, J./Ehlermann, C.D., eds., *Kommentar zum EU-/EG-Vertrag* Vol. 2/I (Baden-Baden, Nomos, 1999).
Groeben, H. van der/Thiesing, J./Ehlermann, C.D., eds., *Kommentar zum EWG-Vertrag* (Baden-Baden, Nomos, 1991).
Haas, U./Reimann, C., 'Das "Fernsehrecht" an Sportveranstaltungen als Abwehrrecht',, 5 *SpuRt* (1999) pp. 182-187.
Hachmeister, L., 'Wer hat Angst vor unabhängigem Fernsehen? Zum neuen deutschen Desinteresse am 'dritten Weg', 22 *Funk-Korrespondenz* (1996) p. 11.
Hancher, L. 'Community, State and Market', Chapter 20 of Craig, P./De Burca, G., eds., *The Evolution of EU Law* (Oxford, Oxford University Press, 1999).
Hancher, L./Ottervenger, T./Slot, P.J., *E.C. State Aids*, 2nd ed., (London, Sweet & Maxwell, 1999).
Haracourt, A.J., 'EU Media Ownership Regulation: Conflict over the Definition of Alternatives', 36 *JCMS* (1998) pp. 369-389.
Hearst, S., 'Broadcasting Regulation in Britain', in Blumler, J.G.,ed., *Television and the Public Interest* (London, Sage Publications, 1992) pp. 61-78.
Heermann, P. W., 'Kann der Ligasport die Fesseln des Kartellrechts sprengen?', 1 *SpuRt* (1999) pp. 11-15.
Hell Hansen, L., 'The Development of the Circumvention Principle in the Area of Broadcasting', 2 *LIEI* (1998) pp. 113-138.
Herrmann, G., *Rundfunkrecht* (München, C.H. Beck, 1994).
Hilf, M./Pache, E., 'Das Bosman-Urteil des EuGH. Zur Geltung der EG-Grundfreiheiten für den Berufsfußball', 18 *NJW* (1996) pp. 1169-1177.
Hoffmann-Riem, W., 'New media in West Germany: The politics of legitimation' in Dyson, K./ Humphreys, P., ed., *The Political Economy of Communications. International and European Dimensions* (London, Routledge, 1990) pp. 171-193.
———, *Rundfunkrecht neben Wirtschaftsrecht. Zur Anwendbarkeit des GWB und des EWG-V auf das Wettbewerbsverhalten öffentlich-rechtlichen Rundfunks in der dualen Rundfunkordnung'* (Baden-Baden, Nomos, 1991).
———, 'Protecting Vulnerable Values in the German Broadcasting Order' in Blumler, J.G., ed., *Television and the Public Interest* (New York, Sage Publications, 1992) pp. 43-60.
Hoggart, R., 'The Public Service Idea', in *British Broadcasting: Main Principles* (London, Broadcasting Research Unit, 1983).
Holzer, N., 'Deutsche Rundfunkgebühr als unzulässige Beihilfe im Sinne des europäischen Rechts?', 4 *ZUM* (1996) pp. 274-285.
Home Office, ed., *Broadcasting: Copy of the Licence and Agreement Dated the 2nd Day of April 1981 between Her Majesty's Secretary of State for the Home Department and the British Broadcasting Corporation*, Preamble and Annexes, 1981.
Hoppmann, E., 'Meinungswettbewerb als Entdeckungsverfahren' in Mestmäcker, E.J, ed., *Offene Rundfunkordnung. Prinzipien für den grenzüberschreitenden Rundfunk* (Gütersloh, Verlag Berteslmann Stiftung, 1998) pp. 163-198.
Houing, R./Colliard, A., 'Politique communautaire de concurrence et audiovisuel: état des lieux', (1998) *RTDE*, pp. 1-33.
Hughes, M., 'Article 86 of the E.C. Treaty – State Monopolies and Competition', 8 *Irish Journal of European Law* (1999) pp. 18-36.

Humphreys, P., *Media and Media Policy in West Germany: The Press and Broadcasting since 1945* (New York, Berg, 1990).
Immenga, U., 'Europäische Kommission: Marktbeherrschende Digital-Allianz', Case note on Case IV/M. 1027, (1999) *Computer & Recht* pp. 424-431.
Immenga, U./Mestmäcker, E.-J., *EG-Wettbewerbsrecht. Kommentar* (München, C.H. Beck 1997).
Ishikawa, S./Murmatsu, Y., 'Quality Assessment of Broadcast Programming: Research Subjects for Future', 27 *Studies in Broadcasting* (1991) pp.207-219.
Jenny, F.Y., 'Competition and State Aid Policy in the European Union', 18 *Fordham Int. LJ.* (1994/95) pp. 525-554.
Jestaedt, T. and Anweiler, J., 'Europäische Fusionskontrolle im Medienbereich', 18 *EuZW* (1997) pp.549-555.
Jones, C./ Gonzáles-Diaz E., *The Merger Regulation*, (London, Sweet & Maxwell, 1992).
Keane, J., *The Media and Democracy* (Cambridge, Polity 1991).
Kelly, M., 'Influences on Broadcasting Policies for Election Coverage' in Blumer, ed., *Communicating to Voters: Television in The First European Parliamentary Elections* (London, Beverly Hills and New Dheli, Sage 1983) pp. 65-82.
Kepplinger, H.M. et al., 'Medientenor und Bevölkerungsmeinung. Eine empirische Studie zum Image Helmut Kohls' in 38 *Kölner Zeitschrift für Soziologie und Sozialpsychologie* (1986) pp. 247-279.
Kevin, D./Schlesinger, P.R., 'Can the European Union Become a Sphere of Publics?' in Eriksen, E.O. and Fossum, J.E., *Democracy in the European Union: Integration Through Deliberation?* (London, Routledge 2000) pp. 206-229.
Kilian, W., *Europäisches Wirtschaftsrecht* (München, C.H. Beck, 1996).
Kischel, U. in Kischel, U., ed., *Rundfunkfreiheit und Rundfunkmonopol* (Baden-Baden, Nomos, 1999) pp. 75-102.
Kleinsteuber, H.J., 'Telecommunikationspolitik und Deregulierung in den USA: Der Fall American Telephone & Telegraph (AT&T)', 24 *Rundfunk und Fernsehen*, (1987) pp. 151-168.
Kleinsteuber, H.J./Rosenbach, M., 'Digitales Fernsehen in Europa: Eine Bestandsaufnahme' in 35 *Rundfunk und Fernsehen* (1998), pp. 24-57.
Klotz, R., 'Auf dem Weg zu einem europäischen Mutlimediarecht. Gesetzgebung und Wettbewerbsaufsicht durch die europäische Union', 6 *ZUM* (1999), pp. 443-455.
Korah, V., *An Introductory Guide to EC Competition Law and Practice* 6th ed., (Oxford, Hart Publishing 1997).
———, 'Collaborative Joint Ventures: the Competition Rules of the Common Market and the Invalidity of Contracts', (1991-92) 15 *Fordh. Int. L.J.* p. 248.
Kresse, H., 'Marktöffnung und Pluralitätssicherung. Eckpunkte zur effektiven Vielfaltsgestaltung im privaten Rundfunk' in Kresse, H., ed., *Pluralismus, Markt und Medienkonzentration: Positionen* (Berlin, Vistas, 1995) pp. 11-94.
Kresse, H./Heinze, M., 'Der Rundfunk: Das "jedenfalls auch kulturelle Phänomen"', 6 *ZUM* (1995) pp. 394-397.
Kronenberger, V., *Le monopole des alcools en Finland: exemple de la mutation des monopoles publices en droit communautaire* (Toulouse, Septentrion, 1999).
Lau, J., 'Das Fernsehen als Feind der Kultureliten. Ein Selbstgespräch' in 9/10 *Merkur. Deutsche Zeitschrift für europäisches Denken* (1995) p. 890.
Le Grand, J. and New, B., *Fair game? Tackling monopoly in sports broadcasting* (Demos Commentary, 1999).
Lloyd, P., 'Trade and Competition Policy' in *Conference on Competition Policy and International Trade* (Brussels, European Institute for Advanced Studies in Management 1998).
Loman, J.M.E./Mortelmans, K.J.M./Post, H.H.G./Watson, J.S., *Culture and Community Law. Before and after Maastricht* (Deventer/Boston, Kluwer, 1992).
Lupinacci, T.M., 'The Pursuit of Television Broadcasting Activities in the European Community: Cultural Preservation or Economic Protectionism?', 24 *Vanderbilt Journal of Transnational Law* (1991) pp. 113-154.

Maggiore, M., 'Audiovisual Production in the Single Market' in *European Cultural Foundation & European Institute for Media, Europe 2000: A Report of the European Television Task Force* (1990) pp. 69, 70.
Majone, G., ed., *Deregulation or Re-regulation? Regulatory Reform in Europe and the United States* (London, Pinter Publishers, 1990).
———, *Evidence, Argument and Persuasion in the Policy Process* (London, New Haven, 1989).
March-Hunnings, N., 'Cable Television in Italy' in (1975) *The Journal of Business Law* (1975) pp. 72-74.
———, 'Annotation on Case 52/79 and Case 62/79, in 17 *CMLRev.* (1980) pp. 564-569.
Marenco, G., 'The Notion of Restriction on the Freedom of Establishment and Provision of Services in the Case-Law of the Court', 11 *YEL* (1991) p. 128.
———, 'Le Traité CEE interdit-il aux Etats membres de restreindre la concurrence?', 3/4 *Cahiers de droit europeén* (1986) pp. 285 et seq.
Marenco, G./Banks, K., 'Intellectual Property and Community Rules on Free Movement: Discrimination unearthed', 15 *ELRev.* (1990) pp. 224-256.
Martin-Pérez de Nanclares, J., *Die EG-Fernsehrichtlinie: Rechtsgrundlage, Kommentierung und Umsetzung in das Recht der EG-Mitgliedstaates sowie Österreichs und der Schweiz* (Frankfurt a.M., Lang, 1995).
Marsh, C.S., ed., *Educational Broadcasting 1936* (Chicago, Chicago University Press 1937).
McDonald, K., 'How would you like your Television: with or without Borders and with or without Culture – A new Approach to Media Regulation in the European Union' in 22 *Fordh. Int. L. J.* (1999) p. 1991.
Mc Lean, N., *Self-regulation in the Broadcasting Sector* (Council of Europe, SEM 3 no. 13, 1998).
Meckel, M., 'Kommunikative Identität und Weltöffentlichkeit: Theoretische Überlegungen zur Rolle der Medien im Globalisierungsprozeß' in 43/4 *Publizistik* (1998) pp. 362-375.
Meessen, K.M., 'Potlitische Identität in Europa', 6 *EuR* (1999) pp. 701-712.
Mestmäcker, E.-J., *Recht und ökonomisches Gesetz. Über die Grenzen von Staat, Gesellschaft und Privatautonomie,* 2nd ed.(Baden-Baden, Nomos, 1984).
———, ed., *Offene Rundfunkordnung. Prinzipien für den grenzüberschreitenden Rundfunk*, (Gütersloh, Verlag Berteslmann Stiftung, 1988).
———, ed., *Recht in der offenen Gesellschaft. Hamburger Beiträge zum deutschen, europäischen und internationalen Wirtschafts- und Medienrecht*', 1st ed., (Baden-Baden, Nomos, 1993).
———, 'Über den Einfluss von Ökonomie und Technik auf Recht und Organisation der Telekommuniktaion und der elektronischen Medien' in Mestmäcker, E.-J., ed., *Kommunikation ohne Monopole II',* (Baden-Baden, Nomos,1990) pp. 13-177.
———, 'Commentary on Article 37' in Immenga, U./Mestmäcker, E.-J. *Wettbewerbsrecht*, Kommentar, Vol. II (München, C.H. Beck, 1997) pp. 1485-1515.
———, 'Offene Märkte im System unverfälschten Wettbewerbs in der Europäischen Wirtschaftsgemeinschaft' in Coing, H./Kronstein, H./Mestmäcker, E.-J., eds., *Festschrift Böhm* (Karlsruhe, C.F. Müller, 1965), p. 345.
———, 'Staat und Unternehmen im europäischen Gemeinschaftsrecht. Zur Bedeutung von Art. 90 EWGV' in (1998) *Rabels Zeitschrift* pp. 526-586.
———, 'The EC Commission's Modernization of Competition Policy: a Challenge to the Community's Constitution', 1 *EBOR* (2000) pp. 499-542.
———, et al., eds., *Der Einfluß des europäischen Gemeinschaftsrechts auf die deutsche Rundfunkordnung* (Baden-Baden, Nomos,1990).
———, ed., *Festschrift Hans van der Groeben* (Nomos, Baden-Baden, 1997).
Meyer, C.O., 'Towards a European public sphere? Transnational Investigative Journalism and the European Commission's Resignation' in Baeren, B./Rauppi, J., eds., *Transnational Communication in Europe. Practice and Research* (Berlin, Vistas, 2000) pp.107-127.
Muchlinski, P.T., *Multinational Enterprises and the Law* (Oxford, Blackwell, 1995).
Nikolinakos, N., 'Strategic alliances in the pay-TV market: The TPS case', 7 *ECLR* (2000) pp. 334-339.

Nitsche, I., 'Collective Marketing of Broadcasting Rights by Sports Associations in Europe', 4 *ECLR* (2000) pp. 208-214.

———, 'Fussball-WM 1998: Missbrauch der marktbeherrschenden Stellung beim Kartenverkauf, 5 (2000) *ELR* pp. 175-177.

Noelle-Neumann, E., 'Medienwirkung und Medienpolitik' in Mestmäcker, E.-J., ed., *Offene Rundfunkordnung. Prinzipien für den grenzüberschreitenden Rundfunk*, (Gütersloh, Verlag Berteslmann Stiftung. 1998) pp. 495-504.

———, 'Das Reizwort "Ausgewogenheit". Über gruppendynamische Prozesse im Rundfunk-Journalismus' in *Franfurter Allgemeine Zeitung*, 8 May 1981, p. 7.

Nossiter, T.J., 'British Television; A Mixed Economy' in *Research on the Range and Quality of Broadcasting Services* (London, HMSO 1986) pp. 1-71.

Núñes Müller, M./Kamann, H.-G., Case note on T-95/96 (1999) *Europäisches Wirtschafts- und Steuerrecht* pp. 332-338.

O'Connell, 'Television without Frontiers: The European Union's continuing Struggle for Cultural Survival' in 28 *Case Western Reserve Journal of International Law* (1996) p. 501.

Ossenbühl, F., *Rundfunk zwischen nationalem Verfassungsrecht und europäischem Gemeinschaftsrecht – Rechtgutachten erstattet der Regierung des Landes Nordrhein-Westfalen* (Frankfurt a.M., Hessischer Rundfunk, 1986).

Otten, R. G., 'Die Gebührenfinanzierung der öffentlich-rechtlichen Rundfunkanstalten im Rahmen des Art. 92 EGV', 11 *ZUM* (1997) pp. 790-800.

Page, A.C., 'Member States, Public Undertakings and Article 90', 7 *ELRev.* (1982) pp. 19-35.

Pappalardo, A., 'Der Europäische Gerichtshof auf der Suche nach einem Kriterium für die Anwendung der Wettbewerbsregeln auf staatliche Maßnahmen' in Mestmäcker, E.-J., ed., *Festschrift für Hans van der Groeben* (Baden-Baden, Nomos 1987) pp. 303-314.

Papathanassopoulos, S., 'Broadcasting and the European Community: the Commissions audiovisual policy' in Dyson, K./Humphreys, P., eds., *The Political Economy of Communications, International and European Dimensions* (London, Routledge, 1990).

Pathak, A. S., 'The EC Commission's Approach to Joint Ventures: A Policy of Contradictions', 5 *ECLR* (1991) pp. 171-183.

Peacock Committee, *Report of the Committee on Financing the BBC* (London, HMSO Cmnd 9824, 1986).

Philips, 'Structure, Conduct and Performance – and Performance, Conduct and Structure' in *Industrial Organisation and Economic Development* Markham, J.W./Papanek, G.F., eds. (Boston, Houghton Mifflin, 1970).

Pernice, I., Commentary on Art. 90, at para 53 in, Grabitz, E./Hilf, M. *Kommentar zur Europäischen Union*, Vol. I (Munich, C.H. Beck, 1994).

Pilkington Committee, *Report of the Committee on Broadcasting 1960* (London, HSMO 1982).

Porter, M.E., *Competitive Advantage of Nations* (London, Basingstoke, 1990).

Porter, V. /Hasselbach, S., *Pluralism, Politics and the Marketplace. The Regulation of German Broadcasting*, (London/New York, Routledge, 1991).

Presburger, P./Tyler, M.R., 'Television without Frontiers: Opportunity and Debate Created by the New European Community Directive', *13 Hastings Int. & Comp. L. Rev.* (1990) p. 495.

Pullen, M./Ris, B., 'Advocate General Reinforces the Principle of Country of Origin Control under the Television Without Frontiers Directive', 8 *ECLR* (1996) pp. 453-461.

Reich, R.B., *The Work of Nations: Preparing Ourselves for 21st Century Capitalism* (New York, A.A. Knopf, 1992).

Ridder, C.M., 'Die Rolle des öffentlich-rechtlichen Rundfunks im kommerzialisierten Mediensystem – Zukunkftsstrategien der BBC', (1993) *Media Perspektiven* pp. 150-158.

Rodriguez-Curiel, W., 'Chronique de jurisprudence: quelques réflexions sur la jurisprudence récente de la Cour de justice en matière d'aides d'Etat', 3 *RIDE* (1993) pp. 433-460.

Rosengren, K.H. et al., 'Quality in Programming. Views from the North', 27 *Studies in Broadcasting* (1991) pp. 21-80.

Ross, M., 'I love Lucy, but the European Community doesn't: Apparent Protectionism in the European Community's Broadcasting Market', 16 *Brooklyn Journal of International Law* (1990) p. 595.

———, 'Article 16 E.C. and services of general interest: from derogation to obligation?', 25 *ELRev.* (2000) pp. 22-38.
———, 'State Aids: Maturing into a Constitutional Problem', 15 *YEL* (1995) p. 79.
Röthel, A., 'EuGH: Dienstleistungsfreiheit für Judoka. Freizügigkeit von Basketballspielern', 12 *EuZW* (2000) pp. 371-380.
Ring, W.-D., *Medienrecht. Rundfunk. Neue Medien, Presse* (Munich, Verlag für Verwaltungspraxis 1990).
Rüggeberg, J., 'Rundfunk als Wirtschaftsgut – Die Europäische Wirtschaftsgemeinschaft im Zugriff auf den öffentlich-rechtlichen Rundfunk', (83 *Verwaltungsarchiv* 1992) p. 330.
Ruß-Mohl, S., 'Kontrolle der Kontrolleure', 2 *Journalist* (1994) p. 41.
Salvatore, V., 'Quotas on TV Programmes and EEC Law', 29 *CMLRev.* (1992) pp. 967-990.
Sarnoff, D., 'Broadcasting in the American Democracy', in Marsh, C.S., ed., *Educational Broadcasting 1936* (Chicago, Chicago University Press1937) pp. 146-155.
Schardt, A., 'Novellierung der Richtlinie "Fernsehen ohne Grenzen": Quoten ohne Ende?', 11 *ZUM* (1995) pp. 734-739.
Schlesinger, P.R., 'From cultural defence to political culture: media, politics and collective identity in the European Union' in 19 *Media Culture & Society* (1997) p. 369.
———, 'Wishful Thinking: Cultural Politics, Media and Collective Identities in Europe', 43 *Journal of Communications* (1999) pp. 6-17.
———, 'Changing spaces of political communication: The case of the European Union', 16 *Political Communication* (1999) pp. 263-279.
Schmitd-Vockenhausen, M., 'Revision der EG-Fernsehrichtlinie. Ein weiterer Schritt in eine europäischie Medienordnung?', 5 *ZUM* (1998) pp. 377-381.
Schwarze, J., *European Administrative Law* (London/Luxembourg, Sweet & Maxwell, 1992).
Schwartz, I., 'Broadcasting and the EEC Treaty', 11 *ELRev.* (1986) pp. 17 et seq.
Scott, C.B., 'European Unification – Broadcasting Law – Eastern Europe and the "Television without Frontiers" Directive: Radio Free Europe – Can Television Unify it?', 22 *Georgian Journal of International and Comparative Law* (1992) pp. 547-566.
Segrave, K., *American Television Abroad. Hollywood's Attempt to Dominate World Televsion.* (Jefferson, North Carolina and London, Mc Farland & Co., 1998).
Slot, P.J., 'Case note on inter alia C-260/89 ERT', 28 *CMLRev.* (1991) pp. 964-988.
———, 'Case note on Case T-95/96', 36 *CMLRev.* (1999) pp. 1335-1344.
Slotboom, M.M., 'State Aid in Community Law: A Broad or Narrow Definition?', 20 *ELRev.* (1995) pp. 289-301.
Steindorff, E., *Grenzen der EG-Kompetenzen* (Heidelberg, Beiheft 65 zur ZHR, 1990).
Stopper, M., 'Wer ist Veranstalter und Rechtsträger im Profi-Fußball?', 5 *SpuRt* (1999) pp. 188-192.
Streinz, R., 'Der Vertrag von Amsterdam', 5/6 *EuZW* (1998) pp. 137-147.
Stuyck, J., 'Case note on C-267 and C-268/91', 34 *CMLRev.* (1997) pp. 1445-1468.
Teeter, D.L./Le Duc, D.R., *Law of Mass Communications. Freedom and Control of Print and Broadcast Media* (Westbury/ N.Y., Foundation Press, 1995).
Temple Lang, J., *Media, Multimedia and European Antitrust Law* (Albany/N.Y., Fordham Corporate Law Institute, 1997).
———, *Community Antitrust Law and Government Measures relating to Public and Privileged Enterprises: Art. 90 EEC Treaty*, (Albany/N.Y., Fordham Corporate Law Institute, 1984) p. 550.
Tracy, M., *The Decline and Fall of Public Service Broadcasting* (Oxford, Oxford University Press 1988).
Tribe, L., *American Constitutional Law*, 2nd ed. (New York, Foundation Press, 1988).
Tridimas, T., *The General Principles of EC Law* (Oxford, Oxford University Press, 1999).
Ullswater Committee, *Report of the Broadcasting Committee* (London HMSO, Cmnd. 4798, 1936).
Usher, J.A., 'The Development of Community Powers after the Single European Act' in White, R./Smythe, B., eds., *European and International Law* (London, Sweet & Maxwell, 1990).

Van der Woude, M., 'Art. 90: Competing for Competence', 17 *ELRev.* (1992) Competition Checklist 1991, pp. 60-80.
Veljanovski, C./Bishop, W., 'Choice by cable: the economics of a new era in television', 36 *Hobart Paper* (1983) Institute for Economic Affairs, London.
Venturelli, S. S., *Liberalizing the European media: politics, regulation, and the public sphere* (Oxford, Clarendon Press, 1998) .
Von Heydebrand u.d. Lasa, 'Free Movement of Foodstuff, Consumer Protection and Food Standards in the European Community: Has the Court of Justice Got ist Wrong?', 16 *ELRev.* (1991) p. 391.
Wachsmann, A./Berrod, F., 'Les critères de justification des monopoles: un premier bilan après l'affaire Corbeau', (1994) *RTDE* p. 39.
Wachtmeister, A.M., 'Broadcasting of Sports Events and Competition Law', 2 *Competition Policy Newsletter* (1998) pp. 18-28.
Waldhauser, H., 'Anmerkung zum Beschluß der BGH vom 11. Dezember 1997 (KVR 7/96) zur Zentralvermarktung der Europacupspiele durch den DFB', 2 *ZUM* (1998) pp. 129-132.
Wallace, R./Goldberg, D., 'The EEC Directive an Television Broadcasting', 9 *YEL* (1989) p. 175.
Weatherill, S., *After Bosman: Tracking a Sporting Revolution.* Amended version of a paper delivered under the auspices of the Sports Law Centre of Anglia Polytechnic University as the First Bosman lecture in the Middle Temple, London, 5 May 1999.
Weiss, G., 'The Concentration and Profits Issue' in Goldschmid, H.J./Mann, H.M./Weston, F.J., eds., *Industrial Concentration: The New Learning* (Boston, Little, Brown, 1974).
Weiler, J.H.H., 'The Transformation of Europe', 100 *Yale Law Journal* (1990) p. 2403.
Wertenbruch, J., 'EuGH: Freizügigkeit von Berufsfußballspielern', 3 *EuZW* (1996) pp. 82-92.
Wiedemann, V., 'Der Zugang zum Rundfunk in Grobritannien' in Mestmäcker, E.-J., ed., *Offene Rundfunkordnung. Prinzipien für den grenzüberschreitenden Rundfunk* (Gütersloh, Verlag Berteslmann Stiftung 1988) pp. 89-102.
Whish, R., *Competition Law,* 3rd ed. (London, Edinburgh, Butterworths, 1993).
Winn, D.B., *European Community and International Media Law* (London/Dordrecht/Boston, Graham & Trotman/Marinus Nijhoff, 1994).
Woods, L./Scholes, J., 'Broadcasting: the Creation of a European Culture or the Limits of the Internal Market?', 17 *YEL* (1997) pp. 47-82.